D1381235

PALLY

© 2008
Published by Know the Score Books
Printed by Cromwell Press

ISBN 978-8-48185-00-5

ACKNOWLEDGEMENTS

Gary Pallister would like to thank Mary, Lauren, Eve, Mam and Dad for all their love and support; Sir Alex Ferguson; Steve Bruce; Bryan Robson; Lee Sharpe; Terry Venables; Tony Mowbray; Bernie Slaven; Cliff Butler; designer Michael March; publisher Simon Lowe; Colin Wilkinson.
Ivan Ponting would like to thank Pat, Rosie and Joe, as ever.

Mixed Sources
Product group from well-managed forests and other controlled sources
www.fsc.org Cert no. TT-COC-2082
© 1996 Forest Stewardship Council
FSC

PALLY

Gary Pallister

with Ivan Ponting

CONTENTS

FOREWORD
BY SIR ALEX FERGUSON

He had to endure a nightmare debut for Manchester United, and he was panned cruelly by the press in his first weeks at Old Trafford, but before very long Gary Pallister matured into the best footballing centre-half in the country, bar nobody.

That was a fantastic achievement, and he can be justly proud of a magnificent career, but what gives me just as much pleasure when I think about Pally is that he has never changed as a character in all the years I have known him.

He has always been a smashing lad, very easy-going and popular with everyone, completely straightforward in all his dealings; and if he's a fellow of simple tastes, he's an extremely intelligent one, too.

But while it's hard to imagine a more terrific bloke, he did have his idiosyncrasies, like so many footballers. For instance, he liked his sweeties, his crisps and his Coke, and we had to keep an eye on all that, though it wasn't always easy.

I remember calling at his house one night to pick him to go to a dinner. He was still getting ready, so Mary asked me in, and there beside the couch in front of the television was a giant bottle of Coke, a bag of mixed Maltesers and Mars bars, and a monster packet of crisps.

I said to her: 'That's not his, is it?' and she said: 'Well, it's not mine!' Next minute Pally comes down the stairs and I had a go at him: 'If I come in here and see them again then I'm going to fine you.' His reaction was typical: 'Mary, I've told you about this before. For the last time, stop eating sweeties all day!'

For all that, Gary was essentially an honest individual, and not difficult to manage. Of course, if I have a player for a long time then I tend to start treating him like one of my family, and that carries with it the odd occasion when a little fatherly discipline is dispensed.

It's like if you have a little boy and he misbehaves at the table then you might give him a clip and tell him to finish his dinner. So from time to time he might have heard: 'Pally, behave yourself now, where were you last night? And get your hair cut!' That's always been my way, and I'm the same now with Ryan Giggs, Gary Neville and Paul Scholes. I've watched them all as they were growing up and I never want to see them alter. When I do see a lad change, then it hurts me a wee bit, and I feel it's some sort of reflection on me. I like to play my part in bringing them up the proper way. If I can meet their mothers and fathers after I've had them with me for years, and hear that their boys are the same lads that they always were, then I feel I've achieved something with them, quite apart from the football.

I like to be able to say: 'These boys have been fantastic people.' Pally was like that, so were the likes of Brucie and Irwin. They were always true to themselves, and that sort of consistency of nature allowed them to stay longer in the game. Similarly with Scholesy and the rest – you couldn't wish to meet nicer blokes. It's a delight to see them now in their thirties, unchanged by all their success, still with nice manners; that gives me so much satisfaction.

Getting back to Gary, he was one of the first players I pursued after coming down to Old Trafford from Aberdeen late in 1986. Middlesbrough had been in receivership, then brought in a new management team of Bruce Rioch and Colin Todd, and there was a real resurgence of energy and optimism at Ayresome Park, epitomised by a young back four of Gary Parkinson, Tony Mowbray, Pally and Colin Cooper. We watched them a lot because, with Kevin Moran injured so frequently and Paul McGrath having his own problems, we were looking for centre-halves. Almost from day one I was keen to buy Pally, but Rioch wouldn't sell.

Then in the summer of 1989 I decided I needed a clean sweep, and got rid of Gordon Strachan, Jesper Olsen, Chris Turner, Graeme Hogg, Norman Whiteside, Moran and McGrath to help finance the new players I needed, but still Middlesbrough wouldn't countenance letting Gary go.

So I turned my attention to Glenn Hysen of Fiorentina, who I knew was a good, experienced operator. After doing the necessary groundwork, I flew to Italy along with the club solicitor, Maurice Watkins, to clinch a deal for the Swede. We thought we had him, but at the last moment he signed for Liverpool instead, which was severely disappointing at the time.

We had made a long journey to complete a signing that we never clinched, and on the way back we shared a flight with John Smith and Peter Robinson, the Liverpool chairman and secretary, who were so smug. It was almost unbearable.

When I got home I told our chairman, Martin Edwards, that we would have to go for broke and pay whatever we had to for Pally, but striking a deal was easier said than done. I suggested that Martin set up a dinner meeting with the Middlesbrough chairman, Colin Henderson from ICI. But when the date was fixed Martin was on holiday, so it was Maurice Watkins and I who headed north to the Tontine restaurant, off the A19, for the fateful meal.

We started by saying we couldn't go higher than £1.5 million. Maurice was afraid that Martin would have a fit if we did. But Colin Henderson turned out to be a born negotiator, hardened by his years of experience with ICI, and I suppose he knew he had us by the balls. Pally was outside in the car park, and the Middlesbrough contingent knew that a deal was going to be done, so they had the whip hand.

It got to the point when it became a real argument, a shouting match across the dinner table. I told 'Boro that they had a serious problem, because if we walked away then they would be left with a seriously unhappy player. I made the point that he was only 22 years old and they were denying him the chance of bettering himself. They had been in receivership and our offer would allow them to recover a lot of their losses.

As the temperature rose, we took a break but when we came back the guy was sticking to £2.5 million and not a penny less. Having gone up to £2.1 million, Maurice and I stepped outside for a last time to discuss the next move. He said: 'Bugger it, we'll make a final offer and if they say "no" then we'll just walk out the door.' So we went back in, offered £2.3 million and made it clear there would be no more movement. They said: 'Okay, but we'll have to be paid in cash.' I thought: 'Bloody hell, take the balls off me too!'

By then we were into the early hours of Tuesday morning. We had to get Gary registered by lunchtime to play against Norwich on the Wednesday. So we went to Ayresome in the middle of the night and got their young secretary up to get the paperwork done. Maurice and I didn't get back to Manchester until 5.30 am and he had a meeting at 8 o'clock.

So it was an expensive and taxing evening out, and I think we even paid for the meal. But was it worth it? Absolutely. Looking back, there is no doubt that we got a bargain, no matter how expensive it seemed at the time.

When I first saw Pally playing for Middlesbrough in a Freight Rover Trophy game at Rochdale I thought he bore a slight footballing resemblance to Alan Hansen. Our chief scout at the time, Tony Collins, had the same view, being impressed at the way the boy carried the ball out of defence, but added the rider that he was lazy and lacked concentration. Those were his very words.

Well, Pally is a relaxed character, and I suppose you could say he could be lazy, if you left him on his own with his Mars bars. But he had a great natural pride in himself, and I felt that he would respond to motivation – and so he did.

Gary had so much going for himself in terms of ability and, though it wasn't widely recognised, he was lightning quick, the fastest man at the club by a mile. We lined up a 100-metres race, and we put him against Giggs, Ince, Parker and Kanchelskis – and he murdered the lot of them. Once he got that big stride going, Pally was a high-velocity athlete.

Still I must admit that when I saw him stripped for his medical, I thought: 'Jesus Christ, he's a bag of bones, a matchstick man. Those skinny thighs, there's nothing there.' So we put him on a weights programme, every day at The Cliff, our old training ground; he developed quickly, soon you could see a massive change in his physique, and he was fine. Mind, he wasn't keen on the weights and he used to try and dodge the extra work by nipping out of the gym door into the car park, but I would catch him and whisper the error of his ways.

Gary was unlucky in his first match as a United man, being turned by Robert Fleck – himself a decent player, quick and aggressive – and it cost us a goal in a 2-0 home defeat. He was unfortunate, too, in that he was a young man attempting to settle into a team containing five new players, and one which soon was hard-hit by injuries. Another new signing, Neil Webb, snapped an Achilles while playing for England, then Bryan Robson did his calf and Viv Anderson his knee. Bryan and Viv brought so much to the side in terms of grit and determination that we lost a lot, and the young newcomers suffered because of it.

For much of that season we were badly fragmented and there was no consistency about us. We couldn't pick a regular team and even though we won the FA Cup, we weren't settled, even having to play one of our new midfielders, Micky Phelan, at right-back in the final against Crystal Palace. It wasn't until we brought in Denis Irwin, then Peter Schmeichel and Paul Parker, that we forged an absolutely superb defensive line, with Pally and Steve Bruce at its heart.

Benefiting enormously from the continuity we eventually achieved, the pair of them struck up a brilliant partnership and became the backbone of the whole team. I think they were made for each other, one complementing the other perfectly. Brucie had a great personality. He didn't have Pally's pace but he was a born leader, he could read a game and he would stick his head in anywhere. Steve was the best attacker of a ball I have known. He must have had his nose broken at least five times, but he never bothered to get it fixed because he knew it would soon be happening again.

As for Pally, he was always worried about getting his good looks ruined but somehow it never happened to him, which is astonishing for a centre-half over so many seasons. It wasn't until his last year with us that he had a head injury, when he needed three stitches above his eye, and then he made a ridiculous fuss about it!

Not that he wasn't brave, because he was. He wasn't demonstrative about it, but he could stand up to any physical pounding, as he did to such telling effect against Wimbledon at Selhurst Park in the FA Cup in 1994. There was huge significance in that game because of all the hype about how they were going to batter us, but Pally put the fearsome John Fashanu in his pocket. He was just awesome that day, playing a gigantic part in our 3-0 win.

By then he was peerless among centre-halves in England, very calm and composed. My only worry about him was that he tended to be a slow starter in some games, but once that first 15 minutes was out of the way then he got into the flow of the action and I could breathe easily.

From this distance, it's not easy to see why he didn't collect more than his 22 caps, although his ongoing back pain didn't help. Of course, the England management valued the leadership qualities of Tony Adams, and it's a fact that the pair of them, though both right-footed, played left centre-back for their clubs. But I could never understand why they weren't given an extended run together, because both could have played either right or left and not much would have got past them.

As for all-round technique, Pally was very accomplished, being a terrific natural striker of the ball, and there was a time when he started sauntering forward to get involved in free-kicks. I have to say, though, that he enjoyed variable success.

When we met Pecsi Munkas on the way to winning the European Cup Winners' Cup in 1990/91, Pally shoved everyone out of the road over in Hungary, so somebody rolled the ball to him and he kicked the ground! Then there was a penalty shoot-out in deep mud in Moscow, and his shot hardly reached the line. We were 2-0 up on penalties and still got knocked out, can you believe that? So I don't want to dwell too long on Gary's dead-ball expertise, though he did hit a good one against Blackburn on the night we received the first Premier League trophy in 1993, and his face as he celebrated was a picture of glee.

In the end, he had a lot of problems with his back and we signed Jaap Stam because we had to look ahead, but Pally's departure represented a big loss to us, both in terms of his physique in the middle of our defence and his phenomenal levels of consistency.

He went back to his beloved Middlesbrough – he always returned to that part of the world as often as possible when he was with us – and more recently he has been doing all right as a television pundit, although there was one game when I had to give him a little bit of stick afterwards. When we played City the other season, he was on the air with Niall Quinn and we had two penalty kicks turned down. Quinn said he wouldn't have given them, and then Pally started to agree with him. The big sook!* When I saw Peter Schmeichel and Steve Bruce a little later, I left them in no doubt as to my feelings: 'You can tell that big lanky so-and-so, he's a ****ing Manchester United man, and he's not to forget it!'

In reality, I know perfectly well that Pally never would forget that. He was always a credit to the club, to the game and to himself, and I'm proud to have been associated with him.

*uncomplimentary Scottish word (used affectionately in this instance!).

Sir Alex Ferguson,
Old Trafford,
September 2008

PRELUDE

I stormed across the Old Trafford dressing room towards Alex Ferguson, and he was advancing on me with the light of battle in his eye. If we hadn't been grabbed and forcibly restrained by the likes of skipper Bryan Robson, coach Brian Kidd and assistant boss Archie Knox I dread to think what might have happened.

The manager had started raving at me at half-time in an FA Cup tie against Queen's Park Rangers and, having suffered his verbal lashings frequently during my first season and a half at the club, this time I just snapped. Anybody who knows me will testify to the fact that I am, by nature, a laid-back kind of guy, but this time he had gone way too far with his insults. In that fleeting, white-hot moment, I was boiling with rage and might even have been ready to go toe to toe.

Such an explosive scenario might not sound like the ideal springboard for a trophy-laden future at one of the world's premier sporting institutions, or for an amicable working relationship between a footballer and his boss, but so it proved.

That unashamedly passionate episode proved to be the watershed in my time at Manchester United. It led to deep-seated respect and genuine warmth, certainly on my side and, I have every reason to believe, the feelings were mutual.

There were rows, plenty of them, in the years that followed, but by then we understood each other, knew in our hearts, in our very guts, that we were singing from the same hymn-sheet. We both wanted to win football matches, to explore the limits of our ability, to take our game to a new level, and to do it in the name of Manchester United.

There follows between these covers the tale of how we did our damnedest to achieve our ambitions at Old Trafford, together with an honest account of my triumphs and periodic tribulations with Middlesbrough, and reflections on my treasured time in an England shirt. If I have whetted your appetite, then read on ...

Gary Pallister
Yarm
September 2008

CHAPTER ONE

ALEX FERGUSON? BLOODY HELL!

There is not the tiniest shred of doubt about who was the dominant figure in my professional life during my trophy-laden years at Old Trafford. As the man who helped me to achieve almost all of my goals, Alex Ferguson stands alone, a truly colossal influence. But precisely what shade of character is the prodigiously successful Scot? It was not always easy to tell, because you were never quite sure what to expect from him.

For instance, I have seen him handle himself impeccably in meetings with the good and the great, exuding dignity and authority as he has been introduced to some of the world's leading politicians. Yet I have played cards with him and had games abandoned because he has thrown the whole deck into the air like a spoilt child. As Choccy McClair put it once: 'You'd give your kids a clip if they behaved like that!'

Usually the card school comprised myself, the Gaffer, physiotherapist Jimmy McGregor, Robbo, Brucie and Denis Irwin, and on practically any bus journey at least four of us would would have a game going in the back seats. It wasn't long before I discovered that playing with the future Sir Alex could be absolute murder. It wasn't a matter of money, it was just that he detested losing at anything. If luck wasn't with him, he could fly into sudden rages, hurling the cards across the aisle, and it could be acutely embarrassing. It was hard to know where to put your face, because he was the manager and supposed to be setting an example. We'd all be trying not to laugh and it would be a case of: 'Has anybody seen the ace of spades?' or 'Where's the two of diamonds?'

Often we played 'Hearts', a game where you have to chase the leader and pass on three cards. Obviously they weren't always favourable and if you gave him bad ones – and invariably that cruel fate fell to me – then he'd have the hump, snapping and snarling across the table. I'd think: 'God, I can't do anything else', but there he was muttering and growling at me as though he wanted to rip my head off. I used to dread it and always tried to manoeuvre the seating so I wouldn't have to pass anything to him. Trouble was, everybody else was doing the same, and usually I was outflanked. The manager's tantrums didn't always end the game, but usually they did because we couldn't find the cards!

I could never quite get my head round these two conflicting images of one of the most famous figures in sport. At one instant he would be taking charge of some mammoth match under the world spotlight, at another he would be chucking his cards like a bad-tempered brat. You had to witness it to believe it, but it was all part of the complex character of Alex Ferguson, arguably the greatest football manager who ever lived.

Such bizarre behaviour was unimaginable as I drove up to the Tontine restaurant on the A19 to meet the Gaffer for discussions about my prospective transfer to Manchester United in August 1989. All I knew about him was strictly second hand. Obviously I'd picked up on his fearsome reputation as the flintiest of taskmasters, a disciplinarian you crossed at your peril, but I'd never witnessed the infamous 'hairdryer' in action and, of course, he was on his best behaviour for our initial encounter as he was trying to get me to sign for his club. There wasn't even the slightest hint of his darker side as he talked glowingly about his ambitions at Old Trafford and the top-quality players he had already acquired. My contract negotiations could hardly have progressed more smoothly.

But when I arrived for work at The Cliff, United's training headquarters before the state-of-the-art installation at Carrington was opened, I soon came to understand the overwhelming weight of his presence. I'm not saying the players were intimidated by him exactly, but when he came down from his office on to the park, everybody snapped to attention and put that little bit extra effort into whatever they were doing. To me, that was a marvellous sign, because every club needs a manager with that kind of aura and authority.

All too soon, though, I began to experience Alex Ferguson in the raw, and I'd be a liar if I said I enjoyed it. Despite vast expenditure, of which I was the single most costly item, things weren't going brilliantly for the team in the manager's third full season in charge and we found ourselves uncomfortably close to the wrong end of the old First Division table. Accordingly he must have been under intense pressure, and he made no attempt to disguise his feelings.

Surprisingly, maybe, the first major eruption was not after my first couple of games, in which we were beaten by Norwich and Everton, nor even after my fourth, the cataclysmic 5-1 defeat by Manchester City. That day at Maine Road I think he was in shock. We expected him to explode but he was too dumbfounded by the whole shattering scenario of being hammered by our local rivals to get torrid with us. Instead, apparently, he went home, went to bed and stuck his head under the pillow.

So he showed a little patience with me, realising that my head must have been in a spin following the painfully protracted process of my transfer from Middlesbrough, but it wasn't long after the City debacle that he was screaming and shouting in my direction, and once started, the storm that raged over my head showed precious little sign of abating as that crushingly disappointing League campaign wore on.

From quite an early stage it was obvious that there were certain players who copped it, particularly the younger ones, and I seemed to cop it the most. It was understandable up to a point because the press were having a field day, singling me out for particular vilification in view of my £2.3 million fee, which equalled the British record at the time. I was being portrayed as his biggest mistake, so perhaps he felt he had to get more out of me. Certainly it's fair to say that throughout our time together he felt I needed to be pushed, and was never averse to giving me a metaphorical (thank goodness) kick up the backside. To be strictly honest, most people in the game have reckoned that I needed a rocket every now and then. It wasn't that I was lazy, merely that I have a relaxed outlook on life.

That didn't make me feel any better, though, when the Gaffer was tearing into me mercilessly after games, in front of the whole dressing room. I'd grown used to this sort of treatment from Bruce Rioch at Middlesbrough, but I was desperate not to get embroiled in another such bitter and ultimately destructive situation.

At this point, I must stress that there was a crucial difference between the Ferguson and Rioch approaches. With the United boss there were no grudges or repercussions, it was all forgotten by the next day. When you met him again it was difficult to imagine there had ever been a barney, because invariably he was upbeat and positive, focusing intently on the next game, whereas with Rioch the resentment tended to simmer damagingly.

Also, it's important to emphasise that Alex Ferguson was magnificent in the way he protected his footballers by always keeping his criticism within the dressing room. No matter what tirades he had subjected us to, in public he would always back us to the hilt, and he told us never to worry about what was being said in the press, much of which inevitably involved his own immediate employment prospects.

Still, being on the business end of the 'hairdryer' was pretty gruesome and during my first few months in Manchester I found it extremely difficult. I suppose I was still awestruck at being there at all, and was reluctant to take issue with my boss. I was desperate not to make things worse and the last thing I needed was to fall out with Alex Ferguson.

That said, my early reactions varied according to the particular situation. If I felt I had made a bad mistake then I would put my hand up, admit the blame, take the brickbats and get on with life. But on some occasions, when I felt he was downright wrong and the other lads agreed with me, I would stand up for myself and fight back. Perhaps he was trying to see how far he could push me – he was due to discover the answer to that on the fateful day we met Queen's Park Rangers in a cup tie – but it was evident that he just couldn't countenance losing any kind of argument, no matter how trivial.

It's ironic that often I am painted as a complete failure during my first 18 months at Old Trafford, yet at the end of my first season, 1989/90, I was voted player of the year by the fans, so I must have been doing something right.

My turning point as a Red Devil, really the crossroads of my entire career, arrived on 7 January 1991, a Monday night, when we were entertaining Queen's Park Rangers at Old Trafford in the third round of the FA Cup. We came in 1-1 at half-time, having lost an early lead shortly before the break, and the manager started having a go at me, saying I was letting their centre-forward Mark Falco push me around. I thought he was wrong, that I hadn't been playing badly, and I told him so. Then suddenly the situation escalated to the very edge of control.

He called me something – I think it might have been a wimp – and it must have caught me on the raw. I just snapped, leapt to my feet and lost my rag totally, and simultaneously the Gaffer blew a gasket. On my part it was as though a dam of frustration had burst. All my resentment about the times I felt he had attacked me wrongly came bursting out with a vengeance, and as I stomped towards him, I was in the grip of an all-consuming rage.

In those few torrid moments, with bitter insults flying in both directions, he was marching towards me, and he wasn't about to kiss and make up. Fair play to the manager, I'm 6ft 4ins while he's a lot shorter and more than 20 years older, but I don't have the slightest doubt that, fleetingly at least, he was bent on lamping me. Luckily Brian Kidd grabbed me – I think it was Kiddo, but I was that mad I can't be certain – and Archie Knox took hold of the Gaffer.

For a long period at Middlesbrough, I'd been at loggerheads with Bruce Rioch and now it flashed across my mind that, whatever the consequences, I couldn't let it happen again, so I was ready to fight back with all I had.

With the restraining hands of Kiddo and Archie still on us, we did not exactly conduct a coolly reasoned debate. He roared at me: 'You're not going out second half, you're a joke, you're a disgrace.' I flung my boots off and informed him: 'I wouldn't f****** play for you anyway.' Or words to that effect. Whatever, we said some terrible things to each other.

Eventually he calmed down a bit as I carried on taking my gear off, but then he started up with another rant and again I responded in kind. For the second time in a couple of minutes we were striding towards one another with violence on our minds, but this time I was seized by Bryan Robson and another of the lads, while Archie collared the Gaffer again.

At this point I was convinced, as I sat on the dressing-room bench contemplating an early bath, that my Manchester United career must be at an end. But Archie had pulled the boss to one side, and I had a fair idea who they were talking about. The gist of Archie's argument was that United needed their centre-half out there for the second period, but I don't think the Gaffer wanted to listen at first. He was growling and muttering and scowling, you could practically see the steam shooting out of his ears.

But the next second he rounded on me and said, almost between clenched teeth: 'You're not getting away with it that easily. Get back out on that pitch for the second half.' At that moment I was not for turning, and while my remarks were not eloquent, certainly they were forceful. I told him: 'Am I f***? No chance am I playing for you. You can f*** off.'

My brain was still buzzing but Archie came over to calm me down and the other players were telling me: 'Do it for the lads and for yourself, if not for Alex Ferguson.' So I was convinced, albeit reluctantly. I did go back out and we won 2-1, thanks to a goal by Brian McClair about 15 minutes from time.

When we came in afterwards I was still boiling from the half-time confrontation, and the manager, though placated somewhat by the victory, was still seething. He had another little dig at me, just in passing rather than a full-blown insult, and I can't remember whether I reacted or not. If I did it wasn't on anything like the scale of our previous clash.

I went home after the game with my mind in turmoil. I knew I couldn't merely allow the incident to pass or it might fester in the manner of my relationship with Rioch at Ayresome Park. We had a day off after the Rangers match so there was plenty of space for me to stew on matters, but time did not prove to be a great healer. After my day away from the club I was still just as upset as before.

In that frame of mind I determined to go and face him after our next training session on the Wednesday morning, though I realised I might not have to initiate the meeting. It seemed more than likely that I might be slammed on the transfer list.

Despite my battle with the Gaffer, and my conviction that I was in the right, I didn't want another confrontation. I didn't want to leave United, but the air had to be cleared after he had pushed back the boundaries of what I considered to be acceptable behaviour. At least if I had to go then I would depart having said my piece.

To that end I worked out what I would say in every conceivable scenario which Alex Ferguson might throw at me. I was going to tell him how I thought I was getting on at the club, what I might be doing wrong, where I thought he might have a point, the whole works. I thought I'd have every base covered when I went into his office.

On the Wednesday I went to The Cliff and the Gaffer spoke to me a couple of times during training as if nothing had happened between us. But that did nothing to put me at my ease. I couldn't really concentrate on my work, which must have been obvious, but nothing was said. As I showered after the session, I psyched myself up by going over ever eventuality yet again, then one of the YTS lads popped his head round the door to say the Gaffer wanted to see me in his office. This was it.

Up the stairs I went, tapped on his door and walked straight in. Usually I would knock and wait for an answer, but I just wanted to get it over with. The Gaffer just stared at me, perhaps shocked that I had strode in without being invited. After that tense moment, he told me to have a seat and I was all up for the slanging match which would inevitably ensue. Then he sat down, gazed at me across his desk and dropped the biggest bombshell I could have imagined.

I can still recall his exact words: 'I want to apologise for what I said at half-time in the game.' You could have flattened me with the proverbial feather! Of all the possibilities I had mulled over, there was never the tiniest thought that he might say sorry. I just wasn't prepared for it and, suddenly, I felt totally deflated. All my brave intentions about talking things through just vanished into the air. With me sitting there utterly flummoxed, no doubt with my jaw sagging, he continued: 'I went too far. I said things that I should never have said. It was wrong.'

I couldn't believe the evidence of my own ears. I knew that Bruce Rioch would never have made such an admission, and Alex Ferguson was reputed to be on a whole different plane, the most vitriolic of all footballing ogres. I couldn't do much more than nod my head, rather dumbly he might have thought, as he went on to explain that he couldn't countenance having fights with his players at half-time.

He told me: 'I've got ten minutes to get my message across, as quickly, clearly and maybe as bluntly as possible. I say things which come off the top of my head and I just fire away. I went beyond the pale this time, but I cannot have players reacting the way you did.'

I understood his point, but I'm sure he also appreciated that he had pushed me too far. He knew I had to react for my own self-respect. Maybe I should have apologised as well for trying to get into what could easily have ended up as a physical confrontation, but I continued my impersonation of a nodding donkey, we shook hands and that was the end of it.

You could say it was a superb piece of man-management because, from that day onwards, he had my total respect. He had been man enough to admit that he had stepped over the mark, and that took real courage.

Is it conceivable that he stage-managed the whole thing to see how far he could push me? Was it all part of his renowned psychology? After all, the possibility – probability, even – that he uses his anger as a tool to motivate people has intrigued observers ever since he moved to Manchester. To this day, I can't say for sure, but I don't believe that was the case on this occasion. Certainly he wasn't above doing things in a calculated way to produce a reaction, but on the day of the Rangers tie he had appeared absolutely livid, spouting venom at me. If he was putting me on, then he must be the finest actor ever to walk the earth.

After that, there was a subtle change in my relationship with Alex Ferguson. I felt a little more comfortable with him, though I still got bollockings from time to time. Evidently he felt he had to be on my case perpetually because of my approach, which some have called laid-back and others, less charitably, described as lackadaisical. It seemed that he had to be at my throat much of the time, pushing me as hard as he could. So in one sense it didn't change anything, but I sensed that now he knew exactly where I stood, that at least I had some fight in me and would not submit meekly to serial lashings. Now, at least, we could respect each other on a more meaningful level than before.

Though I felt he was picking on me at the time, I should emphasise that most of the lads came in for their share of Ferguson flak at one time or another. For instance, there was the famous head-to-head with Peter Schmeichel at Anfield in January 1994 after we had lost a three-goal lead, a truly spectacular contretemps which made mine seem like a mere skirmish. The pair of them were spewing obscenities at each other and it looked like blood would have to flow.

Peter was twice as young as Alex Ferguson, twice as broad, and a supremely intimidating physical specimen, yet still the manager looked as if he wanted to tear our goalkeeper limb from limb. The Gaffer would never back down; he'd front up in any scenario, which was a measure of the man. People call him intelligent, but I don't think he'd have been too intelligent to have fought Peter that day. Once again, it's hard to imagine that the manager was attempting deliberate provocation, such was the naked passion on display, though there's only one person who knows for sure, and that's the Gaffer himself.

Household names were not exempt from a roasting. I've seen tough guys like Mark Hughes and Roy Keane catch it hot and strong, and once or twice he even had a pop at Robbo. Mind, it wasn't often that Bryan had a bad game, so it was very rare for him to feel the rough edge of the manager's tongue, but the fact that the manager was willing to confront his Captain Marvel proved that he wasn't daunted by reputations. Probably the only man to escape altogether down the years was Eric Cantona, and that wouldn't have been because the boss was afraid of him, more that he felt a row would be unproductive where the Frenchman was concerned.

When the Gaffer was handing out a dressing-down, the other players would sit around thinking 'Thank God it's not me.' You would try not to attract attention to yourself in case suddenly he remembered something you'd done wrong and turned on you. An outsider might surmise that such treatment could be destructive to individuals, but I never saw anyone wiped out by it or shrink into their shell as a result. We were all top professionals and no one wanted to be seen as a soft touch by allowing a bollocking to knock him down. Mostly everyone took it on the chin and maybe, now and then, had a dig back. I suppose it's all about bravado – there was a lot of testosterone in that dressing room!

I never had a problem with taking criticism if I felt it was deserved. That wasn't the case when the Gaffer and I had our battle royal following the FA Cup tie with Queen's Park Rangers, but it was a different story at Liverpool in September 1990. I had a shocker as we conceded three first-half goals on the way to a 4-0 hiding, and he took me off at the interval after ripping into me in the dressing room. One of his milder observations was: 'You'll never make a centre-half as long as you've got a hole in your arse.' The Gaffer always had a way with words!

The point was that I knew I was having a rotten game, he was right to take me off and he got no complaint from me. After the game he announced to the press that I'd been injured, which was his way of protecting me from adverse publicity. I guess he was looking after his own back, too, as he had just paid a king's ransom for me, but I was grateful, all the same.

Of course, it wasn't all strife and trauma, far from it. When things were going well, which was most of the time during my nine seasons at the club, he liked to mess about and have a laugh. Sometimes he'd use the overpowering force of his personality and his knack of intimidation to get you going – then you'd realise he was just taking the mick.

Invariably, though, I believe his ruling consideration has always been to make Manchester United the best. He was professional enough to put aside his own dislikes if he had a really good player who wasn't to his taste off the field, always provided that the individual wasn't upsetting the spirit of the team, and he would be ruthless enough to tell anybody if they were not performing to the rigorous standards required at Old Trafford. I've seen people reduced to tears at the prospect of leaving the club, but nothing clouded his judgement if he believed something was right for Manchester United.

Sometimes you wondered if there were any feelings. How could anyone appear so cold and heartless as he did on occasions? But if you're going to run any club successfully then you can't hide from the hard decisions, and Alex Ferguson didn't.

That said, and whisper it softly, the Gaffer does have a nice side which doesn't get much publicity. There have been plenty of instances when he has taken a player under his wing and helped him to solve personal problems. Like Sir Matt Busby before him, Alex Ferguson understood that players had to be right in their private lives to produce their best on the pitch, and he would spare no effort to help. I knew from experience exactly what he was like as an agony uncle, and certainly I felt indebted to him.

He prized loyalty extremely highly, and if people were doing the business for him on the park, then he would give that back in any way he could. It was an appealing part of his nature that many people didn't see.

What lifted him above other managers, made him the most staggeringly successful of his own or any other generation, was the ability to get the very best out of the people under him. He could always recognise born winners, people like Robson, Bruce, Hughes, Keane, Ince and Cantona, individuals with a mental strength which most others simply don't have. And, crucially, he had the golden gift of putting them all together and giving them a structure within which to operate.

Despite the volcanic side of his nature, which is always prone to erupt, sometimes when it is least expected, I do feel a tremendous personal warmth towards him. Undeniably he can be harsh, and a little bit of a bully, but I'll always love to see him. Whenever I go back to Old Trafford he invites me into his room for a coffee and a chat, and even though I'm no longer working for him, he'll still have a pop at me, probably taking issue with something I've said on television a few weeks ago. At least it keeps me on my toes …

CHAPTER TWO

HOW CAN YOU BE A PROPER CENTRE-HALF IF YOU NEVER GET BOOKED?

I'm a Teessider through and through, but the record says I was born in Ramsgate, Kent, so I'd better explain myself. My dad, Ian, was a fitter, who was working on a contract down in the Garden of England in 1965, so I spent the first six months of my life there. When that contract ended, he found more work in the Coventry area for a while but the family moved back to its Teesside base – Dad hailed originally from Billingham and my mother, Pat, from a mixture of Thornaby and Billingham. But though the Pallisters are north-easterners, and would never want to be anything else, Ramsgate held fond memories for Mam and Dad and we used to go back there quite often for holidays when I was growing up.

We are quite a clan, with both my parents coming from big families. Mam's father died when she was very young and when her mother remarried, my mam ended up with two new half-sisters and a half-brother. Dad had three sisters, one of whom, Mary, died in 2005, and three brothers, one of whom passed away many years ago. I have a lot of cousins, so many that I have always found it hard to keep up with them.

Then there is my sister, Karen, who is three years older than me. She was always the brains of the family, which made life difficult for me when I started school. Because she was extremely clever, everyone expected me to do just as well as her academically, but that was never the case. Right from the off I had different interests in my life, namely a succession of sports – football, cricket, athletics, basketball. Sport was my love, my passion, and it totally overshadowed my schoolwork. At that time, I guess, it would have made my mam and dad a lot happier if I had been a little bit more scholarly, but I couldn't change the way I was.

When the family returned to the north-east, my dad worked for ICI in Billingham for many years, and when Karen and I were off to school, my mam went back to work in the tax offices in Middlesbrough. At first we went to live with Nana and Grandad, Mam's mum and dad in Billingham, and stayed there until eventually we found a house in Norton, just down the road, where my parents still live to this day.

As a nipper, I indulged my obsession with sport in general and football in particular at every opportunity. My dad was more of a rugby man, playing for the Billingham club, but he never pushed me into the oval-ball game. He understood that my heart was somewhere else and, anyway, my mam always loved football. They both encouraged me to play, though there was one worrying interlude when it looked like I might have to stop.

When I was seven or eight I developed a limp. I think Mam thought I might be swinging the lead at first, so secretly she followed me to school one day to check up on me. But I would never have done anything like that to escape my lessons – perish the thought – and sure enough she saw me dragging my leg along the pavement, so she took me to see the doctor. He couldn't find anything wrong but thought I might be suffering from TB in my hip-bone. As a result I went to hospital for five days, where they tested me thoroughly but remained flummoxed by the cause of the limp, so they concluded I must have a 'lazy leg', something I would grow out of in due course. Probably there are people in the game who have known me well, notably one or two managers, who might say that eventually the condition spread to my whole body! Anyway, Mam wasn't too bothered because the specialist reckoned it should have no effect on my future life, provided I didn't want to be a professional sportsman, which was rather ironic as things turned out. She never spoke to me about it as I was growing up, not wanting to worry me, and it just seemed to get better. She finally mentioned it to me after I had been with Manchester United for several years, by which time it was irrelevant.

At this point I have a bit of an admission to make. Though I have always been an enthusiastic Middlesbrough supporter – I went to 'Boro games from about the age of six with my Uncle Malcolm, and I'll remain eternally grateful to him for that – it's a fact that as a primary school lad in the early 1970s I had a fondness for Leeds United too.

Even though I only managed to see Leeds in the flesh when they travelled to Ayresome Park, I suppose it was natural for me to have a yen for Don Revie's great side at the time, because they were so successful and so wonderful to watch. It was the glorious heyday of Billy Bremner, Johnny Giles, Jack Charlton, Peter Lorimer, Eddie Gray and the rest. Whenever I was kicking a ball about with my friends, which was just about every minute of my free time, I always wanted to be Peter Lorimer because he had the hardest shot in football. I was a centre-forward in those days, and I dreamed of becoming a sharpshooter like Peter, a fantasy which didn't quite materialise! As for Eddie Gray, who later looked after the youth side when I was at Middlesbrough, what a fantastic player he was, a great dribbler and a truly magical entertainer.

But the player from that fabulous team who made his mark on me, quite literally, was the fiery, dynamic little Scot, Billy Bremner. What a man. I came up against him when he was playing for Doncaster reserves at Belle Vue, at the time when he was managing Rovers. I was right at the start of my career with Middlesbrough while he must have been in his forties, so there was an age difference of more than two decades, and there must have been a difference of about a foot in height, too.

When I went up to get on the end of a long throw-in I was a bit puzzled. Usually you get the little feller standing in front of you, with the big centre-half behind you. Billy was playing sweeper and he stationed the giant stopper in front of me, while he moved to my rear, which I thought was strange. But the next moment I understood his tactics well enough as I received a sudden, violent dig in the ribs from behind me. I could hardly believe it. Obviously I had huge respect for him, but I turned and gave him a quizzical look as if to say 'What are you doing, you little squirt?' Even at that advanced stage of his playing days he was still desperate to win and willing to do practically anything to achieve his aim. He played through his whole career on the edge and he was at it right to the end, even at that level. Billy was a genuinely great footballer, but he had this fearsome side, and sometimes he overstepped the mark.

A lot of great players have that extra bite, that split personality. For example, the likes of Denis Law, Bryan Robson and Roy Keane always walked a tightrope with referees and the laws of the game. Sometimes, undoubtedly, they went a bit far, but that was an unchangeable part of their make-up. Take that spark away from them and they wouldn't have been the brilliant performers that they were. At the opposite extreme there are people like Bobby Charlton, who never got into trouble but still was among the finest players of all time.

Then there was a fellow called Gary Pallister, who didn't accumulate too many bookings. I used to take plenty of banter from the lads about that. The question they always asked me, though not always in such polite terms, was: how can you be a proper centre-half if you never get booked? I must admit that, even after they brought in the rule outlawing tackles from behind, I didn't get carded for a year and a half. I took all the ribbing in good part because I knew the boys weren't being serious. They were happy as long as I was doing my job.

I'm well aware that intimidation goes on in football, but it was never part of my game. On the other hand, centre-forwards certainly tried to put the frighteners on me down the years. Some of them would get on my case, get in my ear, from the first whistle. Soon enough I came to the conclusion that if I reacted to them I was merely rising to their bait, playing into their hands. They wanted to scare me, bully me, anything to disturb my concentration and take my mind off my game. The best policy, for me, was to ignore that treatment whenever possible.

Occasionally, whatever the violent intent, it could be quite amusing. For example, I shall never forget meeting Mick Harford, a feller with a formidably fearsome reputation, for the first time in a game against Luton at Ayresome during the 1980s, soon after I had got into the 'Boro team. About ten minutes into the match I intercepted a ball and tried to take it past him. He clipped my heels, I spiralled over and we were awarded a free-kick. As I was picking myself up from the floor, the referee was lecturing Mick, and his response is still vivid in my mind. 'I haven't touched him …' he said. Then he turned, slowly and deliberately, and looked me in the eye before adding, with his meaning crystal clear '… YET!'

It was a chilling scenario for a young player to be told that by one of the hardest men in the game. But, looking back, it was very funny, too.

Not quite so hilarious were a couple of encounters with another bruising centre-forward, Billy Whitehurst, the first of which was in a Division Two meeting between Middlesbrough and Reading. He had knocked out a long ball from left to right, which was unusual for Whitehurst, and as I'm tracking him into the box he caught me with a forearm smash, really cemented me one. I was on the floor, the referee and linesman had seen nothing, and he was just laughing at me, which told me all I needed to know about Billy.

Then there was a reserve game at Old Trafford when he was playing for Sheffield United. For some reason there wasn't a first-team game that weekend, and the manager had split the side to play in two reserve fixtures, so that all of us would get some match practice.

When the first ball was served up to Whitehurst I headed it away and he said: 'Do that again and I'll smash your nose all round your f****** face.' 'Fair do's Billy,' I thought. 'That's one way of playing football, but it isn't mine.' As it turned out, they won 2-0 and he scored both the goals. There was no point in getting into a battle with the likes of Whitehurst in a reserve game, so on that occasion I decided that discretion was the better part of valour and just let him get on with it.'

Returning to my boyhood, I suppose I'd have relished the chance to watch some games at Elland Road, but the opportunity never came along. Not that I didn't love going to Ayresome Park, because I did. I still recall vividly the team which won promotion to the First Division under Jack Charlton in 1974. They were real heroes to me. I was particularly thrilled by the front-men, like Alan Foggon, who was to play briefly for Manchester United under Tommy Docherty; David Mills, who became the first Briton to cost half a million pounds when he moved to West Bromwich Albion in 1979; and centre-forward John Hickton, who remains a massive idol in Middlesbrough. Then there were superb operators in midfield, Graeme Souness, Bobby Murdoch and David Armstrong, and a magnificent pair of central defenders in Willie Maddren, who went on to be a mentor of mine later in my career, and big Stuart Boam. The full-backs, John Craggs and Frank Spraggon, were terrific, too, an integral part of the team's terrific backbone. These were the people making an indelible impression on me during my early years in organised football, which I had first sampled at the age of seven.

As a little boy I was a centre-forward and, contrary to popular belief later on, I was quite quick in those days. In fact, I was pretty useful at athletics, especially the 100 metres, 200 metres and the long jump. In most football matches I found I would get plenty of one-on-ones with the goalkeeper, mainly because of my pace and because no-one had taught the kids how to defend properly. I loved the games for my junior school, the Frederick Nattrass, and even more after I moved up to Blakeston Comprehensive School. That had plenty to do with being in a team that was extremely successful – we won our league title in four seasons out of five – and with the fact that I was scoring freely as a roving striker who was much taller than most of his opponents. I was always big for my age and sometimes played for the year above me. Then around the age of 13 or 14 it seemed that I'd stopped growing and everybody appeared to catch me up. But when I was 15 to 16 I just shot up again; suddenly I was 6ft 4ins, taller than most people let alone the average schoolboy.

It wasn't until my last year at Blakeston that I became a centre-half. We were playing a local school, who majored on rugby but now they had decided to have a go at football. Week in, week out, they were hammered by all the other schools, but when we faced them our centre-half, a lad named Ian Watson, had been out at an all-night skating marathon. Three times we took the lead, and each time they equalised. So there we were, the best school team in the area, drawing against a side we should have been pulverising out of sight – and our centre-half couldn't keep his eyes open! Our manager, Malcolm Danby, blew his top, ordered Ian off the pitch and told me to move to centre-half. Malcolm was so mad that, at first, he forgot to send a substitute on. Anyway, I lined up at the back, we won the game 8-3, and it's where I stayed. I never played up front again.

My second love at the time was basketball. I'd been introduced to it by my mentor at school, Peter Swan, who was in his first year as sports master. He was a huge influence in the way that I developed and conducted myself. Peter was a stickler for rules, never allowing anyone to appeal against a referee's decision. I guess that rubbed off on me later in my career, because I was very rarely involved with referees, though that might have had something to do with the fact that at United, with the likes of Bryan Robson, Roy Keane, Paul Ince and Steve Bruce, there were always a lot of boisterous people getting involved with referees, so I could afford to keep quiet.

Back in the late 1970s, I had arrived at Blakeston with a little bit of a reputation, having had my fair share of scrapes at junior school. I was a big lad and seemed to attract a bit of trouble. There had been fights with other kids, occasional barneys with teachers; nothing outrageously nasty, but I suppose I was a little difficult to handle. Maybe I had a bit of a chip on my shoulder about being singled out sometimes. I felt it was because my size made me prominent. The situation was exacerbated because I came in as Karen Pallister's brother. The pressure was on to be the next brainbox, but I had other ideas about what I wanted to use school for. I didn't want to disappoint my parents but, as I mentioned before, I was never very interested in academic subjects.

Peter Swan appeared to understand where I was coming from, helping me to settle in and encouraging me with my sport. One afternoon at the sports hall, he sat me down and we had a serious one-to-one discussion about how important it was for me to channel my energies in the right direction, instead of wasting them on getting into trouble. Looking back, for a guy in his first year to have that sort of foresight was deeply impressive. It meant a lot that someone had taken the time out to think about my individual needs, and to care what happened to me. Some see teaching merely as a job, and don't really concern themselves with the development of the youngsters. But Peter was different. His enlightened attitude made a real mark on me, and I have always respected him for it.

Knowing I was quick and able to jump, he got me involved in hurdling and gave me extra coaching sessions at lunchtimes. Then he took me off to the district sports tournament at Middlesbrough athletics arena, where I won the schools hurdles race and went on to finish third in the county. Maybe Andy Gray, who offered the opinion that I had never been quick when I came out of retirement to play in *The Match* for Sky Television in 2004, should take note! Whatever, I was extremely grateful to Peter Swan and to Malcolm Danby, my house master and football manager.

I also played cricket for the school, and in my last year there was a bit of rugby, but it was never for me. We had a big lad called Pud, who must have been 13 stone at the age of 15. One day I was stood on the try-line and he came hurtling towards me. I thought: 'Do I really want to try to stop him?' I made up my mind quickly, just stood to one side and let him put the ball down for a try. That summed up my attitude to rugby. I just wasn't interested.

While playing successful schools football, I also turned out for a club in Norton called Barmoor Boys, though we didn't do too well. I remember us getting beaten 21-0 on one occasion, losing to a side called Nunthorpe, a nursery for Aston Villa. My association with Barmoor lasted only one season, and did nothing to enhance my credentials.

I left school at 16, basically not knowing what I wanted to do with my life. I managed only two O-levels, then I went to college to re-sit some more, which I suppose was nothing more than a cop-out because I didn't want to go out into the big wide world. In practice, college was a waste of time, except that I could still get plenty of football, basketball and cricket.

I was still 16 when I joined a football club called Stockton Buffs, having been recommended by Malcolm Danby. The Buffs operated in one of the higher senior leagues, but their under-18s were an average team at the time, in the bottom half of their table. Still, I must have made a reasonable impression because I played a couple of games for their senior side before the season was out.

Meanwhile college was going pear-shaped. I had started off in their first team, but then I was dropped to the second after only one match, which I couldn't understand because the standard was much lower than Stockton's. After that I fell out with the manager of the second team, who was also the religious education teacher. I got a few choice words off my chest and was promptly relegated to the thirds.

Thus I wasn't too happy as I reached the end of the college year, though I was cheered to receive a call from a guy called Rob Cushley, who was junior manager of Billingham Town. Rob talked encouragingly about my potential, but at first I felt I couldn't turn my back on Mick Lawler at

Stockton, who had been good to me. However, Rob knocked on my door, gave me the spiel and brought a form for me to sign. I was very keen to play at a higher level, I knew some of the Billingham lads, knew they were very good players, so I decided that I would make the move. As it turned out, the Stockton team collapsed anyway, so I didn't feel too bad about it in the end.

Now I left college, feeling distinctly disillusioned and still with no idea of what career path I might follow, beyond a vague and, at the time, seemingly impractical notion that I wanted to become a professional footballer. My next destination was a Youth Training Scheme course which was linked with ICI, and I'm bound to say it was hopeless. The idea of YTS seemed to be to get people off benefit while offering them some sort of useful experience, but basically it was no more than slave labour. I was given £25 a week and treated as a dogsbody wherever I went. I spent two months with a garage, two more with a plumbing and heating business, and two at a paper-packing place. I could raise no spark of interest in any of them, because none of them made the slightest attempt to educate me.

The government was paying to get me off their unemployment list, but then I became no more than fodder to be abused by the people in charge of these firms. It proved of no benefit to me whatsoever. I suppose it gave me something to do, and I met some decent people, but otherwise it was a complete waste of time. Maybe I was unlucky in my employers but, talking to my friends in similar situations, it appeared to be the norm. There was never any effort to give YTS lads any passion for the business, whatever it was. It was nothing more than pure exploitation.

All the while I had wanted to be a footballer, no matter how unrealistic it might have seemed, and that desire never left me through school, college and YTS. I guess I must have retained some sort of belief, too, despite never playing any representative football. My only honours, at district and county level, had been at basketball, and I'd actually turned town trials for a place in the regional basketball squad because they clashed with a school football game. I had to tell Peter Swan that my first love was football, and I think he felt let down, but he understood that football was what made me tick. Although he was disappointed after all the effort he had put in on my behalf, he never showed it, and I really respected him for that.

A week or so later I was in trouble for fighting with a lad in the changing rooms. I was marched into the office of the head of PE, who gave me a dressing down, but also accused me of letting down the school, myself and Peter Swan for not going to the basketball trials. It was a vicious attack which reduced me to tears, and really it was nothing to do with him. He was a joke as a PE teacher anyway. That stuck in my throat for a long time, and remains as one of my more painful schoolday memories.

Back on the football front, I was making progress of sorts, playing for slightly better teams all the time and gradually learning more about being a centre-half. I was thinking that if I could get to the Fourth Division, maybe play for somebody like Darlington or Hartlepool, I'd be made up, I'd have achieved my ambition. But the lads I knocked about with, they'd tell me: 'Pally, it's not going to happen. If you were going to be picked up by a professional club then it would have happened when you were 16, or even earlier. Be realistic and find a regular job.'

But still I dreamed and the move to Billingham Town, a better team with better players, gave me a lift at a crucial time. At least I was moving up the ladder, no matter how slowly, and I still had the eternal optimism of youth. I played my first season with Billingham at junior level, and we were pipped for the championship by a team called Smith's Dock. But we were a good side, we won three or four cups, and during that first season I received a massive boost from an unexpected quarter.

One day there was a knock at the door and standing there was this oldish guy, who said his name was Jimmy Mann. He was a scout for Grimsby Town and he asked me for a trial with the reserves. It came completely out of the blue as I'd never been linked with any professional club before. It sounded almost too good to be true.

Jimmy said Grimsby reserves were playing Doncaster reserves, and he'd pick me up from home to take me to the match. It seemed almost surreal. When he left I was pinching myself to see if I was really awake. I rang Mam at work and told her this guy had turned up on the doorstep to ask me if I wanted to play for Grimsby. I still couldn't really credit that it had happened and soon I was wondering if I had imagined the whole episode. But, sure enough, Jimmy called for me at the appointed time, then said he had to pop into Middlesbrough to get another young triallist. That turned out to be Peter Beagrie, who was still playing for Scunthorpe in 2006, having passed his fortieth birthday, since when he has become a Sky TV football pundit.

I started the game in a state of high anticipation, but was brought rudely down to earth when I gave away a penalty after only five minutes. Still, I felt I did okay for the rest of the game, did myself justice at least, and I was delighted when they invited me back for another trial. So I returned to Billingham on a high, only for my euphoria to be punctured when my club vetoed a further trial because they had so many cup finals coming up.

Perhaps I should have been a bit more determined in standing up for my interests, but I let it go and the Blundells Park connection was put on ice.

As that season wore on, having done pretty well for Billingham's junior side, I was called up by the seniors a couple of times, and again I made a favourable impression. Thus when Brian Hall, the club's stalwart stopper for some 20 years, decided to retire that spring, I was given the chance to replace him.

So I started the next campaign as centre-half for the first team, and I think I did all right, though I was still a skinny lad and not really punching my weight. Really there was nothing of me. I've always been a bad eater, filling myself with junk food but never putting on any weight. All the calories from the incessant crisps, chocolate and pop were just burned off by my sport.

But now, finally, I began to make some meaningful progress towards my heart's desire as, during that first term with Billingham's seniors in 1983, Middlesbrough expressed an interest in me. I got a shout to go down to Ayresome Park, where Malcolm Allison was the manager. I was so excited, thinking this might be my long-awaited breakthrough, so I was absolutely gutted when I felt I didn't do myself justice on the night of my trial.

I was playing for the reserves, and it wasn't long before I noticed that I wasn't as fit as the rest of the players, which was always a worry in my professional career. Extreme fitness never came naturally to me. I played alongside people like Bryan Robson, Roy Keane, David Beckham and Ryan Giggs, and they just seemed so naturally fit, as if they could run all day. But I was a big lad, with weight to carry around, and stamina never came easy to me. I was always struggling to fill my lungs. After long-distance running it took me a lot longer to recover than other lads, so it was a constant battle. In the early days I wondered whether this situation was going to nip my career in the bud.

Certainly, when I came off the pitch that night after making my first appearance for Middlesbrough reserves I was sorely disappointed, and I slumped down in the dressing room, thinking I didn't have a hope in the world. But the reserve team manager Willie Maddren, who had been the cultured centre-half in Jack Charlton's fine 'Boro team and had always been one of my role models, consoled me, telling me how difficult was to impress in a team containing four or five triallists. He put his arm round me and said: 'Listen, I've seen enough out there tonight to warrant keeping a close eye on your progress.' He added that I should go back to Billingham and work on my physique and stamina. I thought he was just being nice, trying to pick a boy up when he was so obviously down, but his interest was genuine.

After listening to Willie I went outside to Mam and Dad, who were supportive, but still I felt glum, thinking that I'd blown my one and only big chance. Dad cheered me up a bit when he told me Malcolm Allison wouldn't have known how poorly I'd played, because he had left the game after five or ten minutes. I thought that was extremely peculiar. How could he make his mind up about five triallists in ten minutes? Whatever, I went back to playing for Billingham and stayed there for the rest of the season, learning how to look after myself in a tough, physical league.

During that spring of 1984, with the club in increasingly desperate financial straits, Malcolm Allison was sacked as manager, and in the summer he was replaced by Willie Maddren. That did nothing to harm my personal prospects and I was a couple of months into my third season at Billingham, living on the dole with a few expenses from the club to help me out, when I got the call from Ayresome Park. This time it came from Barry Geldard, a 'Boro scout who had lived two doors away from us in Fuller Crescent, Norton, when I was much younger.

So I went for another trial with the reserves, at home to Oldham, and this time I felt as if I did well, and straight after the game Willie Maddren, or it might have been one of his staff, said to me: ' You're not working, you're at a loose end, so do you want to come and spend three months with us? Train and play for the reserves, and we can keep an eye on you. No strings attached at this stage, but it's an opportunity.'

I was only too happy to agree, but if I thought I was on a smooth path to soccer stardom then I had another think coming. There wasn't much glamour about sitting with the juniors and first-year professionals in their dressing room, and all the rancour in the air came as a bit of an eye-opener. Then, two or three days after I started my trial, there were a lot of valuables stolen from the players' clothes. I was the new boy and I got the feeling that all eyes were on me, a stranger on the dole. Fortunately it wasn't long before they discovered the identity of the thief and that was a tremendous relief for me. It was difficult enough for me to be fighting for my future in the game, without having extra pressure.

Still, I didn't really enjoy the environment because there seemed to be constant argument. I just didn't like the feel of it and actually thought about walking away from it all at one stage because the atmosphere appeared so negative. I suppose I was a little bit intimidated because most of the kids in the dressing room knew each other well, having grown up together at the club. Maybe they felt I had just come in and was taking away one of their mates' opportunity. I didn't feel comfortable and told my parents how I felt.

But I knuckled down and played the games, became a regular in the reserves and felt I was doing all right on the pitch. When my three months were up, Willie sat me down and said he wanted to put me on a month-to-month contract with Middlesbrough. The only problem was that there was no money, the club was skint. But Willie had found a solution. He'd had a word with a friend, Dick Corden, whose son Steve was also at the club, and the generous businessman was happy to sponsor my wages for however long he needed to.

At the time there was a story that Billingham got a couple of goal nets and a bag of balls out of my move, purely a goodwill gesture because Billingham didn't have any contractural rights beyond an agreement which prevented me from joining another Northern League club. Later on I'm told Billingham might have done even better out of me, receiving a set of strips when I signed for Manchester United! Okay, it's something, but it's still extremely small potatoes for helping a player along the way to a £2.3 million deal. I know Middlesbrough didn't have to do anything, but they might have felt that a few bob would have been a massive help to Billingham at a time when they were looking to get floodlights. 'Boro dragged a lot more money than I was actually worth out of the United deal, so I think they could have managed something more.

Going back to my personal situation in 1984, Willie offered me £50 a week, which did not exactly make me rich a rich man overnight. Considering the money I was already getting elsewhere, including my boot money at Billingham, I was no better off signing as a professional at Ayresome Park. In fact, by the time I had paid for the bus to get to Middlesbrough from Norton every day, I was probably worse off. But after talking at length to my parents, I decided that it might lead somewhere, and I signed a month-to-month deal. I was a bit peeved by the hand-to-mouth nature of the arrangement, but I didn't realise at the time how tough it was for the club. Not too long afterwards, when they went into liquidation, the precariousness of their situation would become frighteningly clear.

CHAPTER THREE

A DEBUT, DARLINGTON
AND DESPAIR

There was a certain air of desperation about Middlesbrough throughout 1984/85, my first season at the club. Cash was fearfully short and, on the footballing front, a disappointing winter turned into a spring of ominous foreboding. While I was continuing to learn my trade in the reserves, the first team nosedived perilously close to demotion from Division Two, scraping clear of the drop only on the final day of the campaign with a nervy victory over Shrewsbury.

I made no personal contribution to that escape, though there was one point during the season when I might have been pressed into senior action as an emergency centre-forward. First-team striker Archie Stephens was injured and, with the side playing direct, route-one football, they needed a big target man to step into the breach. Accordingly they decided to experiment in a reserve game by asking me to play up front in the first half, then trying Alan Kernaghan, another central defender a couple of years younger than me, in the second. The old magic from my earlier days as a spearhead did not resurface, and Alan was picked to face Notts County the following Saturday, retaining his place for several games.

Meanwhile I felt I was settling in pretty well in my principal role and had come to terms with my new life. Certainly, training every day made a huge difference, so I felt a lot fresher and fitter in the games, and it was a pleasure to line up alongside very good players such as Colin Cooper, who played sweeper behind me before he converted to left-back, the winger Stuart Ripley, and my old pal Peter Beagrie, who was soon promoted to the first team.

Still, though, I didn't think the overall atmosphere at the club was a healthy one. It struck me that there were a lot of older professionals who were taking the mick, seeing out their careers in a nice, comfortable berth without putting in the effort or dedication. They didn't seem to have any passion for the club and I don't think they did enough for a marvellous guy like Willie Maddren. All too often I would see a player arrive at

Ayresome on a month-to-month deal and play fantastically well, but after getting a long-term contract he would never be the same again. Willie trusted a lot of people and too many let him down, which I found exceedingly sad. He had such a hard job, with all the financial constraints, that it must have felt like working with his hands tied behind his back. I had tremendous sympathy with his plight.

Willie was such a lovely man, and he put so much effort into battling to keep his hometown club afloat. Some people said he wasn't ruthless enough, and perhaps that was true in some cases where people were taking advantage of him. But he deserves enormous credit for the way he brought through youngsters – like Cooper, Ripley, myself, Gary Hamilton and Gary Parkinson – and that policy was the catalyst for 'Boro's eventual renaissance. In addition it was Willie who brought in goalkeeper Steve Pears and the strikers Bernie Slaven and Archie Stephens, all of whom played vital roles in our resurgence. Always he tried to protect the kids by not throwing them into a relegation battle unless it was absolutely unavoidable; he understood that careless treatment could destroy confidence and entire careers. Later Bruce Rioch had to rely on youngsters, because there was no one else at the club and he had no choice. But they were all lads who had been nurtured by Willie and they proved a fabulous legacy to the next manager.

My association with Willie Maddren was colossally beneficial to me. In a way, he put his reputation on the line for me, after bringing me from non-League football and then pushing me through into the first team. I guess he believed in me. He took me for one-on-one sessions, placed me under his wing and guided me at a time when I needed it desperately. Willie was a footballing centre-half and I like to think that aspect of his play was apparent in my own. Maybe the footballing side of my game was as a result of being a frustrated centre-forward. I always liked to play a bit, to join in the team movement and have some attacking impact other than merely going up for corners. Maybe it would have been coached out of me if I had gone straight into the professional ranks from school, but coming up as I did, I had the chance to develop rather more freely and in my own time.

Eventually I made my senior debut as a 20-year-old at the start of the 1985/86 season. Having had a narrow escape from relegation the previous spring, and with his squad seriously depleted by injuries, Willie knew it was time to blood some of his proteges. Still, when he told me I was in for the opening day at Wimbledon, it took me by surprise because there had been no previous talk of me stepping up quite so soon.

The game was at Plough Lane in front of 2,844 people, two of whom were Mam and Dad. It was the beginning of the Crazy Gang era at Wimbledon, and I was facing Alan Cork, a terrific player, and Stewart Evans, who was about 6ft 6ins. We were battered 3-0, but I received favourable reports in the national and local press, and I was retained for the following midweek meeting with Mansfield in the League Cup. This was not a happy experience: they were two divisions below us, we lost 2-0 and I didn't have a particularly good game, so I couldn't complain at being left out for the next match. Shortly after that Willie pulled me into his office and explained that I wasn't going to be stretched in the reserves, so I'd be better off going out on loan, to play against seasoned professionals in competitive matches. He was right. Returning to the reserves after having a sniff of the first team leaves an empty feeling, so I was pleased when it was arranged for me to go to Fourth Division Darlington.

The Feethams experience was an eye-opener. I joined up on a Friday, had one training session, then was told I was in the first team for the Saturday game with Bristol City at Ashton Gate – and I still hadn't been introduced to manager Cyril Knowles. I got up at 5.30am to be at Darlington to board the bus at 6.15, and when we pulled away I still hadn't met the boss. We picked him up along the way, but he didn't come to the back of the bus to speak to his new player, even though there was plenty of time as we got stuck in traffic and didn't get to the ground until 2.30. We ran into the changing room, got stripped quickly while listening to the team talk, and still he hadn't spoken directly to me. Finally, as we were walking out, he patted me on the back and said: 'Good luck today, son.' That was it, my grand introduction to Cyril Knowles!

The game itself was a backs-to-the-wall job. We put in a sweeper after only ten minutes but we lost 1-0 with a fellow north-easterner, Alan Walsh, scoring the winner. It was a long and pretty sombre journey back, but I still didn't get to know Cyril any better because he made no further attempt at communication.

Later, though, I found he was a real character, both fearsome and funny. Cyril, who had enjoyed an illustrious career as a tough full-back and a cult hero with Spurs in the 1960s and 1970s, could be extremely intimidating, putting the fear of God into some of his players. He signed a right-back, Chris Evans, at about the same time that I arrived on loan, and after several games he told him that if he didn't put a performance in today he was headed straight back where he came from. Not surprisingly, the lad was a nervous wreck.

Sometimes Cyril would lose his head in training if things weren't going right. He was a shouter, a screamer, a bit of a bully who made you feel you were always walking on eggshells. He was a total contrast to Willie Maddren, though I did enjoy playing under Cyril. He tried to buy me when my time was up, but he was offering something minuscule and I'm happy to say that Willie told him I wasn't for sale. Mind, the state Middlesbrough were in, if Cyril had come up with a set of strips or a couple of extra footballs, then who knows …

I played seven games for Darlington and that spell did me a lot of good. My mind would have switched off had I been forced to return to 'Boro reserves. The Fourth Division offered a very physical style of football, I took plenty of hard knocks and that helped to toughen me up. I was facing big battering-rams of centre-forwards who wanted to kick me from pillar to post, and I had to cope.

That said, I have always relished the footballing side of the game. Rather than be in a battle, I liked to pit my wits against skilful opponents. I hate route-one football, always did and always will, but that's what I had to contend with at Darlington, where the aerial bombardment tended to be constant. Still, I look back on my stint at Feethams as a valuable part of my professional education. I'm all in favour of the loan system, especially at a club like Manchester United where so few of the kids break into the first team. Without competitive games in front of lively crowds, they would simply stagnate.

Around the same time as my Darlington adventure I received a call, a strictly illegal approach, from the manager of a Third Division London club offering me a move, and Willie told me that, during my first year at Ayresome, Norwich City had asked if I was under contract. He replied in the affirmative, technically a 'porky' because I was only on a temporary agreement, and the overtures stopped. On such decisions do whole careers hang. If I'd have got wind of it at the time, when I was on £50 a week, I might have been tempted, and I might have ended up playing next to Steve Bruce rather earlier than I did.

On returning to Middlesbrough, that November I won a regular place in the side alongside Tony Mowbray for the remainder of an extremely difficult season. There was no money and we struggled abysmally, with attendances hitting rock-bottom – sometimes we were playing in front of no more than some 4,000 people. Those fans who did remain loyal became really hacked off and, as is the way in football, poor Willie Maddren became an inevitable casualty of the slump. I remember his final game vividly. It was at Charlton on the first day of February, I was substituted, we lost 3-1, and afterwards Willie was taken into the boardroom, where he was sacked.

During the weeks leading up to that sorry occurrence, Bruce Rioch had been at Ayresome Park as a coach and, in retrospect, it seems likely that the club brought him in with an eye to giving him the top job. Certainly I had the impression that Willie felt his authority had been undermined by the appointment of Bruce, and I believe to this day that my old mentor was never offered a fair crack of the whip. Given that he had no financial resources, I thought he did a marvellous job in keeping the club where it was. On a personal level, he had invested vast amounts of time and energy in me, nothing was ever too much trouble for him, and because of my relationship with him, maybe his dismissal hit me harder than a lot of the other players.

Bruce was a stark contrast to his benevolent predecessor, ruling with an iron fist from the moment he took over. He introduced a stringent training programme, bringing us in mornings and afternoons, really steamrollering the boys with his running and fitness work. We expected a tough period as he stamped his authority on the whole football club, and that was exactly what we got. He was a hard man, a strong character, but we could see the need for discipline and, certainly at first, everybody knuckled down and tried to do what he wanted. Certainly, for the rest of that troubled season he didn't encounter any opposition on the training field. Possibly some of the senior professionals muttered behind closed doors because he was no respecter of reputations, and I could see where he was coming from in that respect. A cancer had invaded the club; there seemed to be no hunger to succeed and that was something he was determined to change. However, it would have been unrealistic to expect an instant turnaround and once more the team slid inexorably into the relegation dogfight.

Ironically, for the second successive year, the issue was decided on the final day at Shrewsbury, but this time with the wrong outcome for Middlesbrough. For me it was a particularly catastrophic occasion, as I was sent off in a 2-1 defeat. As it turned out we would have been demoted even if we had won, because Blackburn picked up three points in their last game to lift themselves just out of our reach, but there was everything to play for when we kicked off at Gay Meadow. The omens were bleak as we went a goal down in the first half, and there was rioting among our fans which caused the game to be stopped temporarily. But I managed to flick the ball on for Archie Stephens to equalise early in the second period, and I was still buzzing with the excitement of that when a pass was played through our defence. Unfortunately the Shrewsbury lad got half a yard on me; I stretched to get the ball and I touched it. Admittedly I didn't get a lot on it but I did play it fairly. However, the boy went over my extended leg, the referee judged it to be a professional foul – it was the first season in which players were sent off for that offence – and I received a straight red card. I don't think it was a correct decision. You know yourself whether you have made connection with the ball, and I had, so it was a legitimate tackle.

Now we were down to ten men with half an hour left in a game we just had to win. I had left the lads with a mountain to climb and I was utterly devastated, especially when I heard Shrewsbury's second goal go in as I was sitting in the bath, about five minutes from the end. All manner of thoughts went through my mind. Principally, even though I knew I hadn't committed a genuine foul, I blamed myself for being sent off and realised that the result might have been different had I stayed on the park. It was hard to take for a young kid trying to make his way in the game.

I was fined two weeks' wages by the manager, which disappointed me after I told him I had played the ball. It was obvious to me that he didn't accept my version of the incident, and that hurt. Perhaps he thought he had to impose the penalty to maintain discipline, which was all-important to him. For example, he used to fine us a tenner if we hadn't had a shave, which was all about being clean-cut and projecting the right image. That was a Clough thing, Bruce having played under the great man at Derby, but there was no way that introducing a few petty rules was going to transform Rioch into a second Clough.

There's a thousand and one stories about Cloughie. I'll never forget when I received my award as PFA Footballer of the Year for 1992. He was guest of honour at the ceremony, and he'd said a few nice things about me. Then as I shook his hand he stood on my foot and said: 'Don't get too big for your boots, son.' Of course, the two of us had a bit in common, both having played for Middlesbrough and both being local lads.

I'll always remember when I made my international debut against Hungary and, as a TV pundit, he was asked what he thought of Gary Pallister. Cloughie's response, in that trademark Teesside drawl, was: 'He looks a million dollars, and he's worth a million pounds!' For a guy like that to say such a thing about me made my day. In essence, he was saying we both came from the same place, from non-League clubs in Billingham, and eventually found our way into professional football. I loved that; it was great.

But I'm getting ahead of myself here. Back in the early summer of 1986, there didn't seem much to smile about as I contemplated life in the Third Division the following term. But even that morbid prospect was placed into some kind of perspective when, shortly afterwards, I went on holiday to Tenerife and phoned home, only to be told by my mother that Middlesbrough had gone into liquidation. Never mind worries about playing in a lower league; now, just as I was starting to build a decent reputation, it seemed I might not be playing anywhere, and irrational fears of ending up on the soccer scrapheap flitted through my brain. In retrospect, I don't suppose there was a realistic likelihood of that drastic scenario because, even though 'Boro were facing a potentially fatal crisis, at 21 I was young enough to bounce back somewhere else. All the same, it was a horribly anxious time, and it didn't exactly help the holiday go with a swing.

Duly I returned home to find that the bailiffs had closed Ayresome Park and our training facility at Hutton Road, putting huge shackles on the gates, creating a grim image which summed up a desperate situation. The players sat through the rest of that summer not getting paid, just waiting by the phone for news; then when it was time to resume training, we did so at Middlesbrough college because there was nowhere else to go.

We were told that because we weren't getting paid we could leave on free transfers and some, including Peter Beagrie, did depart. Peter, who joined Sheffield United, was a gifted individual and a big loss to Middlesbrough. He was a bright personality on and off the pitch, a really chirpy lad who always had plenty to say for himself, always looking to take the mick. As a player he could be a bit frustrating at times, because he would beat a defender by checking back, but then instead of crossing he would feint again, and again, and again. But there was no doubting his prodigious natural talent on the ball and there was a point where it seemed he might make a very big name for himself. He did have a terrific run at Everton, but never quite managed to take it to the next stage.

Peter's departure upset some people, but no one could blame him for going, and once we were relegated the fans had to get used to familiar faces using the exit door, the manager getting rid of a lot of the senior professionals, apparently because the club couldn't afford their wages. Perhaps just as pertinent in some cases, though, was the fact that they didn't have the necessary desire.

I was made aware of interest in me from Crystal Palace and was told I was within my rights to speak to them. So, with nobody coming forward to save 'Boro and the clock ticking, I went down to Selhurst Park to meet the chairman, Ron Noades, and the manager, Steve Coppell. Financially their offer wasn't great, especially as it involved moving to London, which I didn't really fancy. Although I had to consider every option, the whole package of heading south, finding a place to live, being on my own in one of the world's biggest cities … none of that appealed to me at the time, so I turned it down.

At that point I was still enjoying my football at Middlesbrough – my difficulties with Bruce Rioch having not yet reached a head – and I was still finding my feet as a professional. Although the team had been struggling, on a personal level I felt I was beginning to make a mark.

CHAPTER FOUR

TRIUMPH AND STRIFE

For a while it seemed as if Middlesbrough would not be allowed to start the 1986/87 season, but we went back to training anyway, hoping against hope that the heroic efforts of two men with a burning passion for the club – Colin Henderson, a leading figure with ICI, one of the area's main employers, and Steve Gibson, a 26-year-old local businessman – would save it from extinction. In the event, they engineered a financial package which was accepted by the League only ten minutes ahead of its final deadline on the day before the opening of the new campaign.

By then I had experienced the first of my serial dust-ups with Bruce Rioch. It was a hard time for everybody, with the lads receiving no wages and stuck in limbo about their future, but the manager was cracking the whip in training, apparently making no allowances for the situation. One day he blew up at me. I can't remember the precise details, but we were in a group and he told me he wasn't happy with the way I was working so I might as well go home. I up and left, just walked away. That was the first of many rows between us. I came back into training the next day but he hadn't forgotten the incident. He was in the habit of carrying on such things for far too long. As I mentioned, I had plenty of rows with Alex Ferguson over the years but he would put them behind him. With Bruce, you could walk past him down a corridor where you had to turn sideways to get past each other and he would ignore you.

For the rest of my time at Ayresome Park, there was always an uneasy truce between the two of us. We were two contrasting characters who couldn't get along. He was brought up with a military background and might have been a regimental sergeant-major, a real martinet of a disciplinarian, while I was laid-back and easy-going. He wanted to change my outlook on life, for me to become similar to him, and that was never going to happen so there was a clash of cultures straight from the off.

That said, I admired him as a coach and I thought that what he brought to the side was worthwhile. He wanted his team to play football, he organised us cleverly and he instilled a belief that we could do well. Bruce bullied young kids into believing that they could play and, unquestionably, he frightened a lot of people. Our average age at that time was about 20; he was a big name as a Scottish international, carrying a fearsome reputation as a midfield tackler and hard man who could also play a bit. I knew that what he was teaching was right; he was a good coach who spoke a lot of sense. But at times he was too overpowering and as people grew up then they began to ask more questions of his style. In all fairness, though, Rioch deserves credit for a hell of an achievement in getting us promoted back to the Second Division in 1986/87, given his chronic lack of resources. True, he had the benefit of a wave of talented kids coming through, thanks to Willie Maddren, but still he had to mould them together into an effective team – and he did.

The season got off to a distinctly surreal start as we had to play our first home game, against Port Vale, at Victoria Park, Hartlepool, because the gates were still closed at Ayresome Park. I was suspended for the first two games following my dismissal against Shrewsbury at the end of the previous campaign, but then I was reinstated in central defence alongside Tony Mowbray and we were comfortable together right away. In fact, with full-backs Gary Parkinson and Colin Cooper also playing tremendously well, we had a terrific back line and conceded only 30 League goals all term, easily the best record in the division. Given that degree of solidity, and with both Bernie Slaven and Archie Stephens scoring loads of goals, it was hardly surprising that we were in contention at the top of the table for most of the season. There was a little bad spell in February and March when we lost three out of four, but we finished with a fabulous burst to come second, only three points behind the champions, Bournemouth.

My first game of that season was away to Wigan, which proved something of a watershed. We were a very young side now, with lots of experienced men having left because of the financial position, and we suffered a terrible chasing in a goalless first half. As we headed for the dressing room at the interval, I remember one of their players shouting: 'Come on lads, this team's shite.' But somehow we managed to keep them at bay and we won 2-0. That was the game that raised our confidence and lifted us for the rest of the season. We had gone away from home, and won through sheer grit and determination. The funny thing was that their man had done Rioch's job for him at half-time by motivating us with his few well-chosen words. The crowds remained very small at first – after all, we'd sunk as far as we could sink – but as our momentum built, so the public responded to our effort and to the fact that there were so many local lads in the team.

That spring I managed my first League goal in an important 1-0 win at Carlisle, who were struggling against relegation and put up sturdy resistance against us.

I've always been the butt of jokes for not scoring enough goals for a lad of 6ft 4ins. I've always liked to attack the ball but I've been better in my own box than the opposition's, but this time was different. Bernie Slaven took a corner from the right, swinging the ball into the near post with his left foot, and I was completely unchallenged to head in from a yard out. I was that excited about breaking my scoring duck that I think my celebration ended down in our own goal. I don't know where I got the energy from. After that, I was anxious for the game to end, with my goal being the winner. I didn't want anybody else to score, not even a second for us!

At that point, during our promotion run-in, the whole team was on a high. We conceded only four goals in our last 15 games and I couldn't have been happier with my partnership with Tony Mowbray. Mogga was a wonderful lad, only 23 at the time but a natural leader, and one of the great things Bruce Rioch did was to make him captain. Bruce came out with the famous quote: 'If I was going to fly to the moon then I'd want Mogga alongside me.' So when somebody started a fanzine it was called *Fly Me To The Moon*.

In character Mogga could be compared to Bryan Robson, Tony Adams or Steve Bruce. He was always the biggest influence in our dressing room, a fantastic motivator. He was mature beyond his years, a born organiser and an inspiration to the rest of us. That was terrific for me because I was never a great talker on the park. I was always too tired to be shouting and pointing, but Tony certainly made up for my quietness. He was a fine player, too, and helped me to learn about being a centre-half in my early days. All my managers said somewhere along the line that I needed a kick up the ass, and I was lucky that I played alongside two great captains and motivators in Tony Mowbray and Steve Bruce.

Regarding Tony, even back in 1987 it was obvious to everyone who knew him that he was management material, and duly that has come to pass. He coached at Ipswich for three years, waited for the right job to come along and eventually took over the reins at Hibernian, where he forged an impressive reputation. I always felt that he would return to England eventually, though, and sure enough he moved into the hot seat at West Bromwich, ironically as the successor to Robbo. I'm delighted to see that he's making the most of it. Few would disagree that during

2007/08 West Brom were the best footballing team in the Championship and they fully deserved to win their title. Mogga is similar to Sir Alex in his footballing beliefs. He's always wanted his sides to express themselves by playing smooth passing football, attacking football. He wants them to entertain and he won't change that for anyone. He doesn't go for success at all costs, but sticks to his principles and he has emerged as a breath of fresh air in the modern game. Readers will gauge that I'm not the greatest fan of Bruce Rioch, but I must give credit where it's due and say that he had his Middlesbrough team playing the right way, and I think Mogga learned a lot from him.

As a personality Tony is a very understated type and some reckon he comes across as being too serious, but actually he's got a keen sense of humour. I must say, too, that he's an extremely strong person, having survived the tragic loss of his wife Bernadette during his time as a player with Celtic. Now he's got his life back on track; he's remarried to Amber, started a family and moved on.

As the 2008/09 season began he was facing a tough challenge in re-establishing West Bromwich Albion in the top division, but nobody should doubt that he was ready for it. I'll be watching his progress with a great deal of interest, and with immense confidence in his ability. Any club could count itself lucky to acquire his services and I'm certain that Mogga is destined to become a major figure in the game.

Returning to 1986/87, Middlesbrough clinched promotion in our penultimate game with a goalless draw at home to Wigan in front of more than 18,000 fans, and only then did the true scale of our achievement strike home to me. What a sea-change there had been in the fortunes of the club. One summer we were facing liquidation and the next we were celebrating a return to the Second Division. It seemed like a near-miraculous salvation after so many people had predicted we would slide straight down to the Fourth when we started the season with a crop of youngsters. So many were making their debuts, and there were plenty of others with only two or three games to their credit. Most of the older players, whose inexperience might have been invaluable in lifting us out of the division, had been released because of financial constraints. There was plenty of talent in the club but the odds against promotion were astronomical. As the wiseacres put it: 'You win nothing with kids.' Sound familiar?

Now Bruce Rioch was looked on as something of a miracle worker in Middlesbrough and, for all my personal differences with him, that was fair enough. He didn't want us to play kick-and-rush football. He had a system that he had drummed into us, all about passing the ball on the floor, working through midfield, making sure that the forwards got good quality of passes. We stuck to it all season, entertaining the fans at the same time as remaining solid, and we got our reward.

Yet for all the joy engendered by our success of 1986/87, there was no shortage of observers who reckoned we might come down to earth with a bump in 1987/88. The only major signing we had been able to make was midfielder Dean Glover from Aston Villa and it's fair to say that most of our fans expected no more than consolidation in the Second Division, especially when we made a shaky start, with only one win in our opening five games. We kicked off against Millwall and I found myself facing one of the guys who'd given me a rough ride in the Third Division, Tony Cascarino. When we'd played his former club, Gillingham, near the end of the previous campaign, we'd clashed and there had been a bit of spirited chat between the pair of us. With eyes blazing, he'd said to me: 'See you next time.' I responded with: 'You won't see me because you'll still be stuck in this f****** division.' But then he joined Millwall, where he was to form a superb partnership with Teddy Sheringham, and there he was standing in the tunnel for the first game of the new season, giving me a devilish grin as if to say: 'I'm back to haunt you!' We drew 1-1 that day and Tony and I had our usual battle, but he might claim the last laugh as Millwall pipped us for the title.

After our sluggish beginning we needed a big result and we got it in the form of a 1-0 win at Villa in September, which appeared to transform our fortunes. I don't think many people expected us to get anything there but, much as at Wigan during the previous term, this was a turning point, one that inspired a lot of confidence in the team. We grew as the season went on, as we got used to playing at a higher level, and through the autumn and early winter we went on a fantastic run, losing only one game in 20. Then came the inevitable blip, as we lost three on the belt around New Year, before we picked up the pace again on the run-in.

When we faced Leicester in the last game of the season, we only had to do as well or better on the day than Aston Villa to secure automatic promotion. There was a carnival atmosphere at Ayresome Park, with the fans thinking everything was done and dusted, especially as Leicester were stuck in mid-table with nothing to play for. But the Foxes hadn't read that particular script, taking a two-goal interval lead through Gary McAllister and Peter Weir. Bernie Slaven got it back to 2-1 with a goal which looked five yards offside, and after that I think everyone in the ground was totally confused. Whether or not we contrived an equaliser, everything depended on Villa's result at Swindon, and as play continued we were getting conflicting reports from the terraces. As we tried to do complicated sums about goal difference, we didn't know whether to go gung-ho to try and force a draw or hold on to what we had. In the end we lost, Villa drew and the two clubs had the same goal difference, but Villa claimed second place because they had scored more goals. What an anti-climax! Success had been viewed as a foregone conclusion, there was a cut-glass trophy to commemorate the day, a presentation ceremony had been arranged ... and then nothing had happened. Instead of celebrating our arrival in the top flight, we had been condemned to the play-offs by the tiniest of margins.

When we went back into training on the Monday, Bruce told everybody to go home. We were that down, that deflated. He told us to have Tuesday off, come back in on Wednesday with our heads right, and that we could still do it. When we returned he stated his belief in us and said he was going to have a bet that we would win promotion. Did anyone else want to do the same? We put £100 each on ourselves and that proved a tellingly effective extra bond to our team spirit.

Our first play-off opponents were Bradford City, who had already defeated us home and away in the League. They beat us yet again, 2-1, down at Bradford, but in the second leg we were winning 1-0 at the end of normal time, then Gary Hamilton scored from outside the box in extra-time to put us through to the final. That was the only time we beat them all season, but it was enough.

Still, to attain that coveted place among the elite, we had to overcome Chelsea, who had finished fourth from bottom in the First Division, which in those days was enough to suck them into the play-offs. It proved a bit hairy as we beat them 2-0 at home, through strikes from Trevor Senior and Bernie, but then Gordon Durie scored early in the second leg at Stamford Bridge and, from that moment, Chelsea expected to win. Bernie had a great chance to settle it, but he missed, and in the end we were reduced to hanging on as they battered us. We did it, though, which gave the players a fantastic feeling of having triumphed against overwhelming odds. I believe it was an absolutely colossal achievement by a club which had recently been so close to extinction. We had started the season thinking about consolidation and ended it in the top flight of English football. We could hardly believe what we had done, we were all pinching ourselves. It was such a shame that the moment was soured by

Chelsea fans, who pelted us with rubbish as we went down the tunnel. That part was a nightmare, spoiling the occasion to a certain extent because we couldn't celebrate on the pitch in our moment of triumph. We went out again about 20 minutes later, with all our fans still in the ground, and that was wonderful in itself, but still it was not the same as when you get that first buzz.

Everyone in the team played a significant part in our unlikely rise from the Third Division to the First in successive seasons, but I believe the mammoth part played by our goalkeeper, Steve Pears, tends to be overlooked. He never received much publicity but he was good enough to be picked for a full England squad at one point and I count myself as being lucky to have played in front of him. I'd say Steve was unfortunate not to have forged a career with Manchester United, the club he joined as a teenager. During his stay at Old Trafford he found himself behind Gary Bailey, and then manager Ron Atkinson turned his attention to Chris Turner, but for my money Pears was better than either of them. He's a lovely lad, too. He lost part of one of his fingers after trapping it in a door and we had plenty of craic with him about that. We'd ask him how good a 'keeper he might have been if he'd had all his fingers, and we'd tell him he might have tipped a few more of the high ones over the bar!

There was a top performer at the other end of the pitch, too, where Bernie Slaven, who remains one of my closest friends in the game, was a massive influence and could always nick us a goal. When 'Boro signed Bernie from Albion Rovers he was a part-time gardener in the local parks. He wrote away to all the clubs in England asking for trials and I think 'Boro was the only one which responded. As an out-and-out finisher he was up there with the very best I've played with, but he didn't have lightning pace and always played on the threshold of offside. He grew used to taking stick from the crowd for wandering offside, but he always had to steal what yards he could. In truth, he wasn't the bravest and he wasn't keen on heading the ball, but he was an artist at sticking it away. He used to say you don't have to smash the ball into the net, just place it, that's enough. Bernie had neat feet, it seemed he could slide the ball in from any angle, and he had this priceless instinct for being in the right place to take the chances.

Beyond all that, the boy Slaven is an incredible character. You might call him totally daft. I know I do. He doesn't drink, being the only teetotal Scotsman I've ever met, and that suited me perfectly because whenever we went out, he was willing to drive everywhere – so there was no hanging around for taxis. There were occasions, too, when he was a saviour for me because there are always so-called fans who like to tell football clubs that their players are out on the town. Now if a letter came in to Middlesbrough claiming that Messrs Pallister and Slaven had been seen on the toot, drunk as lords, then I had an unshakeable get-out. Bruce Rioch knew that Bernie didn't drink, therefore there could be no substance to the allegation. My reaction was always: 'If this informant thought Bernie was drunk, how can you believe a word he's written? Let's be fair, Gaffer.' Over the years, I'd say that Bernie saved me more fines than I was actually forced to pay by the manager.

I think the reason that he never touched booze was that he had seen a lot of his friends struggle with drink and drugs back in Glasgow and was determined never to go the same way. Bernie used to laugh at the rest of us, telling us we talked a lot of crap when we were drunk. I'd say it was like having a normal conversation with him. The funny thing was that when Bernie was out, you'd think he'd had a drink, because he was so lively, buzzing, full of life.

As far as I know, he had an alcoholic drink only once in his life. Bernie had a morbid fear of flying. We were on tour of America after getting promotion, and he was having to take valium to calm him down to get through flights. One day he had been unable to get his valium and I was sat next to him on the plane, holding a brandy. I told him to have a shot to relax him, to chill him out. He was having none of it and I got fed up listening to him, so I turned away to talk to whoever was on my other side. When I turned back for my drink it had gone and Bernie had this big grin on his face. I don't think it had the desired effect, though. He was far too nervous, and would have had to down a few more before he might have stopped worrying.

That fear of Bernie's was very pronounced, as I found out when the team went to Bermuda during a break. We travelled down to London by bus, getting there late at night ready to fly out first thing in the morning. We were in our hotel room and Bernie was pacing up and down, unable to sleep. I was trying to calm him but he was getting worse and threatening to get the bus home. Eventually his father phoned me, asking me to make sure he stayed in his room, then got on the plane. I was at my wits' end, telling my mate I'd have to call the manager if he didn't pull himself together. By now it was past midnight and I was desperate for some sleep, as we had to be up at 5.30 am. I made sure he got into bed, put the lights out and the next thing I remember is hearing the alarm in the morning. I rubbed my eyes, snapped the light on, looked across the room and saw that Slaven's bed was empty. I walked into the toilet and there was a note there that read: 'Sorry Big Man, couldn't face the flight, gone home.'

I couldn't believe it. I thought Rioch would go berserk. I knocked on Bruce's door and it was answered by the assistant boss, Colin Todd, who must have been there for a meeting. At first Colin flat-out refused to believe me, but it was all too true. Soon I started getting phone calls from the local newspapers. The story was: 'Bernie goes missing on Bermuda tour'. The big question was: 'Has he disappeared into the Bermuda Triangle?' I just dead-batted, said I thought he had a bit of an injury; another lad said he'd seen Bernie suffering from sickness. The trip went ahead, we were in Bermuda for a week and when we got back we thought our centre-forward might be kicked out of the club. The thing was, he was difficult to replace because he scored most of our goals. In the end he was fined, but I think it made the club understand just how real his horror was. He did fly again, but after that he always remembered to pack his valium.

I could empathise with Bernie's problem because I suffered my own fear of flying. It dated back to when I was 11 and I went to Austria with the school on a skiing trip. I'd never been on a plane before, and the closer we got to the journey the more terrified I became. I'd built up this terror of flying and, well, crashing. It scared the living hell out of me, the thought of being in a little metal tube full of people up in the sky. To me, it just defied the laws of nature. Over the years, too, I came to dislike the noise the thing makes on take-off, and the surge of power you feel as it speeds along the runway, forcing you back in your seat. No matter how much I hear that it's the safest mode of transport, I feel that my fate is totally out of my own control.

All those years ago I was actually praying as we flew into Austria, and what happened on my next excursion – to Majorca, again with the school, when I was 15 – was not calculated to ease my apprehension. At about half-distance, the captain came on the Tannoy and said we had to make an unscheduled stop at Barcelona. I thought nothing of that, but as we were taxiing on the tarmac, the captain came on again to tell us that a crank has phoned up to say there was a bomb aboard. I didn't think much of the timing of the announcement. Why didn't they get everybody off first? I was sat at the back of the plane and the steps were at the front, but I think I was the third person off. I was down that gangway and off the aircraft like a rat up a drainpipe. It could have been done in a more orderly fashion if he'd just sat on that information for a bit longer. I was really shaken up.

Then they had to search all the luggage before we were given the all-clear. All our bags were on the tarmac next to the hold; we had to claim them and give them to the security man to put on the plane. Bear in mind that I was in a nervous state, and I picked up the wrong suitcase, which was identical to mine, before boarding. Next thing I knew a teacher was screaming 'Pallister, get out there and get your case.' I didn't know what was going on. But in front of everyone I had to get off the plane, down the steps and find my case; I was alone on the tarmac, except the collection of armed gendarmes which surrounded me. That accomplished, I had the lonely walk back to my seat, with countless pairs of eyes boring into me. It was like a scene from a thriller, and I don't think it helped me come to terms with flying. As I grew up and became a professional footballer, I got used to air travel, but I have never liked it, and still suffer sweaty palms before take-off.

My worst experience on an aeroplane in adulthood was on a Manchester United flight to Norwich on an unbelievably windy day. As we flew in to land the turbulence was chronic – as it had been all the way down from the north – and all the lads were looking over at the likes of myself, Giggs and Incey, who were known to be nervous flyers. They were all chuckling and taking the mick mercilessly while we were hanging on to the seats. As we were about to touch down we were hit by a massive gust of wind, a freak apparently, and it tipped the plane towards its right-hand side. Suddenly everybody shut up; all the laughing and larking stopped. As the plane banged along and eventually righted itself, there was not a sound. Everybody was schtum. The piss-taking had stopped. We taxied to a halt, everybody looked at each other, and I said: 'You're not f****** laughing now, are you?'

We got off and by then Ken Merrett, the club secretary, had spoken to the pilot, who'd told him: 'You'll never come that close to disaster and walk off a plane.' It seems the wing-tip had nearly caught the ground, which would have been calamitous. The incident was reported briefly by the media but no big deal was made of it. I promise you, though, it was a very big deal for us at the time, a massive shock to our systems.

To me, the fact that we were always flying was one of the most serious down-sides to being a top footballer, and the number of flights grew ever more numerous. At first it was just when we were playing in Europe, but then we started flying to the likes of London, Southampton and Norwich. It was all about saving time and conserving energy, rather than being stuck on buses for hours on end. That was all very well but, me, I've always preferred four wheels.

Yet while I look back on that near-miss en route to Carrow Road with a feeling of pure terror, it does not qualify as the most hair-raising airborne episode of my life. That dubious distinction goes to a little entertainment initiated by United's security expert Ned Kelly, and furthered wickedly by a certain Brian Kidd, whose job I had believed – with a naivete that now strikes me as pathetic – was to look after the footballers in his charge, not scare the living daylights out of them!

We knew that Ned, whose main brief was to look after the players, had been in the Army but we weren't sure whether or not to believe his claim that he had been in the SAS. Even when he organised a team-bonding day out to the group's base in Herefordshire we remained unconvinced until we were shown an introductory video in which we spotted him acting as a bodyguard to a top foreign statesman. We were well impressed by that, but I wouldn't say it prepared us for all that followed on what might be described as a thrill-packed day. Actually, I would use another description; I would call it bloody terrifying.

After the video we were taken on a tour of the base, starting at a place called 'the killing house', where we were treated to a demonstration of hostage rescue. They persuaded Alex Ferguson and Ryan Giggs to act as hostages, a couple of SAS people took the roles of terrorists and the rest of us were shepherded into a corner of the room. Suddenly the lights went off, then came back on in the blink of an eye, by which time the Gaffer and Giggsy had been pushed on to a table with guns held to their heads. Meanwhile each of us was confronted by a guy in infra-red goggles, who was stood two inches from our faces. The speed with which it all happened was unbelievable, and while it was fascinating, it was even more startling.

Next we were taken to a building into which a flash bomb was thrown – the sort employed in the siege at the Iranian Embassy – and were told that if we had been inside the target room then we would be totally disoriented; our eardrums would feel like they were bursting and the blinding flashes would scramble our minds. After that came an enjoyable session firing live ammunition with different types of guns, before our hosts announced the piece de resistance of the day's entertainment. They would take us up for a gentle ride in a helicopter.

My immediate reaction, being a poor flyer, was 'No chance', and Incey, Giggsy and Brucie agreed with me. But all the other lads went up two or three times, with apparent enjoyment, and for the rest of the day they gave us relentless stick, goading us to have a go. In the end we relented, but told the SAS men to go easy because we didn't like flying at the best of times. What in the name of God made us think they would pay attention to that?

No sooner had we climbed aboard the helicopter and strapped ourselves in than Kiddo, our friend and protector, came on the radio to the pilot with the instruction: 'Give 'em the works!' Believe me, the man at the controls needed no second bidding. The engine roared and right from take-off he started throwing his machine around, speeding over fields and hedges about ten yards off the deck, swerving sickeningly from side to side at breakneck speed. It felt like the worst rollercoaster ride I'd ever been on, but it was as nothing to what was in store.

Without any warning, he took us soaring almost vertically into the sky, nose-first. I had no ideas that helicopters could do that. We were all screaming our heads off and holding on to our guts. Even Ned Kelly looked uncomfortable. He was kidding us that he was okay, but his face was as white as a sheet and he fooled nobody. After it seemed we had been climbing forever, the pilot levelled out, then we just had time to catch our breath and gasp for mercy before he dropped us out of the blue. We just plummeted towards the earth and it didn't seem as if anything could possibly stop us. It was the most awful thing I've ever been through. Of course, at what seemed like the last split-second before we hit the ground, he levelled out again, before chucking us around some more. We were just abusing the guy, calling him all the names we could think of, but we didn't want to put him off his work! He was only about 4ft 2ins tall but probably he could have killed any of us with one finger. Looking back it was a truly fantastic experience, but I didn't feel like that at the time – and I have never forgiven that man Kidd.

That night we went to the SAS mess for a meal, and to share a few stories, and I'm delighted to report that, tough cookies though they were, they couldn't drink our lads under the table. They went to bed before us, so we won in the end and raised the United victory flag over their mess!

To return to my Middlesbrough days, a lot of the most vivid memories are tied up with that crazy Scottish gardener, Slaven. One that is brief and simple but which sums up my ever-deteriorating relationship with Bruce Rioch followed a defeat at Ayresome Park. Bruce stormed in and just ripped into Bernie and myself about our commitment in the game, an attack which we both thought was monstrously unfair. We just walked out of the dressing room into the big bath and let him get on with it. We were always together and we were invariably the two he took issue with.

Then there was the time we got into trouble at the swimming pool in Billingham, when we were there one afternoon with Bernie's dad. We were horsing around, nothing significant or disruptive, when the pool manager told us to get out of the water. We were surprised at his over-the-top reaction and informed him that if he wanted us out, then he'd have to come in and drag us out. There was a letter of complaint to the club, but I can't remember whether or not we got fined – probably we did.

What irked us hugely was that Rioch had his favourites. For example, there was Tony Mowbray, a great lad and a mate of mine, but Bruce doted on him and it showed in many ways. I remember when we were negotiating new contracts, Tony and I both asked for sponsored cars and were promised we would get them when we had signed. Sure enough, within a week Mogga was in possession of an XR3i Cabriolet, brand spanking new and wholly desirable. I was thinking: 'Wow, happy days, it's my turn next!' But weeks went by, they turned into months, and still I got nothing. Finally I was presented with the keys of a Citroen with my name plastered all over it in huge red letters, just the sort of thing guaranteed to make anyone feel self-conscious, while Tony was driving his lovely little sports number decorated with sleek, tasteful script. Bruce had sorted it out for me, and it told me all I needed to know about my relationship with the manager and my status at the club. I just knew he was taking the mick.

As for Tony, he could always stretch the limits with the boss in others ways, too. For instance, one day he arrived to get on the team bus with Steve Pears and they were five minutes late so Bruce made a joke of it. A week or so later Bernie and I climbed aboard about a minute late and Bruce went: 'You're fined, you're an absolute disgrace, blah-blah-blah.' That sort of thing tended to get our backs up and we were rarely out of his bad books.

Back in the Third Division days, before balanced diets dominated the lives of most professional footballers, we used to go mad with chocolate on a Friday night. We would go down to the local baker's and fill up with cakes, crisps, boxes of chocolates, then shove it all in our towel bag to eat later on. The only problem was that the rest of the lads would get to hear about it and were always trying to infiltrate our supplies. Some nights we'd get back to our hotel room to find our goody-bags had been raided. Maybe they'd have left one Mars bar, just for effect, and it became open war. We would defend our sweets at all costs, using the only weapons at our disposal ... water pistols. I know it sounds silly now, but we were only young lads and although the water fights could get pretty wild on occasions, no one ever did anything malicious.

Admittedly, I can see that it must have been annoying for the hotel staff who had to clear up, and one day the club did receive a complaint that we had drenched one of the rooms, clearly in a battle to the finish. By the time the communication arrived I had finished training and had gone off to play snooker. This was before mobile phones made everyone accessible, so they couldn't contact me and I went home at about 4pm, having had a relaxing afternoon on the tables. Just after I walked through my front door the phone went, and I was told to get down to the ground because the manager wanted to speak urgently to all the players. I was mystified, but imagined that there must have been a big new signing he wanted to tell us about.

Not so. It turned out that most of the lads had been there for several hours, all having been summoned individually by Bruce Rioch, who was hopping mad and now read out a letter from the hotel manager, saying that a room had been waterlogged. Now this was not Bruce's idea of how model professionals should behave and he went off the deep end. He asked who had been involved and Bernie, myself and a couple of others put our hands up. In fact, there were others who should have done the same, but they kept their mouths shut and got away with it – we could hardly believe that they didn't have the balls to own up. Predictably, we were fined heavily and I think the incident might have coloured the manager's view of me a wee bit!

Things might have been better between Bruce and myself if we could have had a laugh together occasionally, but obviously my sense of humour did not correspond with his. Another apt illustration of that came during a trip to Devon, when we were due to play Plymouth. We were staying in a big, old hotel that conjured up visions of a haunted mansion; it really was a spooky gaff, almost like something out of The Addams Family, and it had a massive staircase with huge bay windows at every level.

One night Dean Glover, Bernie and myself were walking down to go for our meal when Deano remembered that he'd left something in his room. As he disappeared along the corridor to get it, Bernie and I jumped on to the wide shelf in front of one of the windows. The plan was to hide behind the curtain, then leap out and give him the fright of his life as he came back downstairs. We knew he wouldn't be long because his room was close by and, sure enough, soon we heard the shutting of a door and footsteps coming down the stairs. When he reached the bottom we threw the curtain open, screamed at the top of our voices and jumped on his back. Of course, it turned out that Deano had taken longer than we had expected, and the unsuspecting figure we had hurled ourselves upon was none other than Bruce Rioch …

The manager just stood there and looked at us, then walked away. Of course, we felt really embarrassed, about two inches high, but we composed ourselves and strolled into the dining room. There was Rioch, letting the other lads know what had happened, but it all seemed very stiff in the telling. Like: 'Was I scared? Of course not.' Somehow, even in a situation like that, he couldn't quite unbend.

While my problems with Rioch worsened towards the end of my time at Ayresome Park, often it was Colin Todd who kept me sane. His character was totally different to Bruce's and they operated what was almost a 'good cop, bad cop' routine. Bruce would give me a bollocking and Toddy would try and pick me up. I learned a lot from Toddy. He had been a magnificent central defender in his heyday, and he was still terrific when he trained with us, taking part in the five-a-sides. He wasn't the biggest but he read the game brilliantly, always nipping in front of his striker to nip the ball away. His ability to anticipate what would happen next was just fantastic and he retained that as a coach in his forties.

I could sit and talk about football with Toddy, whereas there was never any satisfactory dialogue with Bruce. I found him constantly antagonistic. There was always an edge between us and we didn't trust each other. Toddy was more like a father confessor, a fellow I could talk to about anything, someone who put me at my ease. Whether he reported the contents of our conversations to Bruce, I wouldn't know.

Once, though, Toddy got upset with me when I came back to the club for a visit as a United player. Bernie had been in contract talks and wanted to know what kind of money I was on before I left. I told him and he asked for the same sort of deal. The Middlesbrough negotiators said they never paid such a figure, but Bernie was able to reply: 'You do, because Pally told me you did.' After all, Bernie was my mate and I was going to help him as much as I could. A while later I was in the dressing room at Ayresome and Toddy, by then the manager, walked in and kicked me out because he reckoned I was influencing his players. But he was fine with me when we were outside, and I know he understood that I would always stick up for my mate.

I think Bernie's experience points up the need for a player to have a reliable agent, although I didn't have one until John Smith of First Artists starting looking after my interests when I was leaving Middlesbrough. I'm convinced that young footballers need somebody they can trust to deal with all sorts of issues because it can be intimidating for boys who aren't used to dealing with high-powered businessmen, which a lot of chairmen are. Naturally enough, the chairman is out to get the best deal for the club, and you've got to get the best for yourself. Especially when you're young, and playing football for the sheer enjoyment of it, you don't really look to the future or think about how short your career might be. You need a professional on your side, someone who can judge what your worth is in the market-place.

Leon Angel has been my agent ever since I was a couple of years into my stay at Old Trafford. He takes a fair day's pay for a fair day's work, and there was never a feeling that he was taking chunks out of the game as agents do today. He was just as tough in negotiations as United chairman Martin Edwards and thoroughly deserved every penny I paid him. That said, I think it's obscene that an agent can receive £1.5 million for negotiating a contract. It's impossible for any middle man to justify that sort of reward. After all, he's not the performer, and it's money that football could use for better purposes, perhaps putting it into the grass roots of the game. Then there's the added danger that agents have the power to influence their clients into which club to join. I know it's really difficult to change but controls are needed because a lot of the agents don't have too many morals. People like Leon are worth their weight in gold, but there are others who just see the player as a commodity. What scares the fans is when agents influence players to move just to get a percentage of the fee. It all boils down to footballers, and their representatives, being strong enough to know their own minds.

It might surprise a lot of fans to learn that Manchester United were never the best payers when I was there. Despite all their success on the field, they were behind a lot of other clubs in terms of wages. That's been the case down the years, and top players like Bryan Robson, Mark Hughes and Brian McClair could all have got much more money elsewhere. What you have to balance is your desire to play for United and your need for a fair wage.

Sometimes United's parsimony has worked against them. I'm told that Alan Shearer might have joined the club from Southampton in 1992, but the difference between his likely wage at Old Trafford and what he was offered by Blackburn was huge. He could have said no to Jack Walker, but it's a hard balancing act between financial rewards and football considerations, and I can understand his decision. Four years later he had the same choice when he went to Newcastle, but I don't think Blackburn wanted to sell him to Manchester United and Tyneside was his spiritual home. That accepted, it makes the mind boggle to consider what United might have achieved had we had the Premiership's most prolific marksman at a time when we were so dominant anyway.

CHAPTER FIVE

WHY I *HAD* TO LEAVE MIDDLESBROUGH

Let me get this straight; I'll always love Middlesbrough FC. I cheered them from the terraces at Ayresome Park from the age of six and the reason I left them for Manchester United in 1989 had nothing to do with greed or selfishness or disloyalty, as some people appeared to believe. It was simply that I was woefully unhappy with my life at the club. It got to the stage where I dreaded getting up in the morning and going in to training, because I could no longer bear to be around the manager, Bruce Rioch. Our relationship had broken down irretrievably, and I had to get out.

But before going into detail about my departure, I must deal with the 1988/89 campaign, which we approached with cautious optimism, having confounded the pundits by rising from the Third Division in successive years. We knew that taking on the top flight was a tall order, especially as we went into the new season with only one major addition to the squad, Mark Brennan, a cultured England under-21 midfielder who arrived from Ipswich.

The gulf between the Second and First proved far greater than between the Third and Second, and there were games in which we were given right chasings. From operating what we thought was a tight defensive unit at the lower level, we just didn't have the quality to deal with the likes of Peter Beardsley, John Barnes and Ian Wright.

I found it especially hard after missing a lot of the pre-season with a thigh problem. When that happens you can be chasing your fitness throughout the rest of the term, never quite feeling comfortable because you lack that solid base of fitness to stand you in good stead, and that's how it was for me in 1988/89. For all that, we didn't drop into the relegation slot until the last game of the season; of course that's the one that matters most. We paid dearly for picking up only one point in our last four games, culminating with a 1-0 final-day defeat at Sheffield Wednesday when we needed a win to be safe.

During the autumn Peter Davenport was signed from Manchester United, but he struggled to settle. Ironically his first goal was against his old club when we beat them on the second day of 1989 at Ayresome Park, less than 24 hours after they'd had a wonderful win over Liverpool. Alex Ferguson had tried to get our game put back but Rioch wouldn't let him. He knew United would be tired from their efforts against Liverpool and, understandably enough, he wanted every advantage he could get.

From a personal point of view, I believe that was one of the key occasions on which I captured the Manchester United manager's notice. Certainly I saw it as one of my most convincing performances in a season which I don't believe was one of my best. To some extent on that day I was making up for a clanger back in September when the two clubs had met at Old Trafford. I had tried to keep the ball in play near the touchline but I lost possession and it was crossed for Bryan Robson to score the only goal of the game.

During that same encounter, there was a horrible moment when I thought Mark Hughes had broken my leg. I'd played a simple ball back to Steve Pears and Sparky just came in and smashed me from behind. For a few moments I lost the feeling in my right leg, and couldn't put any weight on it. He'd whacked the nerve at the side of my knee, an injury which I still have difficulties with to this day. Cheers, Mark!

When we met again at Ayresome Park he started in similar physical vein and we had a terrific battle, with him clattering into me at every opportunity while I gave as good as I got. After one particularly ferocious challenge on me, which I thought was a diabolically bad one, he was booked. Now, I'm known to be quite a calm character, and I don't usually get involved in revenge tackles, but for the first and only time in my career, I set out to do someone. A pass was laid up to him and I thought to myself: 'Forget about the ball, he's having it.' He must have known it was coming because I just went straight through and he rode the challenge. The referee booked me anyway. I can safely say that's the only time I ever lost my rag like that. The way I saw it, Sparky had got away with absolute murder in both games and I had had enough. He knew the score, but it didn't make the slightest scrap of difference to his approach. Still, we had the last laugh because we won on the day.

Later Alex Ferguson said that when he saw me in this match he knew I could play at the top level, and that I was one for the future of Manchester United. Certainly in retrospect, that was one of the key performances of my career. Funnily enough, years earlier he'd seen me play for Darlington in a Third Division match at Rochdale, and mentioned my name to his chief scout, who wasn't over-enthusiastic. Had that fellow made a different decision, he could have saved United a few quid, that's for sure.

Almost straight after the game that confirmed our demotion to the Second Division, Tony Mowbray and I had to join up with the England 'B' squad for a tour of Iceland, Norway and Switzerland. Thus it was difficult to gauge the Middlesbrough manager's reaction, though it was not hard to imagine. The rest of the lads went back to Ayresome where all but three were invited by Bruce to have a drink and chew the fat about our plight. The exceptions were Paul Kerr, Mark Burke, and my regular partner-in-crime, Bernie Slaven. I'm sure I would have made it four if I'd come back on the bus, too. I think I understood pretty conclusively where I stood.

For all that, during the season I had been talking about a new long-term deal, to keep me at Middlesbrough for the next four or five years. There had been lengthy negotiations with the manager and the chairman, Colin Henderson, which I had conducted myself because I didn't have an agent at the time. I was playing for England by then and was talking to other players, finding out what they were earning in the top flight, but I wasn't asking that sort of money from Middlesbrough because they were still under financial constraints. Still, I told them what I wanted and I was told: No chance.

They made me an offer and I told them I would not be signing their contract. Bruce Rioch started getting uptight about it and we got to a stage where he gave me a week to make up my mind. The ultimatum was: either agree to our offer or we'll withdraw it. He cornered me in the car park after a game at Middlesbrough and asked me if I was going to sign. I said no. He said I wouldn't be offered that contract again and that I'd have to stay at Ayresome Park on my existing wage for the rest of my current contract, which was maybe a couple of years. I refused to buckle, but eventually we did find some kind of common ground. I didn't get exactly what I wanted, but I got more than their original offer, and I signed a deal covering four or five years during 1988/89. However, the protracted unpleasantness during that process brought all my negative feelings about Bruce to a head.

At this point, having just gone down, it was an appropriate moment to step back and take a long, cool look at my career and where it was going. I was coming up to 24 and had been involved with England but then seemingly forgotten about in an international context.

I'd always said that as long as things kept moving forward, and we kept progressing, then I was happy to stay at Middlesbrough because I was a local lad and happy in the area. On the other hand, I had been linked with the likes of Newcastle, Celtic, Liverpool and Manchester United. At the time I never knew how much truth there was in these stories, particularly as I didn't have an agent to act as a go-between, but I felt I had to be fair to myself and my professional aspirations.

So here was my situation: Middlesbrough had just dropped out of the First Division, which was a devastating blow to all of us. I didn't have a satisfactory or even workable relationship with the manager. I wasn't enjoying my football – and that said it all. If you can't enjoy your football then you can't express yourself, you can't show the best of your ability. It all seemed to be pointing the same way, but I didn't make a snap decision there and then. I went to Spain on holiday and tried to put it all into perspective.

Clearly it was a crossroads in my career and I had to make a decision football-wise. As I mulled it over, it became pretty apparent to me that I needed to make a move, that I had no option but to leave Middlesbrough, though I'd had no specific overtures at that point. I had spoken occasionally to the agent John Smith when I was away with England and he had offered his services should I ever need them. So I got in touch with him when I got back from Spain, told him I was unhappy and asked him to see what was out there for me.

He came back in a couple of days and said: 'I think I might have got you a club. It's Liverpool.' They were still very successful at the time, maybe just starting to wane but still one of the major forces in the game. Kenny Dalglish was the manager and, apparently, he wanted to bring me to his club. I was delighted. I couldn't have expected more than that.

So I went back for pre-season and went to Bruce's office. I think he knew what was coming. I told him that in terms of my career I felt I had to move. At this point he was quite civil, calm and realistic. He listened to me, said he didn't want me to leave, but that he'd have a word with the chairman and then get back to me. I was pleasantly surprised by his reasonable reaction. But then one day passed, two days passed, a week passed and I heard nothing, so I went back in to ask him what was going on. This time he snapped at me: 'You're not going anywhere. You've signed a five-year contract. You're staying here. I don't want to sell, the club doesn't want to sell, end of story.'

Now I put in a written transfer request, which was duly knocked back. Then I put in a second one, saying I didn't feel as though it was beneficial to my career to stay in such adverse circumstances, and that I was adamant I was leaving. I left it on his desk and then I went out to train. Afterwards I got a message from one of the youngsters saying that the manager wanted to see me before I trained. When I went in he was holding the letter and he started screaming and shouting at me. It was along the lines of: 'I've told you you're not going anywhere, you've signed a five-year contract, where's the loyalty?' I looked at him and said: 'Well, how many clubs have you had?' In fact, I knew full well that he had played for Luton, Aston Villa, Derby, Everton, Derby again, Birmingham and Sheffield United on loan, then Torquay and Seattle Sounders, so I was on pretty firm ground there. Obviously he had moved whenever it suited his career, and I couldn't blame him for that. The point I was making was that people did move on in football, so why should it be different for me?

He leaned across the desk and I thought he was going to try and punch me. At the time probably I hoped he would so I could have a go back. But he just carried on abusing me verbally. I thought I'd given him the best answer I could, an honest appraisal of what I needed to do to further my career, like anyone else in any other walk of life. I didn't feel guilty at all about what I was doing, but that meeting ended on a very bad note.

Around then John Smith told me that Liverpool wouldn't pay the type of money that Middlesbrough were looking for. At the same time the Swedish central defender Glenn Hysen had been talking to Manchester United about a transfer from his Italian club, Fiorentina. I think he'd met Alex Ferguson, even stayed at Bryan Robson's house, so everything looked done and dusted. He was a proven world-class performer and United seemed happy with the situation, but at the last minute Liverpool hijacked the deal, taking Hysen to Anfield. That was a little bit worrying for me because now I felt in limbo. It seemed clear that if Liverpool had acquired Hysen, then they would not be wanting me as well. However, only another day went by before John rang and said: 'Brace yourself. I've found you another club. It's Manchester United.' Phew! The biggest club in Britain, if not the most successful at that point. I was absolutely delighted.

By this time I'd started the new season with 'Boro and played three more games for them in the first week, finishing with a defeat by Sunderland. Next I got a message to go and see Bruce Rioch, who informed me that United had made a bid, which was going to be discussed at a board meeting that afternoon. He said he would recommend that they didn't take the money, which was his prerogative, that was fair play. He added that he would let me know the outcome, so I went home and sat there all afternoon waiting for a phone call.

None came, and I was watching TV in the evening when it was announced that United's bid had been rejected, and that I would remain a

Middlesbrough player. That was how I found out about it, even though Bruce had said he'd let me know, and it riled me a wee bit. I faced him with that the following day and asked him why he hadn't let me know the board's verdict. He said it had nothing to do with me, this momentous decision about my own future. All I got out of him was: 'You're an employee of the football club, you're under contract, that's that.' That just got my back up even more, so I told him I still wanted to leave. His treatment of me merely underlined everything I felt about Bruce Rioch, everything that was going wrong in our relationship.

The next development was a call from John Smith to say there was to be a meeting that night between Manchester United and Colin Henderson, whom I'd been trying unavailingly to get in touch with throughout this business. I liked Colin and I wanted to speak with him face to face. I'd left messages with his secretary and I felt let down by him because he hadn't got back to me. I thought he was a straightforward guy who would understand my position, not only the footballing considerations but also the personal ones concerning Bruce Rioch. I wanted to explain myself fully, let him know that the Pallister-Rioch relationship had run its course, that all sensible dialogue with Bruce had long ceased, that now it was just pure conflict.

The meeting was held at the Tontine restaurant between Thirsk and Middlesbrough on the A19. I was extremely pleased when John Smith asked me to be there, because it would give me the chance to say my piece to the chairman at last. So I met my agent and we drove to the restaurant but then Bruce Rioch saw my car, which was emblazoned all over with the sponsor's name, and went ballistic. He said that if I went into the room then the whole deal was off, the negotiations would not even begin.

So while Colin Henderson, Alex Ferguson, Bruce Rioch, John Smith and United solicitor Maurice Watkins (who was there because the Old Trafford chairman, Martin Edwards, was out of the country) were discussing my future, I had to sit outside in the car, on my own. The meeting went on for about six hours, well into the wee small hours of the morning as the details were thrashed out, and Alex Ferguson is on record as saying that he had never dealt with anybody as hard as Colin Henderson. I think United started by offering £1.3 million with 'Boro demanding £2.5 million and utterly refusing to budge. There were bids of £1.5m, then £1.7m, then £1.9m, then £2m, and still no agreement was reached. It was something like 3am or 4am before they finally agreed a deal for the British record £2.3m.

All the while I was going through so many different emotions. My mind was in turmoil as I slumped in the car seat listening to the radio, with so much time to agonise. Would I be good enough for Manchester United? Was I making a mistake? Would it be easier and more comfortable to stay at Middlesbrough, where I had a five-year contract? For the first time, possibly, I doubted the wisdom of what I was doing. Earlier that afternoon I had played against Sunderland and, after so much delay, now everything was happening in a rush. When finally John came out with the glad tidings, Colin Henderson and Bruce Rioch had left, and I was able to meet Alex Ferguson and Maurice Watkins.

They explained the wage structure at the club and this part of the proceedings was concluded pretty swiftly. I was told I'd be on the same contract as Bryan Robson, so I didn't dare ask for more than the captain of England was getting. That said, the pay rise wasn't as astronomical as some people imagined. I was offered £160,000 a year, compared to the £125,000 I was on at 'Boro, while I knew from the England camp that players at other clubs were getting £250,000. Meanwhile there was some tapping going on from various sources that left me in no doubt that I could have achieved that figure elsewhere.

Obviously, players within clubs discuss their pay, that's human nature, but I didn't know too many of the United players at that time. I accepted the word of honour of Alex Ferguson and Maurice Watkins, and I signed a six-year deal. I was 24 years old and the deal gave me stability, but when I went back to Bernie and the lads at Boro, I'm sure they thought I was on more money than I actually was. Admittedly, my new agreement represented a decent rise, but it was not a major advance on what I'd been getting at Ayresome. Still, the decision to move had not been about money. It was based on career ambitions, what I wanted to achieve in the game. I could never have forgiven myself if I hadn't accepted the challenge of joining United. I'd have been saying to myself for the rest of my life: 'What if ...?' I couldn't have lived with that.

My honest feeling about the fee was that Middlesbrough were taking the mick by asking for that amount of money. To be sure, it was a superb deal for them but being the subject of the record transfer between British clubs was always going to heap a pile of extra pressure on me, and they understood that perfectly well. Given my standing in the game at that time, I was worth nowhere near that grossly inflated sum and it disappointed me that Middlesbrough held out, insisted on breaking that record. Why could they not have accepted £2.1 million, which would have not exceeded Tony

Cottee's fee when he joined Everton from West Ham a year earlier?

In the following week's Middlesbrough programme notes, Bruce Rioch attacked me, saying that I'd refused to play for the club. That was never the case and it left a very sour taste in my mouth. It was Bruce's parting shot at me and it was totally unnecessary. What was he looking for? Revenge? There was no mention of the fact that we didn't have any kind of relationship any more, thus making it impossible for me to work with him. The manner of parting stuck in my throat for a long time and I don't think my side of the story has ever been told properly until now.

The situation between us was absolutely appalling during the last two or three months of 1988/89. I was growing to hate my football for the first time in my life, and it couldn't go on. Every day in training, Bruce was hammering us, and in my opinion he had lost the script. He was trying to make us fitter and fitter towards the end of a season, a time when players tend to need rest between matches. Certainly I did. We were being driven too hard and it was not productive, but Bruce was getting more and more cranky. You could say that he lost his own discipline in that he wasn't managing to apply traditional football logic to his training methods. I don't think he could bear the thought that we could drop out of the First Division after we had done so well to get there. I could sympathise with that, but his reaction was beyond reason.

So I had to leave, partly to take my career as far as it could go, but also to escape an intolerable personal situation. In any walk of life, whether you're a policeman, a bus conductor or a waiter, if you can't work in a happy environment then you have to go. Now, at last, I hope people will finally understand that.

It grieved me that I didn't have a chance to say a proper farewell at Ayresome Park. Funnily enough, I don't think Bruce left me a note when I went to pick up my boots, and I didn't see Colin Henderson for many years.

Eventually, I'm glad to say, I bumped into him in a restaurant in Yarm, where he congratulated me on my career and said he was proud I'd done as well as I had with Manchester United. True, I saw some of the 'Boro lads out on Saturday nights after games when I came back to the north east, where my family was, and I was pleased that the banter was the same as always. There had been a good rapport in the side when things were going well, partly because there were so many local lads, and this spirit, and a sense of growing up together, was a huge part of our armoury, gave us a great deal of strength as a team. A lot of the lads socialised together, had a few beers, an approach that was even more prevalent at United when Robbo was the skipper.

Happy to report, I have stayed close to Bernie Slaven, who was great in fielding my phone calls during my early days in Manchester when I was stuck in a hotel by myself, and to Tony Mowbray. Mind, I don't know if Bruce thought I was a good influence on Mogga. Maybe he hoped Mogga would be a good influence on me!

No matter what happened at 'Boro, though, I can say sincerely that it has done nothing to dent my long-term affection for the club, and even at the time I left I was sorry to see them struggling. The problem was that Bruce Rioch had lost his grip on the team. Earlier in his reign at Ayresome Park he was dealing with young kids and he got the very best out of them to achieve the two promotions. All credit to him for that, but he achieved his aims through a mixture of bullying, cajoling and pushing boys who were not yet strong enough to stick up for themselves. As they got older, they didn't take as much crap; it was as simple as that. Later Bruce brought in some senior players to try and help the club survive in the top division, but they wouldn't take bullying, either. Of course, the youngsters saw that and they reacted by being less malleable themselves. As a result Bruce lost impetus and was sacked in March 1990. Middlesbrough almost went down again, all the way back to the Third Division, only surviving against Newcastle in the final game.

Did I leave with any regrets? Only in that I hadn't been able to put across my side of the story – partly because I didn't want to get involved with a slagging match with Bruce; and partly because I didn't want to upset the people at Middlesbrough, some of whom were upset anyway, merely at the fact that I'd left. That said, I think there were plenty who understood that 'Boro had done a wonderful deal, receiving a record fee for a footballer who hadn't had the greatest season of his life. That left me to look forward, to see just how far I could push myself in the game that had obsessed me for as long as I could remember.

CHAPTER SIX

THE START OF SOMETHING BIG

My first season at Manchester United was unforgettable, and it ended on a glorious high, but not before I had ridden a rollercoaster of contrasting emotions. My move from Middlesbrough had happened in something of a blur and, for a lad who had led a comparatively unobtrusive life in the north-east to that point, initially it was a bit difficult to take in the grandeur of Old Trafford, especially while coping with mammoth expectations as the costliest player in British transfer history. After signing on the Monday, training on the Tuesday and making my debut on the Wednesday, I could hardly believe the pace with which events were overtaking me.

I was one of five expensive new players whom Alex Ferguson was in the process of acquiring – along with Neil Webb, Micky Phelan, Paul Ince and Danny Wallace – and although I was joining one of the biggest clubs in the world, I was also part of a team in transition.

In addition to all that, there was almost a fantasy feeling about the place, because this was the time when the extrovert businessman Michael Knighton was attempting to buy United. A week or so before I arrived, on the first day of the new season, he had publicised his takeover bid by juggling a football in front of an astonished Stretford End. Then the side had extended the feelgood factor on a sunny afternoon by drubbing the reigning champions, Arsenal, by four goals to one, with Webby cracking a terrific goal on his debut.

In the end it turned out to be an embarrassing interlude in United's history as the buyout never materialised. I never knew quite what to make of it all. Knighton was talking about purchasing the club for £10 million and was trying to raise the money. A little later, when the deal had gone dead, it seemed a weird situation because he would come on trips with the team, but you didn't often see him talking to any of the directors. There seemed to be a distance between him and the others. He seemed perfectly pleasant, but you didn't know whether it was wise to strike up a relationship with him. But whatever the financial rights and wrongs of a bizarre affair, in retrospect it is clear that anyone who had put together a consortium to buy the club at that point, for the sort of figure being mentioned, would have been pulling off one of the greatest coups imaginable.

Far more relevant to me, though, was what was happening on the field, and I could have wished for better than a 2-0 home defeat by Norwich City on my first outing. Afterwards I took more than a bit of stick from the pundits, and while I'm always ready to own up for my mistakes, I reckon I was treated harshly on this occasion. I was blamed for the first goal, but I had been left marking two men, Robert Fleck and Dale Gordon, and to this day I maintain it wasn't my fault. I was trying to hold the pair, the ball came over to Fleck and he nodded down for Gordon to score. Then I gave away a penalty with a rash challenge on Robert Rosario and Fleck converted the spot-kick; I had no problem in admitting full responsibility for that one.

Whatever, losing 2-0 was not the most auspicious of starts for the record transfer. I was disappointed because I had wanted to get the fans on my side straight away, and that probably wasn't the best way to do it! As I trudged off, I thought about all the money United had spent on new players, and reflected ruefully that being beaten by Norwich at Old Trafford was not part of the master plan. The manager didn't say too much to me, just something along the lines that I'd be better for getting that game under my belt and out the way. He knew that I was straight in at the deep end after only one day of training, and that I needed time to settle.

Certainly it didn't help that I had to cope while being away from home for the first time in my life. For the moment I was on my own in a hotel – although Micky Phelan and Danny Wallace were in the same establishment, they had their families with them – and I found myself feeling rather disoriented. Fans see players as one-dimensional beings on the Saturdays, and have no notion of what off-the-field difficulties or side issues they might be facing. In fact, of course, they are ordinary people with ordinary problems just like everyone else. Often they have young kids, who get them up in the middle of the night, though that didn't apply to me at the time. Not that I'm complaining, because the supporters pay their hard-earned cash to be entertained, and shouldn't have to worry about other factors.

After training I would go back to the hotel, then probably pop out for lunch at the *Pizza Hut* in town, by myself like some saddo. Then it was back again to the hotel, where I would like as not just lie on the sofa and watch TV all afternoon. Soon, though, Paul Ince arrived and then we spent the afternoons at the bookies – hardly an ideal lifestyle. It made me think that clubs could do more to look after people in whom they have made such a massive investment, and I think they are more aware of the situation now. These days, too, agents help to manage more of their clients' everyday business.

Back at work, we suffered my second successive defeat, at Everton, but then we thrashed Millwall 5-1, with Mark Hughes scoring a hat-trick. I came off the pitch that day thinking: 'This is what it's all about, this is how we should be demolishing sides like this at Old Trafford. People won't fancy coming here, we've got this player and that player. Norwich was clearly a freak result.'

But a week later the roof fell in when we lost 5-1 at Maine Road. Brucie and Robbo were both out injured but that was no excuse for one of the most traumatic results in United's history. The funny thing was that we started off really well in the game, playing lovely football. But then there was trouble behind one of the goals which spilled over to the side of the pitch, and the players were taken off. From that moment the script went drastically wrong. Everything City hit went in, while we had our chances and plenty of ball with nothing to show for it bar a typically spectacular strike by Mark Hughes. I'm not saying we deserved to get anything, but I don't think 5-1 was an accurate reflection of the play, and the outcome was a bit of a freak. They had about half a dozen shots on target and five of them went in.

I must admit, though, that I didn't have the best of games. There were a couple of goals which I looked back on and knew I should have done better. To lose so comprehensively to our arch rivals after so much money had been spent was totally unacceptable, and I'd say it was the lowest point of my entire career. I think the manager was in shock after the game, practically speechless. Apparently he went home, went to bed and stuck his head under a pillow. I drove back to Middlesbrough with members of my family who had come down to watch the game. Thank God I had them around me. I sought solace at home for the rest of the weekend, but then was confronted with a menacing situation when I returned to training on Monday.

At that time there was no security at The Cliff, and when I walked from the dressing room after training there were three or four burly United fans waiting for me outside the door. As I moved towards my car they told me I wasn't fit to wear a United shirt, we shouldn't have sold Paul McGrath, I was a disgrace to the club, the whole treatment – I caught it hot and strong. I thought it was just me but I found out later that all the lads got abuse from those guys. They really ripped into us and it was quite frightening. There was nobody there to look after us and if they'd have wanted to lay into us physically then they could have done. Such a thing would be unthinkable today, with the fans being unable to get anywhere near the players.

As the personal pressure on me continued to mount, I desperately needed something to break my way, and it did in a home game with Nottingham Forest in November. One of their lads sprinted away from the edge of their box and I ran almost the length of the pitch, tracking another of their players in the middle. As he delivered his cross I got a toe to the ball, nipping in front of the lad I was marking and making a half-block, and it bobbled agonisingly beyond our 'keeper, Jim Leighton, before shaving the post and going out for a corner. After all the criticism I'd been getting, if that had gone in I'd have gone even lower in the estimation of the punters, but almost straight away I went up the other end, Brucie headed one across goal and I stuck it over the line. It was going in anyway, but I had to make sure, and it turned out to be the winner in a tight contest, which earned me some much-needed positive publicity. It was my first goal for United and I look back on it as a defining moment.

Still, as the season progressed, and our results were patchy to put it mildly – we suffered a particularly bleak midwinter, with no wins in 11 League games – there was a genuine fear of relegation about the place. A turning point of sorts arrived in February when we went to Millwall, with a team weakened by injuries. The Den was not the place you want to go in that condition, but we came from a goal behind to win thanks to strikes from Danny Wallace and Mark Hughes. If we'd lost that we'd have been in the drop zone in February, which would have been a nightmare.

Of course, the story goes that Alex Ferguson would have lost his job had Mark Robins not scored the goal that put us through against Forest in the third round of the FA Cup at the City Ground. I'm not sure it was as simple as that. It wasn't just a question of what the first team were doing; he was leaving his stamp of authority on the entire workings of the club, from the bottom upwards. The youth system, for example, was flourishing where previously it had been moribund, and I believe the board understood the direction in which he was working, knew what he was doing for the club in the long term.

True, many of the fans had turned on him, which is always dangerous, and he was taking some murderous flak. I recall a piece in a fanzine, I think it was *Red Issue*, which made their point by publishing *Fergie's*

Takeway Menu. On it were two black puddings and a dumpling, complete with extortionate prices, and they were talking about Danny Wallace, Paul Ince and myself. That was one of the funniest observations I've ever seen, and I remember the three of us having a laugh at it, despite ourselves. But we knew the situation was serious and if we stopped to think it could have made us despair because, after all, that was the fans' genuine voice. Oh dear God almighty, what a time that was.

Nobody knows for sure whether the Gaffer would have been sacked if we hadn't had the FA Cup run. Only Martin Edwards and the board knew that, and they always maintained that it was never an option because they felt he was turning the whole club around. They realised that United had lapsed into bad ways and he had livened everything up, given the place a new life.

Alex Ferguson had been at Old Trafford for nearly three years before me, so the revolution was well under way, and I felt there was a positive attitude there when I arrived. We didn't think we could win the championship, but with five new players coming in we felt the right kind of change was on the way. No way were we prepared to be in the lowly position we found ourselves in for so much of the 89/90 season. The manager was marvellous at deflecting the flak away from the players, taking the responsibility and protecting us in public as much as he could. Unfortunately that didn't stop us being savaged in the newspapers and, as the British record transfer, I was the easiest target.

The League season continued spiralling out of control until we won four on the belt in late March and early April, against Southampton, Coventry, Queen's Park Rangers and Aston Villa, but, praise be, the FA Cup offered salvation. Before the televised match at Nottingham we received an unexpected gee-up when somebody came into the dressing room and told us that Jimmy Hill had informed the nation that we looked like a beaten side, and that was only in the warm-up! Everyone was predicting that the Gaffer would be out if we lost and that meant that we were playing for our own futures, too, because no player likes the manager who has bought him to leave.

On the day, we confounded expectations by producing a fine and spirited performance, capped by the only goal of the game from Mark Robins, a neat header set up by a beautiful pass from the outside of Sparky's right boot. After that Mark II, as he was called in the press, became like a lucky charm for the rest of the season, and at one point he was even picked ahead of Mark I.

In the fourth round we faced a potential banana-skin at Hereford, where we met our Fourth Division hosts on a cold winter's day, up to our ankles in cloying slush, the same Edgar Street mud in which Ronnie Radford unleashed his famous long-distance screamer to knock Newcastle out of the cup in 1972. It turned out to be a real blood-and-guts battle with no opportunity for pretty football, and we were on tenterhooks until the 85th minute, when Micky Duxbury crossed for Clayton Blackmore to score the winner from close range. That came as a terrific relief to me, especially as I was feeling ill after suffering mild concussion following a whack on the head, and I was sick all the way home on the bus.

Next up was a memorable confrontation with Newcastle at St James' Park, and when we lined up for the kick-off the roar from their crowd was unbelievable. The sound seemed to roll down from every corner of the stadium and it was one of the few times in my life when I've felt the hairs stand up on the back of my neck. Such fabulous supporters deserved an exciting game and that's what they got, only they wouldn't have been pleased to see us prevail by the odd goal in five. Danny Wallace played a blinder that day, one of his best displays for the club, topping it off with a brilliant individual goal, with Mark Robins and Brian McClair supplying the others.

The quarter-final against Sheffield United at Bramall Lane proved a really tight affair with a whiff of controversy. They claimed the corner that led to the game's only goal, nodded in by McClair, should never have been given, but over it came, I flicked it on at the near post and Choccy knocked it in at the second attempt after the 'keeper had blocked his first effort.

For the semi-final we were paired with Second Division opposition for the third consecutive time in the form of Oldham, whom Joe Royle had developed into an attractive attacking side. Sure enough, they put up a tremendous struggle and it took two matches, both at Maine Road, to get past them. Maybe because it was one of the most important games of my life to that point, I was unfeasibly nervous before the first encounter. I went to trap the first ball that came to me and I misjudged it, allowing it to creep under my foot, but I got away with that and soon settled into the cut and thrust of a truly gripping contest.

As was the case virtually every time he walked on to a pitch, Robbo was immense, even though he was nowhere near fully fit. Making light of the pain, he was utterly indomitable, confirming my view that he was the best all-round footballer I've ever played with. He had been out for half the season and we'd had to learn to live without him. Other people had stepped forward, gradually assuming responsibility, but when he came back there was a huge collective sigh of relief. We always wanted him out there because he was so influential. Bryan was the manager's eyes and voice on the field, he just took care of everything, and I guess we might have relied on him too much.

That first game finished 3-3, with Robbo, Webby and Danny scoring for us, then Choccy and Mark Robins grabbed the goals that saw us through 2-1 after extra time in the replay. Oldham deserved massive credit for their part in a splendid spectacle, and they had some eye-catching players in the likes of former United marksman Andy Ritchie, defender Earl Barrett and winger Rick Holden. Of course, their man who would make the greatest impact on the football scene was a certain Denis Irwin, a fellow who didn't get the fans on the edges of their seats, but who just did the business efficiently and with a minimum of fuss. We didn't know it then, but following his transfer to Old Trafford in the summer of 1990, he was to become one of the greatest Manchester United full-backs of all time.

As the FA Cup Final neared, with our lingering fears of relegation finally laid to rest, our thoughts turned to our Wembley opponents, Crystal Palace, who were managed by former Old Trafford favourite Steve Coppell. In particular, I wondered whether Ian Wright would be lining up against me, because I knew he was a terrific player, and I was delighted when I found out he would be on the bench. As it turned out, though, he was to have quite an impact, and in later years, whenever I have mentioned my bad back, he has offered the opinion that I'd had it ever since he turned me for Palace's second goal!

All week long the United camp had talked about Palace's powerfully effective set pieces and how we would defend against them by pushing up to keep them out of our box. But when their first free-kick came in I went up with Gary O'Reilly, there was a ricochet off both our heads and Jim Leighton got nowhere near the ball, which looped slowly into the empty net. I have to take part of the blame because I didn't win my header cleanly, but I suppose if Jim hadn't left his line then the ball would have dropped to him.

We fought back strongly and Robbo equalised, then Sparky put us in front and we were favourites to win. Enter Wrighty, who did me on the edge of the box and curled a great low shot past Jim. Some blamed our 'keeper for that one, too, but I think that's harsh. In fact, I take full responsibility because Ian turned me like a kipper.

In the last of the 90 minutes I injured my ankle, but I started the first extra period, which had barely begun when John Salako crossed from the left and Wrighty put Palace back in front. Once again, blame was heaped on poor Jim Leighton. Soon afterwards I limped off to be replaced by Mark Robins; there were 28 minutes left and we had a match to save. Sitting on the bench, thinking we had lost the FA Cup Final, I felt increasingly gloomy but Sparky threw us a lifeline with just seven minutes to spare after being put in cleverly by Danny Wallace.

We couldn't quite force a winner, though Robbo went close, but as we walked to the dressing room the overwhelming feeling among the players was one of relief at living to fight another day after being 3-2 down in extra time. At that point we hadn't thought of the goalkeeping issue at all, though obviously it was exercising the manager's mind. Jim Leighton had done really well after arriving from Aberdeen the previous summer, proved himself solid and become the undisputed number-one at United. But as the season wore on it seemed there was a chipping away at his confidence. He began to take stick from pundits and fans alike, and that seemed to eat away at him. Perhaps it was a telling factor that he was playing behind a back four that was being changed a lot but, whatever the root cause, it wasn't a matter of concern for his team-mates before the final.

In the training sessions between the first game on the Saturday and the Thursday replay, we didn't have an inkling that Jim wasn't going to play. I would never have dreamed it. All my attention was taken up with my own situation, as I was having intensive treatment, morning, noon and night, on the swollen ankle that was threatening my own place. In fact, it wasn't until the day of the game that I was sure I would play, when Jim McGregor fitted a stirrup strap for support.

The night before the replay I was grappling with an ice-pack upstairs at our hotel when the pre-match meeting began between players, manager and the rest of the staff. I was five minutes late, which normally would have earned a ticking-off from Alex Ferguson but not on this occasion, because of my treatment. When I walked into the room I could sense a strange atmosphere. It was distinctly sombre; everybody seemed a bit low and downbeat, but I couldn't fathom out the reason for it. Eventually we got up to go, and still everybody was really subdued, so I asked Brian McClair what was wrong with everybody. When he told me that Jazza was left out of the team and that Les Sealey was playing, it absolutely staggered me.

Not surprisingly, Jazza took it really badly, signalling the end of a fruitful relationship which he and the Gaffer had enjoyed since their

Aberdeen days together. We all had so much sympathy for Jim. If he had played as badly as people said then obviously he was desperate to have the chance to put it right in the replay. But the manager thought the pressure on him had been too great, and his was the opinion that mattered. We were all professional enough to understand the reality that Les was playing and that we had to concentrate on our own jobs. It wasn't going to be an easy match, and I wondered if Les was going to be nervous. How would he respond to such a sudden and enormous challenge? After all, he'd not had a lot of football lately, so were we going to have to protect him, what with Palace being such a direct side?

We knew they would be out to test him, which they did, clattering him repeatedly in the early part of the game. They tried their utmost to upset him, but he rose to the task magnificently. In fact, they were far more physical in all areas than they had been in the first match and there were a few wars going on out on the park. I think that they lost their focus in that they tried to target Les individually and, possibly, that was their mistake.

Alex Ferguson has indicated that, given his time over again, he wouldn't have dropped Jim because of the demoralising effect on his fellow Scot's personality and career. But was the manager right? It was a monumentally tough decision and I don't think it's one I could have made. But that's something the manager has done all his life; he's never been afraid of it. As it turned out, Les had a great game, and we won, so I suppose what the Gaffer did was right for Manchester United. He was vindicated in his choice, but there was a fearful price to pay – the permanent loss of the long-established friendship and respect between the two men. It finished Jim at United, there can be no doubt about that. I think the manager wanted him to stay, but Jim was so destroyed by what had happened that he had to go. The damage had been done and there was no way back.

I could understand it from Jim's point of view. It doesn't bear thinking about how he must have felt at that time. Normally he was a nice, affable kind of guy who just got on with his job. He was laid-back, good to be around, just a lovely, genuine fellow. He had never known disappointment on anything like this scale before, having been a big player in the Aberdeen side which had broken the stranglehold of Celtic and Rangers on Scottish football. He had proved he could handle the pressure of really big games, both for club and country. He had started off well at United, too, looking at home in the cauldron of Old Trafford, and it seemed certain that he would be there for a long time to come.

As to the replay itself, it must have been a terrible game for neutrals to watch. Palace seemed hell-bent on trying to out-muscle us, intimidate us, and they didn't play anything like as much football as they did in the first game. I think they were sidetracked by the Les issue, being obsessed with putting him under as much pressure as possible. But Les was an ebullient character, certainly not the type to be intimidated. He had a happy-go-lucky air about him which was great for the dressing room, and on the night he fronted up superbly, took the knocks, wasn't found wanting in any area. Players such as Mark Bright, Andy Gray, Andy Thorn and Gary O'Reilly were persistently aggressive, but their efforts to frighten him were completely wasted. We were at the referee all night long to protect him, but it's an immense tribute to Les himself that he didn't flinch at any stage, and to keep a clean sheet in the face of such tactics was truly admirable. He was an unorthodox type of keeper and no one would have guessed that Alex Ferguson would have brought him to the club as cover for Jim, though the manager does likes chirpy characters, people with something about them who are lively about the place. Most important of all, though, they have to hack it on the pitch, and there is no doubt that Les did that at Wembley.

It was also a gigantic day for Lee Martin, our young left-back who scored the game's only goal. He was the last person you would have expected to net the winner in a cup final, even more unlikely than me! I shall never forget my joy, but also my astonishment, when he rampaged into the Palace box to get on the end of Neil Webb's beautiful, raking crossfield pass. He took it down perfectly on his chest and in the next stride he had planted it unstoppably into the top corner of the net. Lee's a lovely lad and it's such a crying shame that his career was sabotaged by back problems. He was a terrific player, extremely assured and a very intelligent reader of the game, and the football world looked to be at his feet until the injuries set in. That game also represented the peak of Webby's time with United, just when it looked as though he, too, was an integral part of the club's future.

In retrospect, their cases offer vivid illustrations of the fragility of a footballer's career, but at the time there was nothing sadder than seeing the forlorn figure of Jim Leighton walking away after we had collected the cup, then slumping disconsolately on his seat in the Wembley dressing room while the celebrations went on around him. Understandably, he was inconsolable; there was nothing we could say to pick him up. We hoped that he would be able to put it behind him and carry on at United but the damage proved to be irreparable. It was overwhelmingly distressing to witness the breakdown of a relationship between two people who had meant so much to each other throughout most of their lives in football.

But even the poignant plight of Jim Leighton could not disguise the glorious fact that the FA Cup win was pivotal to United's renaissance. It gave us a taste of success and it gave us belief that we could achieve it, thus proving a crucial factor in the growth of the team and the personalities within that team. It must be remembered, too, that the FA Cup was a much bigger deal at the time. Since then the gloss has been taken off it by the onset of the Premiership and the Champions League. You might even say that the game's oldest senior competition has been consigned to the back-burner of history.

On a personal level back in 1990, collecting that famous old trophy was a euphoric way to finish my first campaign at Old Trafford, exactly the kind of achievement I'd come from Middlesbrough to enjoy. Mind, the glee was tempered by the fact that we knew we had been under-performing throughout most of the League season. We understood that we hadn't yet arrived as the finished article, and that there was still a lot of hard work to do to make sure there was no such balls-up again. But now there was a feeling that we had the capability, and that if we could click consistently then we could go a long way together.

CHAPTER SEVEN

THE BEST BUZZ ...
AND UTTER DESOLATION

It was one of those times that you wanted never to end, an unbelievable high, probably the best buzz of my entire football career. I'm talking here about the protracted celebrations after Manchester United had lifted the European Cup Winners' Cup by beating Barcelona on a dank, foggy Rotterdam night in May 1991. I suppose we were lucky not to fall off the open-topped bus that drove us through Manchester because, believe me, the drinks had been flowing freely. The camaraderie was unsurpassable, the whole thing was an awesome experience and I only wish I could have bottled it, so I could break it open every now and again to have another taste.

There had been immense anticipation at Old Trafford ever since it became known that the ban on English sides competing in Europe, which had been in force ever since the Heysel tragedy of 1985, was being lifted for 1990/91 and that United, as the FA Cup winners, were to be one of the new trailblazers. Somehow it was appropriate that the Red Devils should be at the vanguard of the return as they had pioneered the path into continental football in the first place, back in the 1950s when Matt Busby had defied the authorities to lead his brilliant Babes into the Champions Cup.

European nights at Old Trafford have always been extra special. They seem to generate a unique atmosphere, with the lights, the surrounding darkness, the overwhelming expectation of something out of the ordinary. This was especially true a while ago, before the Champions League increased the number of games and before there were so many Europeans playing regularly in this country, thus reducing the novelty value to fans of seeing top talents from overseas at first hand.

Back in 1990 excitement at the club was at fever pitch, at least it was until the draw for the opening round was made and we were paired with Pecsi Muncas, a little-known Hungarian side. The general reaction was: 'Who? Where?' It proved a gentle reintroduction to continental competition with a comfortable 2-0 home win; then, unusually for United but partially because we had injury problems, we set out to stifle our opponents in the away leg

81

and won a pretty dull game 1-0. It certainly wasn't one of the glamour nights we had been looking forward to so avidly, though the scene was brightened by a few Father Christmas outfits in the crowd as some of our fans found a different way to wear red and white.

Santa in October? Surely that would be the most bizarre note of the campaign, but no, it wasn't. In the next round we drew Wrexham from the lower reaches of our own Fourth Division, who were to finish the season as the Football League's bottom club, but I won't let that deflect any of the glory from a picture-book goal I scored against them in the first leg, a 3-0 victory at Old Trafford. We were already two up when one of their defenders headed the ball out to me. I think I was just inside the penalty box, though some would say the distance grows every time I tell the story. My first thought was to hit it on the full, but some instinct told me to let it bounce, so I took a step back before volleying it into the roof of the net. It was an absolute peach and I told the lads that was the turning point of our whole season. They wouldn't have it, for some reason.

The tie produced another surreal note when we were forced to spend the night before the second leg in a Welsh hotel, because the rules stated that clubs had to arrive in the host country at least 24 hours before each game. It seemed daft, because we ended up sleeping less than an hour away from Manchester. But for that inflexible regulation, we could have driven down on the day of the game and spent the previous night tucked up in our own beds at home. It didn't make much difference to me because I didn't have a family at the time, but it was frustrating for the lads who did. We spend so much time away as a matter of course, and this seemed unnecessary.

After cruising to a 2-0 win at the Racecourse Ground, we found ourselves facing genuinely formidable quarter-final opposition in the form of the French club, Montpellier. We didn't have a lot of European experience between us and the manager warned us that in Europe, just when you felt things were going according to plan, the roof could fall in without any warning. Sure enough that happened at Old Trafford, where an own-goal by Lee Martin left us with a 1-1 draw which was barely adequate, especially given the away-goals rule.

The atmosphere was soured when 'cheat' claims were levelled at Sparky after Montpellier defender Pascal Baills was sent off for aiming a head-butt at our fiery Welshman. Their chairman milked the controversy for all he was worth, reckoning that Mark had gone down too easily, adding that he wouldn't be welcome in France, where he would get his come-uppance.

That really stoked up their fans for what proved to be our toughest battle on the way to the final, but soon Clayton Blackmore quietened the crowd, getting us going with a long-distance free-kick in the second minute, then Brucie clinched our place in the last four with a penalty just after the interval.

Now United faced Legia Warsaw, nominally the weakest of the semi-finalists but clearly no pushovers, having recently conquered Sampdoria of Italy. We had avoided both Barcelona and Juventus, either of whom would have offered a mouth-watering prospect, but we were not complaining and set off for Poland with our hopes and confidence high.

I don't think many of us were prepared for the bleak, grey country which awaited us. It was a real eye-opener to see the hellish conditions in which the people had to live. There was so much poverty, with most of the locals walking around in drab clothes. It was as though we had blundered into the Dark Ages. Certainly it put the pampered world of professional football into sharp perspective and made us think about the general amenities of everyday life which we take for granted. Warsaw was depressing to visit, so it must have been horrendous to live there.

Football-wise, too, we were in for an initial shock as Legia took the lead after about half an hour. There seemed to be no danger, then 'Bang' we were behind. Fortunately we came back with three goals from Choccy, Sparky and Brucie, which set us up nicely for the home leg. We drew that one-apiece and now Manchester United were truly back in the European big time, facing Barcelona in the final in Rotterdam.

That was easily the biggest occasion of my career to date, the first time I'd come up against one of the true giants, and I felt uncharacteristically nervous on the bus on the way to the ground. Normally I managed to be pretty composed, but this time there was so much running through my head and I couldn't stop it from bubbling up. How was I going to perform against mighty Barcelona? How would I cope with Michael Laudrup, one of the world's top strikers? I was desperate not to let myself or my family down, and I was trying to feed too much information through my brain, which didn't suit me. After a while, though, I managed to calm myself down by shutting everything out, not talking to anybody. Somehow I found an inner peace, went into some kind of mental zone where I could just forget everything.

I'd been stirred up a little bit by the fact that the Barcelona coach, Johan Cruyff, had said his team should win and that our two centre-halves couldn't pass the ball. It's not nice being dissed by one of the legends of the game, and I was determined to prove him wrong. I don't know why managers and coaches make such statements when there's every chance it will just wind up the other side. Maybe he thought it would have a detrimental effect on us, but if he did then he got it wrong. Perhaps it was merely a throwaway comment that he didn't think twice about. Whatever, I remember releasing one slide-rule ball for Brian McClair in the first half and I felt like running over to the bench and saying 'Who can't pass the f****** ball, Johan?' Unfortunately Choccy blasted it over the bar, so the point would have been lost. Still I never tire of watching that pass on video. It was probably one of the best balls I ever played.

It was a soggy night in Rotterdam, a really miserable Manchester night, and that suited us far better than it did Barcelona. The atmosphere was fantastic, with our fans filling about three-quarters of the stadium, and that gave us a terrific lift. We were very much the underdogs – I believe they were quoted at three-to-one on to win – and although they were missing Hristo Stoichkov, the brilliant Bulgarian, their side was packed with top stars.

But we got our approach pretty right on the night, performing well as a team, with Choccy playing up against sweeper Ronald Koeman, stifling the Dutchman's superb ability on the ball and his range of passing. Then there was Sparky; what a great night he had against his former club. I'll never forget that second goal. The commentator said: 'He looks as though he's taken it too wide,' then he absolutely smashed it in, in true Mark Hughes-style, from an unbelievably acute angle. He had to put lots of pace on his shot, otherwise it would have been cut out by a recovering defender, but it fair rifled into the net.

For our first goal, Robbo floated a free-kick, and Brucie met it with a header which was going in but Sparky nipped in to touch it over the line. He had to make sure, because he'd have looked pretty stupid if someone had nicked it to safety while he was being polite to Brucie. Two up after 75 minutes, we were cruising, but then suddenly, with 11 minutes left, the outcome was back in the melting pot when Koeman squeezed a free-kick under the body of Les Sealey. To tell the truth, I'm not sure that Les was fit enough to be playing at all. He had received a serious knee injury in the League Cup Final defeat by Sheffield Wednesday, the wound became poisoned and then it was a race against time for him to be ready for Rotterdam. In the end he was asked if he was okay, and he said yes, taking the field with his leg heavily bandaged to avoid further infection. Still, most of the lads didn't think he was fit and they weren't sure whether he should have played, though it's hard to say whether he would have stopped Koeman's effort if he had been 100 per-cent fit. True, it was in the corner of the goal, but he seemed a tad sluggish in going for it, there was no way that his mobility was perfect. I can't deny that I was worried at that stage, and I guess the manager must have been, too, because he had Gary Walsh warming up on the touchline, ready to go on.

After conceding that goal the team owed a huge debt of gratitude to Clayton Blackmore for a momentous goal-line clearance. Certainly I felt thankful towards Clayton, but not as thankful as Brucie. He hadn't put a foot wrong all night but then he chested the ball down and tried to hit it back to the 'keeper with his weaker left peg, and left it short. Laudrup evaded Les and, in that instant, the horrible thought flashed across my mind that we were going to extra time after dominating so much of the play. But then, as if by magic, Clayton popped up to save us, capping a season of magnificent displays at left-back. That term I'd say he was probably our most consistent player, undoubtedly it was the biggest season he ever enjoyed at Old Trafford, and it didn't surprise me when he won quite a few player of the year awards from the various supporters club branches.

But sadly for the amiable little Welshman, Paul Parker arrived, Denis Irwin was switched to the left and Clayton found himself the odd man out. We missed him when he went – he was a bright presence in the dressing room as well as a tremendous player – but at least he could depart in the knowledge that he had a major hand in one of United's most memorable triumphs.

His heroic clearance took the stuffing out of Barcelona. From that instant, the night was ours – and what a night it was. We had so many of our fans there, chanting and swaying in the fretty mist that engulfed the stadium, and when most of the Barcelona supporters left at the final whistle, the United contingent had the place to ourselves. There was an unforgettable lap of honour, then one of the directors, Mike Edelson, made a home video of the dressing room celebrations, the singing in the bath, the drinking of champagne from the trophy, the whole incredibly joyful scene.

Then, just as we were getting the bus back to the hotel for more partying, my room-mate Micky Phelan was called in for a routine drug test, but he was so dehydrated that he couldn't provide a urine sample for ages. Most of the lads disappeared, but I couldn't leave him on his own, so I stayed behind and, fair play to Incey, he waited as well till Micky managed his little potful. Later, when we saw all the video footage of the boys on the bus having such a great time, then maybe we regretted hanging around. Given our time over again, I don't know if we'd have stayed with you, Micky!

We ended up getting a taxi back to the hotel, where the party was already getting into full swing, and soon we were making up for lost time. God knows what time we got to bed. It seemed that no sooner had my head touched the pillow than I was being woken to head for home. Some of my memories of the knees-up are hazy, but I do recall Alex Ferguson coming round with a box of cigars, which seemed a trifle surreal, and I wondered afterwards if I had been hallucinating. Normally I didn't smoke, but I think I made an exception and puffed a cigar that night. A lot more champagne was consumed on the plane journey home – that was one flight that didn't bother me, I guess I was pretty well anaesthetised – and then there was that unforgettable progress through Manchester on the open-topped bus.

When I was able to step back and put what we had achieved into some sort of perspective, I felt proud. For United to go back into Europe for the first time in half a decade, and to win a trophy, in the process announcing that English football was alive and well, was quite incredible, a massive statement of intent. Also the Cup Winners' Cup was one of the few trophies that the club had never won before, and it's one which no longer exists, so there's a real bit of history there. I feel privileged to have played a part in creating it.

Although that season will always be remembered primarily for European glory, we also made splendid progress on the domestic front, vastly improving our League form to finish sixth in the table, albeit no fewer than 24 points behind the champions, George Graham's Arsenal. In the FA Cup, I must admit my most vivid memory was of my up-and-downer with Fergie at half-time in the Queen's Park Rangers game. We survived that, but exited the competition rather limply to Norwich at Carrow Road in the fifth round.

There was ultimate disappointment, too, in the League Cup, when we lost the final 1-0 to Sheffield Wednesday, the game in which Les Sealey's knee was cut wide open and he refused to leave the pitch, which was utterly ridiculous. There were some terrific wins along the road to Wembley, though, with our victims including Liverpool, Arsenal and Leeds, three of the top four clubs in the League table. Unarguably the pick of those victories was at Highbury, where we thrashed the champions-to-be by six goals to two, with Lee Sharpe plundering a sensational hat-trick and Danny Wallace playing out of his skin. Our momentum was beginning to pick up and there was a definite sense that we were building something worthwhile. We had always been capable of isolated brilliant performances, but now our consistency was improving markedly, and we all felt confident that, before long, we could end the club's championship drought, which had lasted a barely credible quarter of a century.

As we kicked off 1991/92, the team changed significantly with the advent of goalkeeper Peter Schmeichel, full-back Paul Parker and winger Andrei Kanchelskis, who had made his debut at the end of the previous term. All three of them made a vastly positive impact and helped to move Manchester United closer to realising their title ambition.

Peter was hardly a household name when he arrived, though we did hear something of his reputation in his Danish homeland as a bit of a shouter, even a bit of a nutter. At first, though, we didn't see what that was all about, because he was a little bit taken aback by the physical nature of the Premiership. He wasn't used to so many crosses being pumped in at him, or some of the ferocious challenges which strikers were allowed to get away with in this country and, perhaps as a result, he seemed quite subdued in his first couple of months at Old Trafford. But as he got used to the English game, and grew in stature, then the shouting and screaming and obscenities that we came to know and love started to become an integral part of his approach.

Right from the off we had the feeling that he was a top-notcher. Being 6ft 4ins tall and bulky with it, he cut an intimidating figure, and he had a huge presence, which a defender always likes in his goalkeeper. As a youngster Peter had played a lot of handball, and you could see that in his game. He used to throw himself at opponents, just spread himself as large as he could in one-on-one confrontations, employing the star-jump technique which I don't think had been seen too much in this country before his arrival. When you saw a forward through on Schmeichel, you didn't feel that the attacker was the favourite because our 'keeper presented such a formidable barrier to pass. Beyond any doubt, once Peter had adapted his game to English conditions he became, for a number of years, the best goalkeeper in the world.

Parks, too, was a marvellous addition. He'd been a regular member of the England squad, had played in Italia '90 and clearly was one of the finest defenders in the country. A full-back was needed because poor Lee Martin was struggling with injury, so the Gaffer slotted Paul in at right-back and moved Denis Irwin to the left flank, where he adapted magnificently. With two such reliable performers on either side of Brucie and myself, and with Peter behind us, it's fair to say we developed into a pretty solid and reliable defensive unit.

As for Andrei, who I'll discuss in more detail a little later, he was a pure entertainer who got the supporters on their feet, and gave us a thrilling extra dimension. Much more would be heard of the hitherto obscure Ukrainian.

Having assembled a terrific squad, the Gaffer made the unusual step, at the outset of the 1991/92 campaign, of predicting that we would win the League. Some thought his words were a trifle rash, given United's 25 years in the championship wilderness, but I agreed with him. I thought we were more than ready, and for most of the season it looked as if we were going to prove him correct. In the end, we were pipped by Leeds, who had fought it out with us every step of the way, and I must pay tribute to them for their resilience. They won the title fair and square, and good luck to them. But that didn't shake the belief in our dressing room that we were now the best team in the land. We felt we had enough in our locker to have taken the crown, though it might have been argued that maybe we still lacked that little bit of something – flair, unpredictability, imagination, inspiration, call it what you will – to break down opposing defences. Before too long, of course, that would be rectified, and from the unexpected quarter of Elland Road itself.

Ironically, in 1991/92 we drew Leeds in both major domestic cup competitions, which was not ideal because when you're going for the title you can do without extra major tests. As it turned out we beat them in both the League Cup and FA Cup, but in the game which mattered most to us, on their ground just after Christmas, we threw away a crucial lead near the end. To be more precise, it was me who threw it away. We were a goal up and looking comfortable when I brought down Gary McAllister for a clear-cut penalty. Well done, Pally!

We took a lot of stick that year as being bottlers, for getting twitchy towards the end, and that hurt, but I don't think it was a fair criticism. We lost some influential players on the run-in, key figures such as Robbo and Incey, which left a chronic gap in the centre of midfield, but possibly even more destructive was the insane fixture congestion. Certainly I don't think we were given a fair deal by the Football League, who ordered us to play four vital games in the space of eight days at the climax of a hectic campaign.

The one that cost us dearly was losing to Forest at home. We dominated that match, poured all over them for the whole 90 minutes, but they broke away twice and scored both times. Two days later we travelled to West

Ham, who were already doomed to relegation, and we lost to a freak goal. I hammered the ball away to the edge of the box, it cannoned into the knee of Kenny Brown and somehow bounced back past Schmeichel. Beyond that, West Ham played out of their skins on the night. If they had put that much effort into every match then it's hard to see how they could have gone down. I just couldn't understand them.

Next we went to Liverpool, feeling pretty dismal, as Leeds had been taking advantage of our setbacks. Such is the intense rivalry between United and Liverpool that Anfield is the last place on earth we would have chosen to lose such a big prize. We knew that if we waved goodbye to the championship there, we would remember it for the rest of our lives. At that point practically all hope had gone, though we were not quite out of it mathematically, even when Leeds had a lucky win against Sheffield United that same morning. But we lost 2-0 and it was purgatory for our fans at Anfield, with so much spite and vitriol pouring from their Liverpool counterparts.

For me it was a thoroughly painful afternoon physically as well as emotionally, because I was forced to leave the action with a horribly sliced foot. But the sheer hate that we encountered made the more lasting impact. Alex Ferguson wanted us to remember it, to imprint it indelibly on our memories so we would make damned sure we never experienced it again. That desire came from within the players, too, and it was a key building block for the success that was to follow in the not-too-distant future.

Most of all we didn't like being called bottlers, and that was a jibe which was rammed down our throats repeatedly. It was an easy line to chuck in, but there was never any mention of the cruel injuries we had suffered in the engine room of the team at such a crucial time, or the ridiculous pile-up of fixtures sanctioned by the Football League. Looking at it in retrospect, maybe both the Liverpool supporters and the authorities were doing us a favour, because their attitudes made us all the more determined. We knew we were good enough to win the title, and that for a club the size of Manchester United it simply wasn't acceptable to keep missing out, year after year. Accordingly we resolved that we were NOT going down in history as merely the next bunch of players who failed to capture the club's modern equivalent of the Holy Grail.

Not that 1991/92 was devoid of achievement as we won the League Cup, something United had never done before, and the campaign was especially memorable for me because we beat Middlesbrough over two legs in the semi-final. It was a hard situation because, as an old 'Boro boy,

I wanted my former club to win a major competition for the first time in their history. That said, I couldn't let emotion stand in the way of my personal ambitions and what I wanted to achieve with United.

After all, it was a semi-final, therefore a very big deal, and I was desperately keen to return to Wembley, so I had to put all my previous loyalties to one side. I was facing a lot of my old mates, and inevitably there was plenty of banter between Bernie Slaven and myself. I remember winding up Bern and defender Curtis Fleming in advance of the tie when I'd gone home for the weekend and we were out on a Saturday night at a club in Yarm. Flem and I had had a drink, though teetotaller Bernie hadn't, of course, and at the end of the night we settled down for some craic about the game. Deliberately provoking them, I said: 'How can you boys expect to beat Manchester United?' They both got a bit tetchy for a while, but I managed to calm them down, it was all a laugh. Bernie kept telling me how he was going to score against me, and so he did in the Old Trafford leg, after a tremendous run by Stuart Ripley. Bernie never lets me forget that goal, or the one he snatched in another League meeting with United at Ayresome Park.

In the semi-final, we drew 0-0 at 'Boro, then we prevailed 2-1 at Old Trafford after extra time, but it all might have been so different. When the game was locked at 1-1, John Hendrie broke through, rounded Peter Schmeichel and tried to put ball into empty net. But just as it was bobbling over the line, I managed to hack it away. Had that gone in then United might well have lost, and 'Boro supporters have reminded me of the incident many times over the years. Then, in the last minute of normal time, Schmeichel made one of the best saves I've ever seen, pushing a downward header from Willie Falconer around a post. We went through in extra time thanks to a strike from Ryan Giggs, and I was a much relieved individual, because I'd never have lived it down if we had lost. I think United fans believed it would be an easy task against a Second Division side, but 'Boro were a good team, well organised by Lennie Lawrence, and they stretched us all the way. I did feel for them after the game, but everyone should understand that professionals can't let sentiment get in the way of doing their job. I couldn't have been more pleased, though, when my old team won promotion that season, a prize that was thoroughly deserved.

As for the League Cup Final against Nottingham Forest, it goes down as the final everyone forgot. We were hot on the trail of the title at the time and people tended to treat the knockout competition as incidental, which was a bit unfair as there was rather more importance attached to it in those days than there is now. To us it was another major trophy, our third in successive seasons, and another sign that we were on the right track.

In all honesty, the game against Forest was not the greatest, but it's remembered vividly by the United lads for playing against the young Roy Keane, who was then in the process of making a name for himself. That afternoon at Wembley, I think he must have had a stand-up barney with every one of our players. He was constantly kicking and snarling and scrapping, always trying to inspire his team-mates and nettle the opposition. Ultimately, though, an early goal by Brian McClair, who was put through by Giggsy, was enough to win it for us. For some people, the enduring image of the match was not the football or even the result; they remember it as the *J-Cloth* final, because United were wearing shirts with a blue-and-white squiggly pattern. I have to admit, they weren't very nice.

For me, that season carried an extra personal significance in that I began to experience injury problems which would dog me on and off for the rest of my career. I was getting pains behind my knee, especially when I was doing long runs, so that although I was able to play I couldn't do the stamina work. I was sent to all sorts of specialists but they could find no damage to the knee, so it was related to the back. It turned out that the heavy plodding involved in the long-distance stuff was playing on the discs and irritating a nerve in the back, which caused the knee trouble. After that, for the rest of my career I wasn't able to do long runs, which was hardly a catastrophe for me because I never enjoyed them anyway. Instead I had to train in other ways to build up my stamina.

But the event which staggered me most profoundly, and most pleasurably, in 1992 was being voted as Player of the Year by my professional peers. When Brian McClair, United's Professional Footballers Association representative, approached Steve Bruce and myself in training one day and asked us if we could go to the PFA ceremony, I didn't have the faintest glimmer of expectation that I might be in the running for the main award. I'd never attended the event before because it is staged in London, too far to drive on a Sunday night ahead of training the next morning. So we both shook our heads; there was no way that we could make it. But then Choccy grinned and said both of us were among the six nominations, which rather changed the picture. Obviously we were delighted, if totally surprised, and we could see that it was important for the club as well as for ourselves that we went down.

So we did, and we were having an enjoyable night with some terrific craic, when Steve and I got chatting about the award. He looked round and said: 'You realise something?' I said 'What?' He said: 'None of the other nominees are here.' Out of the six, who also included Stuart Pearce, Paul McGrath, Ray Houghton and Gary Lineker, there was only Steve and me at the do. So we deduced, as Sherlock Holmes would, through all the clues that we were given, that one of us was going to win it. We didn't miss a lot!

As the enormity of the situation hit home, it changed the entire atmosphere of the evening for us. I became so nervous I couldn't eat my dinner. I was petrified about making a speech if I won it. I was not prepared for it in any way. Delighted as I was to be nominated, never for a moment did I think I might win. As we sat there, Steve was saying: 'It's you.' Of course, I was going: 'Nah, it's you!' As the minutes ticked by we became more and more apprehensive until, eventually, they read out my name. Genuinely, I could hardly credit it. Nobody had pre-warned me in any way; there had not been the slightest hint from Choccy. I was just dazed, which Cloughie might have realised when he stood on my foot! I forgot to thank Mam and Dad, but I did thank the manager and the players, said it was the proudest moment of my career, all that type of stuff, but all the while my head was buzzing. I can't remember exactly what I came out with but almost certainly it was deeply embarrassing.

It was one hell of a tribute to be selected for the PFA award. There can be no bigger honour in football than the one you get from the people that you play against week in and week out, the people you gauge yourself against. Somehow it was the final justification of everything I'd done since leaving Middlesbrough. I had played in big games, in finals, won trophies, represented my country, and now this. I had to pinch myself to realise how far my career had developed in such a short period of time. I'd gone from non-League football to achieving this previously unimaginable height in the space of six or seven years. It must go down as the most satisfying personal achievement of my life.

CHAPTER EIGHT

DEEP, DEEP EMOTION

As the 1992/93 season began it was not immediately apparent that Manchester United would fare better than in 1991/92, which had finished on such a devastatingly dismal low point. We lost our first two games, against Sheffield United and Everton, then managed only a draw with Ipswich.

During the summer Alex Ferguson had been searching for a centre-forward and eventually brought in Dion Dublin, who didn't linger too long at Old Trafford but who remains a close friend of mine to this day. He'd scored lots of goals, and lots of different sorts of goals, at Cambridge; the manager saw a video of them and took a chance for £1 million. Dion scored on his full debut at Southampton, supplying the goal that gave us the first win we needed so desperately, but very soon his leg was snapped in a challenge by Eric Young of Crystal Palace at Old Trafford and his momentum was gone. We all felt so sorry for Dion, but the Gaffer had no alternative but to look for a replacement.

Before signing Dublin, the manager had received a knockback from Alan Shearer of Southampton, and had also made an approach for Sheffield Wednesday's David Hirst. One night on the team coach he had asked Steve Bruce and myself who we thought was better, Shearer or Hirst. We both went for Shearer, while it was clear that the Gaffer favoured Hirst. Sadly, David suffered a succession of debilitating injuries which prevented him from fulfilling his potential, so we'll never know what he might have achieved. Or, for that matter, who made the most perceptive choice, Brucie and myself or Alex Ferguson.

What is sure is that the two of them were neck and neck, and that Shearer was one terrific centre-forward. When we faced Southampton in the FA Cup in 1992, he played up front on his own and made a gigantic impression on Steve and me. He was only a kid of 21, but he had a perfect attitude, wonderful willingness to run and work for his team, and there was an intelligence about his play, too. He wasn't wasting energy with stupid runs, but operating cleverly between the pair of us. It might be imagined that the two would easily dominate the one, but he caught us out persistently, never really being sure which of us should pick him up.

Alan was a great finisher, too, though we could never have dreamed just how prolific he would turn out to be over the next dozen or so seasons.

I'd have been more than happy to see him arrive at United. What he might have achieved with us fairly beggars belief. He was so strong, a tremendous target-man who could hold the ball up and bring others into play; he worked like a Trojan to chase down lost causes, and he could score goals from outside the box or poach them from close range. He had everything, there wasn't a weakness that I could see, but in the summer of 1992 he chose Blackburn Rovers instead of Manchester United. Mind, I have to wonder, if Shearer had joined us, then what would have happened to Sparky, who was to prove such a perfect foil for Eric Cantona? Mark, too, retained the ball brilliantly, adding so much to the team by feeding the likes of Giggs, Kanchelskis, Lee Sharpe and Eric. True, he wasn't the most prolific of scorers himself, but he made up for that in other ways. So, judging by what we won, it might have been just as well that Shearer didn't come and that Sparky stayed!

As it was, shorn of Dion, United soldiered on through the autumn, not losing again until a shock home defeat by Wimbledon at Hallowe'en, but drawing too many, and by late November we were in sixth place in the First Division table, not disastrously off the pace but not appearing to threaten too much, either. We had plenty of top-quality performers, but somehow there was still a missing link. We needed something, or more accurately someone, to ignite us – and then it happened.

More by luck than judgement, it would seem, we signed Eric Cantona from Leeds, and Manchester United were never the same again. It seems that our chairman, Martin Edwards, was approached by his Elland Road counterpart with an inquiry about Denis Irwin, which was rebuffed out of hand. Alex Ferguson happened to be in the room at the time, and indicated that the chairman should ask about Eric. To the Gaffer's astonishment, Leeds were ready to do business and he brought off the deal of his life.

We had played against Eric the previous season when he'd come off the bench for Leeds and nearly scored with an overhead kick from the edge of the box, which epitomised exactly the kind of unpredictable player he was. As he had consulted us about Shearer and Hirst, now our manager asked Brucie and myself what we thought of Cantona and our reaction was: 'Yes, he's a player, he's got something, and it's something different.' I don't know how much impact that conversation had in bringing Eric to the club, but I hope it helped in some way.

Not long afterwards a journalist called me at home and his opening sally was: 'What about your latest signing?' I didn't know we'd made one and he put me through a guessing game in which I mentioned any number of strikers before I gave up. When he revealed it was Cantona, I was stunned. That name had been nowhere near the front of my mind.

When he arrived we could see straight away that he was a showman. Not in the sense of being a circus act, but in that he needed to express himself through his football. He was always trying things in training, astonishing little flicks and touches that the rest of us wouldn't dream about, and we loved that flair. Beyond that he had a unique aura about him, a certain arrogance, so that when he walked in his chest was always puffed out. I suppose it could have upset some people, but it didn't upset us. We'd heard that he was a difficult character, that he wasn't trustworthy, that you couldn't rely on him, but we were determined to take him as we found him and welcomed him to the club as we would have done any other player.

During Eric's settling-in period we were watching, monitoring, assessing him, and gradually it dawned on us that he was having a profound impact on the side. This was illustrated vividly on Boxing Day when we were three down to Sheffield Wednesday at Hillsborough, then he played a part in setting up two goals for Brian McClair before scoring the equaliser himself. When you get a draw in those circumstances, in terms of morale it's like a win, an unbelievable lift. In all fairness, Lee Sharpe was brilliant that day, too, but there was a feeling that it was Eric who was supplying the final extra ingredient which was transforming the team.

Now we really began to hit our stride and reached the top of the table in early January with an emphatic home victory over Tottenham in which Eric was nothing short of majestic. To many people it was surprising that United's two main rivals for the title were Aston Villa and Norwich, rather than Arsenal, Liverpool or Leeds, but the two less-fancied clubs showed little sign of wilting as winter became spring. Thus we were still engaged heavily in a three-horse race when we visited Carrow Road in early April with only seven games left, and we reacted like potential champions by blowing the Canaries away with three goals in the first half-hour. Our pace and movement that night were phenomenal and although our former team-mate, Mark Robins, pulled one back in the second period, the strikes by Giggs, Kanchelskis and Cantona offered a sweeping statement of our intent and our resolution as the race hotted up.

That left us a point clear of Norwich but we remained one behind Villa so there was still plenty to do, and we came perilously close to slipping up in our next game, at home to Sheffield Wednesday, which as some wag put it, was memorable for its three halves of football. I'd better explain.

Despite the superb display at Norwich, we were tense during a goalless first half against Wednesday, and when John Sheridan put them ahead from the penalty spot midway through the half, a lot of people feared the worst. It had all the hallmarks of the Forest meltdown in the previous season and a few of our fans got up and walked out, unable to face another devastating disappointment. Had we lost, I cringe to think what might have happened to our title prospects, but we were not finished yet. With four minutes of normal time remaining, Brucie nodded an equaliser from a Denis Irwin corner and Old Trafford went wild with relief. At least that meant we could leave the pitch feeling positive, although knowing deep down that we had let an opportunity slip.

However, the drama was not yet complete. During the game the referee had been injured, and had to be substituted, so there was a fair bit of injury time to come. Perhaps when nearly seven minutes of it had elapsed, even our most optimistic supporters might have settled for the point, but then we won another corner. This time Denis's delivery was glanced out by Phil King but I was the first to react and picked up possession near the right-hand corner flag. What else could I do but knock it back into the crowded goalmouth with a bit of pace, a bit of whip – just the sort of cross young Master Beckham would specialise in one day – and it was deflected off Nigel Worthington on to the head of Brucie, who planted it firmly past Chris Woods in the goal.

Old Trafford just exploded, the joy was unconfined. Kiddo charged on to the pitch and on to his knees, embarrassing himself for eternity in front of the United faithful while the manager bounced up and down like a six-year-old. That pair's celebrations showed more clearly than anything else just how much that win meant to us all, and I think the genuine passion they displayed that day moved them closer to the fans than ever before. It was a huge, huge moment in the breaking of our title hoodoo, maybe the moment when most people truly believed we were going to do it at last. To win a game in the seventh minute of injury time was enough to make anyone feel their luck had changed. This was our year, surely.

Of course, much was made about the seemingly never-ending period of added time, but I believe sincerely that it was justified because the substituting of the referee had taken ages. Whatever, that was the afternoon when the legend of Alex Ferguson and his fervent time-keeping was born.

As uplifting as that victory was for United, it would have had Villa and Norwich spitting blood. Because we were running so late, probably they were sitting in their dressing room when it came through that we were being beaten. Their reaction would have been gleeful; what a day for them. Then it would have been a bit of a downer when our equaliser came through, but still they would have been happy at United dropping two home points, which could tilt the championship race significantly in their favour. But then, perhaps as they were getting out of the shower, they would have heard of our winner and it would have been a hell of a psychological blow. They must have felt they were facing an invincible force, a team who would not be denied no matter what the odds, and such a feeling can play havoc with anyone's confidence.

As for us, we felt we were walking on water and reeled off three smashing wins on the trot, against Coventry, Chelsea and Crystal Palace, the last of them particularly telling because Villa lost on the same night. That left us four points clear of Ron Atkinson's side with two matches to play so, with Norwich already out of contention, we were on the very brink.

We could clinch the championship in our next match, against Blackburn at Old Trafford on the following Monday night, but Villa were entertaining Oldham on the Sunday afternoon, and if they were beaten then we would take the title without kicking another ball. The manager had told us not to watch that game because he didn't want us caught up in the emotion of it all. He wanted to spare us the stress and the emotion ahead of the fateful meeting with Blackburn. But did we watch it? Of course we did! Wild horses wouldn't have stopped us, so what chance did Alex Ferguson have?

He took his own advice and went out on the golf course, but there was no way I could do that. I saw the game at home, with Mary and my parents there to help me cope with my nerves. Mind, I couldn't sit down and watch every kick. I was in and out of the house, taking myself off for a short walk then popping back again a minute later; it was unbearable. Some people reckoned it would be preferable if we had the chance to win it at Old Trafford, but we wanted it over as soon as possible, we wanted it dead, we wanted to celebrate.

The game was goalless for a long time, but then Nick Henry put Oldham ahead and we were so, so close to our hearts' desire. Even then a Villa equaliser would have meant we needed something the following night, but it never came. After what seemed like an eternity, the final whistle went and Manchester United were champions.

The initial feeling was more relief than joy. What flashed through my head was: 'Thank God we've done it, it's all over, we've laid to rest the ghost that's been haunting the club for more than a quarter of a century.' Next came the pride that I felt, and I shared the emotion with Mam, Dad and Mary. We were all soaking in this great moment when, ten minutes after the final whistle at Villa Park, Brucie came on the phone with: 'Right, it's a party at my house.'

I was amazed because of the match the following night, but he assured me it was okay, he had phoned Alex Ferguson. According to Steve, the Gaffer had said: 'As long as you don't go mad, you don't have too many, and you're home for a reasonable time, then there's not a problem. Just be sensible and have a good time.' Of course, by the time we'd all left Brucie's house at 4am we were all steamrollered. Everybody came to join in, every member of the team. The press were parked up down the road and people kept coming up to the door to celebrate, but we wanted it to be just the players together with their families. One extra fellow who would have been welcome was Nick Henry, but he didn't show up. We were singing his name all night long, too. 'One Nicky Henry, there's only one Nicky Henry ...'

It was an unbelievable night. We had to order in more beer and champagne, so it was a good job the manager wasn't there. I'm sure Steve would have invited him round, but he might have wanted to send us home before midnight. I don't expect he thought it was the right place for him to be. It all felt a bit weird because we never let our hair down on the night before a game, but the title was in the bag and this was special circumstances. We were on an incredible high and felt a vast sense of achievement.

I've got to admit that I felt a bit groggy when we turned up for the Blackburn game later that day, three hours before the eight o'clock kick-off. The Gaffer was at the door of the grill room where we always had dinner, and he must have been overwhelmed by the smell of alcohol. He could see it in our eyes, and he was shaking his head. He must have looked at us one by one and thought: 'He's had a few ... and he's had a few ... and he's had a few.' Not like us at all.

We were all sat there looking at each other and saying: 'How the hell are we going to deal with this tonight?' We knew Blackburn weren't coming to lie down; Kenny Dalglish's side would have been more than happy to spoil the party, so we knew we had to come round and get our heads on pretty quickly. It would have been dreadful if we had served up our worst performance of the season on the night all our fans had turned up to celebrate. The Gaffer emphasised the point, stressing it was important that we should finish the season playing like champions.

Walking out on the pitch was quite incredible. Banners, flags, scarves, everything was waving, it seemed the very stands were waving. There was just so much deep, deep emotion, and we were bursting with pride. It was like 11 Eric Cantonas going out there with our chests puffed out, we were on top of the world, an indescribable feeling. As well as the joy, we could sense the relief from the fans as well. It was like the whole club was giving two fingers to everybody who'd written us off as bottlers, and to those who had poured their venom on us a year earlier. For many supporters of a certain age, that was the biggest night of the whole Ferguson era. In view of what was to follow in 1999, I know that's a lot to say, but it was true. Those people had suffered 26 years of abuse, being forced to bow before Liverpool's serial supremacy, and that hell was over at last.

But only five minutes into the action it felt like another nightmare was beginning as Kevin Gallacher nipped across me at the near post to put Blackburn in front. I groaned: 'Oh no, here we go!' But soon we got a free-kick, Ryan buried it in the top corner from 30 yards, and from that moment we felt it would be our night after all. It was still 1-1 by the half-time interval, during which the lads started giving me stick for being the only regular outfielder who hadn't scored a League goal that season. 'Even Parks has scored; it's a joke, man!' This was a long-running wind-up and I thought it was time to assert myself, so I told them: 'Right, if we get a free-kick this half it's mine, my free-kick, nobody else's, I'm going to take it!'

We went out again, totally relaxed and in control now with the alcohol out of our systems, and started playing some lovely football which led to Eric and Incey combining for our second goal. We were really enjoying ourselves in front of that lovely crowd, with all the pressure lifted, and I thought to myself: 'Life doesn't get better than this.' But suddenly it did.

As if it was scripted from above, in the 90th minute we won a free-kick on the edge of their box. I think both Incey and Giggsy fancied it, but for the first and only time in my career I barged forward, letting them know who was boss, and said: 'No, I'm having this. Step out of my road.'

I put the ball down, spotted a little gap in the corner of the net and thought to myself: 'If I can shank this in the right direction I might be all right here.' So I hit it hard and low, it took the slightest of deflections and skidded past goalkeeper Bobby Mimms in exactly the intended spot. Afterwards the lads reckoned I couldn't believe my eyes when it went in, but I never had any doubts; well, not many! As the pictures showed, my face lit up like a man who'd won the lottery. It was such a perfect way to cap the season for myself. It was the fun element more than anything, having a laugh with the lads. The craic went on for ages and it was great for the team, though I couldn't understand why I wasn't being offered the free-kick job for the next season.

After that we had the joyous experience of picking up the Premiership trophy in front of our own fans and embarking on a phenomenal lap of honour which seemed to go on and on. It was a perfect evening as we gave ourselves up to a mixture of pride in our achievement and overwhelming relief.

The most touching, and appropriate, moment came when the team skipper, Steve Bruce, insisted that Robbo went up with him to receive the trophy. Although he'd made enough appearances to qualify for a medal, that night United's Captain Marvel had been used as a substitute, as he had been for most of the season. But the club and the players owed a massive debt of gratitude to that man. He had carried the team for so long, he'd been a leader and an inspiration, yet he had never really got that close to winning the title, at least until 1991/92. Bryan had suffered chronic injury problems in 1985/86 after United had started with ten straight wins and not been beaten until the 16th game, and it must have been agonising for him to see the prize slip away. At the presentation ceremony Robbo didn't push himself forward in any way, refusing point-blank to go up at first. But Brucie cajoled him into doing it and nothing could have been more right. Six days later, as if to underline his indestructible qualities, Robbo started our final game at Wimbledon and scored his only League goal of the campaign in a 2-0 victory which stretched the title-winning margin to ten points. Fabulous.

Between our dates with Blackburn and Wimbledon, the players enjoyed a blinding day at Chester races. We had a high old time, never getting out of the champagne bar. I can safely say it was the first time I ever went to a race meeting and never saw a horse. Mark Hughes did an interview on TV and it might have been in Welsh, because nobody understood a word he said.

It's wonderful to be among the players in that type of situation. The camaraderie is unbeatable, and once you're out of the game, that's the thing you can never replace. Only the people who had won the title, the first one as a team, could understand what it was all about, and it was one of the greatest times of my life. Taking the club as a whole, it had been building over a period of years, and I felt immensely privileged to have been one of the boys who put Manchester United back on the pinnacle. Without a shadow of doubt, of all the four championships that I played a part in winning at Old Trafford, that first one gave me the most intense enjoyment.

Naturally in the circumstances, our cup exploits in 1992/93 were overshadowed, which was just as well because they were pretty negligible. We went out early in both domestic competitions, which was disappointing, while our first-round exit from the UEFA Cup proved particularly embarrassing to me. We lost to Torpedo Moscow in a tie which didn't produce a single goal until the penalty shoot-out. There we were, at the end of extra time on a freezing night in Moscow, huddled in the centre circle with blankets around us while the spot-kicks were being taken. I think Incey, Denis and Robbo had scored for us, and maybe Brucie had missed and Neil Webb was psyching himself up to take the crucial fifth with us a goal behind. Now poor Webby had missed the decisive penalty when we had lost an FA Cup shoot-out to Southampton the season before, and I could see he was apprehensive over this one. Naturally enough, he didn't fancy being the villain again, so – and I don't know what came over me – I offered to take it for him. He was going through a difficult time at United anyway, so volunteering seemed the right thing to do. Even so, I expected him to brush me aside, to say that of course he had to take it, but like a shot he said: 'Yes, all right then.' I thought: 'Pally, Pally, what are you thinking about? What have you done?' Hell's bells, I had never taken a penalty before at senior level so this was risky, to say the least. But there was no way out so I tried to give the 'keeper the shifty-eyes routine, looking one way and shooting the other, that old favourite; unfortunately it was the perfect height for him to make a save, he threw his cap on it and we were out of Europe, leaving me to wish the frosty earth would open and swallow me up. Mind, there are never any recriminations from team-mates when you lose a shoot-out. They know it's just a matter of having the balls to stand up there and have a go, so I was not exactly scarred for life by the experience. What did puzzle me, though, was why I was never asked to take another penalty …

CHAPTER NINE

WHAT GREAT TEAMS DO

Alex Ferguson kicked off our preparations for the 1993/94 season by demonstrating his genius – and I don't use that word lightly – at managing a group of footballers. He walked into the dressing room and commended us on our efforts in the previous campaign. He was full of praise for the delightful football we had played and for the manner in which we had conducted ourselves under intense pressure; he talked at length about the laying of the championship jinx, which had hung over Old Trafford like a black cloud for such an unacceptable length of time.

But, having patted us on the back, he revealed that he was disturbed by a nagging doubt about the future. He knew he had a squad with all the quality needed to lift the game's great prizes, but was it possible, he asked us, that there were some among us who were content to rest on their laurels, who felt that the job was done now that the title had finally been won? Did everyone in that room have the desire, the raw hunger to go on, to do it again, and again, and again? Because, he assured us, with fire in his eyes and thunder on his brow, that's what great teams do.

Then he came up with his masterstroke. He told us: 'I've got a sealed envelope in my office drawer. In it is a piece of paper on which I've written down the names of all those players who I think might be satisfied with last year's success, and who might not have what it takes to go on again. It might make interesting reading at the end of the season.' With that, he took a long, hard look around the dressing room, and he walked out.

The first reaction of the players was to have a good laugh about it. But pretty soon somebody said: 'Who do you think he's got on his list, then?' Straight away he'd got it into our collective psyche that we had a lot of work to do, because no one wanted to be shown up as a name in his envelope in ten months time. Alex Ferguson was, and remains, a master of mind games. I don't know if he thought this one up himself, or whether he had learned it from somebody else. What I do know is that it was mightily effective.

As it turned out, the Gaffer needn't have worried unduly about anti-climax in 1993/94, and he didn't need to fish out his envelope, as we went one better than in the previous momentous term, winning the League and

FA Cup double for the first time in the club's history. In fact, we went agonisingly close to lifting the domestic treble but we lost the first leg of it, and deservedly so, to Ron Atkinson's Aston Villa in the League Cup Final. At the time of writing, still nobody has won all three English honours in the same season, and nobody has come as close as we did in '94. It's a shame we didn't quite manage it because it would have meant more in those days, when managers were less inclined to field weakened teams in cup competitions, and certainly the League Cup had far more stature than it does in the early years of the 21st century.

Our prospects of renewed glory had been strengthened immeasurably in the summer of 1993 by the acquisition of Roy Keane from Nottingham Forest. Some time earlier, the manager had canvassed the views of the lads, asking: 'If there's one player you could bring to this club next year, who would it be?' It was no contest: everybody said Roy Keane. We'd all had bitter fall-outs with him on the pitch at one point or another, but players relish that type of competition. Of course, Roy was a monumentally talented footballer, but what made him stand out from the crowd was the raw edge of his desire to win every time he took the field.

We were delighted when it was announced that United had signed him, especially as Blackburn, a club on the up, had believed that they had him in the bag. In fact, Roy had told Blackburn boss Kenny Dalglish that he would go to Ewood Park, but then Alex Ferguson came in and snuck him away. I don't think Kenny will ever forgive Roy for that, and I know he gave him an earful down the phone. The outcome was hardly surprising, though, because Old Trafford is a dream destination for any young footballer, especially if he hails from Ireland, where United have a phenomenal following.

It was apparent from his earliest training sessions with us that Keaney was a fantastic player, but his influence at the club built up gradually. The energy and drive were always apparent, but already we had two massive central midfield influences in Bryan Robson and Paul Ince, performers of a similar ilk, and at first Keane thought it wasn't his place to be the snarling, screaming motivator that he'd been at Forest. Possibly it was a case of the Irishman showing the two Englishmen a bit of respect, which they had certainly earned. Happily, there was no restraint in his performances on the pitch, which underlined his stature as soon as he came into the side.

He gave off the same kind of aura as Robbo. Indeed, the most meaningful compliment I can pay Roy Keane is that he's the closest thing to Bryan Robson I have ever seen. That throws up the old debate over which of the two was the best. Well, Fergie's been quoted as saying Roy's the finest he's seen, but maybe I would just give my verdict to Robbo if I had to choose one. That said, I wouldn't want to split them. Both of them were thoroughbreds who made the game look so easy, and it seemed that they could do every job on the park with equal facility. They could pass the ball beautifully, they could win it, they could score, they could defend, they were good in the air, they could lead. Both were absolute diamonds. You are privileged to play with one of them in a career, let alone two. Yet we actually had the pair in the same team at the same time, and Incey was high quality, too. What all of them brought to the table was phenomenal.

Frequently I am asked what Roy Keane is like as a person and, certainly in his early days at Old Trafford, I would sum him up in two words – mad Irishman. He always had a very short fuse and there was the odd explosive incident. In his own book, he has written of his drinking and I don't intend to dwell on that here. Suffice it to say that we had a couple of temporary differences, but even though there were periods when we weren't speaking to one another, there was always an essential and mutual respect. Certainly we had some terrific times together, both on and off the pitch.

One of our arguments started off as a nothing thing, but grew bigger than it should have done. Afterwards neither of us was going to be the first one to speak in case it was construed as a sign of weakness, or whatever. Daft, really.

I don't want to exaggerate the situation because, I must stress, there were only two real disagreements, the first during a winter break in Marbella, when we had a bit of a spat, probably due to the involvement of alcohol. The second was on a pre-season tour of Japan in 1997. After that one the ice between us didn't thaw until 1998, when I agreed to rejoin Middlesbrough. I was walking down to the Old Trafford changing rooms to pick up some of my belongings, and bumped into him in the corridor. He looked at me; I looked at him; we both smiled. I just said: 'I'll see you later, I'm off.' He wished me luck, we had a bit more of a chat in the treatment room, and that was it, the war was off. I've bumped into him many times since then and you wouldn't think there had ever been a problem. In fact, there was never any real malice, just two people refusing to give an inch.

Down the years Roy has fallen out publicly with a few people, not just me. Happily, with the passing of time he's calmed down, he's not as fiery as he was, and I think he's on the wagon, not least because he wanted to prolong his playing career as long as possible. He's got a big family now and I'd say the responsibility of fatherhood has matured him. Also, no doubt becoming a manager with Sunderland will further that process. There was a time when he lived on the edge, not only in his professional life but also off the field, yet despite our run-ins, there was never anything vindictive between us. Basically I always liked him as a lad.

Meanwhile, as a player he was awesome, and I was always overjoyed that he was on my team. When Manchester United had to come to terms with losing Bryan Robson, what a bonus it was to have Roy Keane to take over his mantle. Who is his heir apparent in the modern game? Nobody. There isn't one. Patrick Vieira, once of Arsenal, or Liverpool's Steven Gerrard are the closest you could hope to get, but I'd still pick Keaney in his prime.

Going back to 1993, it was a contrasting type of player, the altogether cooler Brian McClair, who made way for Roy at first, though after finding himself on the bench for much of 1993/94, Choccy bounced back into contention for the following campaign, perhaps helped by various injuries and suspensions but basically because he was a damned fine all-round footballer himself.

Primed by Alex Ferguson's psychological gee-up, we started that new term with a gigantic burden of pressure lifted from our backs, so that we could express ourselves more freely than ever before. There was a new confidence about the side, a certain poise and assurance that had been missing previously. The movement was slick, the passes were made at great pace, everything seemed to gel perfectly, especially on the bowling-green pitches of early autumn. I felt we were playing the best football I'd ever been involved in to that point; in retrospect, it was probably the finest during my whole time at United.

Highlights included a superlative performance at home to Arsenal, when we won by only a single goal, an Eric Cantona rocket from a free-kick, but played out of our skins; and a rip-roaring comeback from two goals down to win 3-2 at Maine Road. Eric scored twice and Keaney got the late clincher, which was so sweet because we were still being taunted mercilessly over the 5-1 debacle of four years earlier. Actually we never fully erased the dismay of that day until we walloped City 5-0 in the so-called Demolition Derby at Old Trafford in November 1994, when Andrei Kanchelskis ran them ragged and scored a hat-trick into the bargain.

Most dramatic of all, though, was a game we didn't win, when we infuriated the manager by giving away a three-goal lead at Anfield. Given the form we were in at the time, seemingly running away with the championship race, it seemed inconceivable that we should be guilty of such a lapse. But fair play to the Liverpool lads, they didn't wilt when we were rampant and they managed to salvage a point. If the score had stayed at 3-0, or if we'd gone on to win by more, the Liverpool team would have been in for fearful stick from their supporters, and I suppose it was down to a combination of guts and pride that they fought back so memorably. Nigel Clough pulled back two goals before half-time, the first with a speculative shot from distance which seemed to move through the air in slow motion. As for the second-half equaliser, I was implicated myself. When Stig-Inge Bjornebye crossed from the left I thought Paul Ince was going to clear and hesitated for a fraction of a second. That enabled Neil Ruddock to say 'My ball' and he powered over the top of me to bury it.

That was the night when Alex Ferguson had a titanic row with Schmeichel, which at one time looked like costing Peter his job. The Gaffer was ranting about the 'keeper's kicking in the game, kept nettling him about it, and suddenly Peter reacted by exploding back at him. The insults that passed between them were quite astonishing, even hysterical, going way beyond the cut-and-thrust of normal dressing-room argument. It would be mortally embarrassing to repeat even the milder remarks, so I'll leave that well alone, but it culminated in Fergie telling Peter he was out of the club because no manager could take that kind of abuse in front of the other players. In the end, Peter apologised to the lads and to the Gaffer, which saved him. Whether Alex Ferguson would actually have gone through with his threat to sack the best goalkeeper in the world, I couldn't say. Certainly it would have taken a brave man to do so, but the Gaffer is all of that, so we can only wonder.

The other issue for which that meeting with Liverpool is remembered is its implication in the betting scandal which broke about the head of Liverpool's extrovert goalkeeper Bruce Grobbelaar. It was alleged that the Zimbabwean let in goals deliberately to influence the result, but I must declare that I had not the slightest inkling that any funny business was going on. In fact, I thought he played well, because he pulled off a two or three exceptional saves. Regarding the goals that he conceded, Steve Bruce's was a well-nigh unstoppable downward header from close range, Ryan Giggs' was a terrific chip – true, Grobbelaar might have advanced too far off his line, but you see that all the time – and for the third Denis Irwin placed a picture-book free-kick right on the stanchion. At the time there was no talk about the 'keeper having a nightmare, and as far as I know nobody has ever come up with concrete evidence of wrongdoing.

I'm happy to say that the matter of bribery never raised its ugly head anywhere throughout my career. There were never any rumours of problems in the modern age; if the subject ever cropped up in conversation, it was all about the early 1960s, when quite a few players were banned. Equally, while we're talking of corruption, much is made about the problem of drugs in sport, but I was never offered any illegal substances, nor did I hear of any other footballers using them. Perhaps I'm naive, but it was never a thought process for me to deal with. I underwent routine tests at Old Trafford but nothing more, and probably they were instituted only because the manager couldn't believe how unfit I was much of the time. Maybe he wanted to find what was wrong with me!

Seriously, I find it a chronic weakness that anyone in a sporting walk of life could be tempted by using drugs, socially or otherwise. Why put a whole career at risk? It would never enter my head to try a line of coke, or whatever the party animals use. You'd be risking everything, it doesn't make sense. Why ruin a fantastic life for the sake of a ten-minute or twenty-minute or one-hour high?

Back in the real world in '93/4, United built up a formidable Premiership lead early on and sustained it into the New Year, when Blackburn crept up on us. It looked as if we were coasting – at one point we were 15 points clear and the bookies stopped taking bets – but then Kenny Dalglish's side enjoyed a real upsurge in form and reeled it back to goal difference by mid-April. They beat us at Ewood Park and the force seemed to be with them, but the turning point arrived for us in the form of another FA Cup semi-final against Oldham.

We were white-hot favourites for the game, which was played at Wembley, but when we were a goal down just a couple of minutes from the end of extra time, it looked like we were finished. By then I had been shunted forward to play up front for the closing stages, but although we were mounting pressure, nothing seemed to be breaking for us and an Oldham victory appeared inevitable. When the ball was pumped into their box one more time I expected it to be nodded out again, but somehow Sparky stretched for a well-nigh impossible volley, the sort he had no right to reach, and it crashed into the roof of their net.

That equaliser felt like a winner. It lifted everybody and proved to be the pivotal moment of our entire season. Had we been dumped out of the FA Cup there's no telling what debilitating effect it would have had on our already indifferent League form, but here, thanks to Mark Hughes, was a chance of salvation. Just after the semi-final, we had been due to go to Leeds, a difficult task at a trying, tiring time, especially after the drain of playing at Wembley. As it was the Leeds game had to be postponed because of the semi-final replay, which worked heavily in our favour. When we did fetch up at Elland Road some two weeks later we had already beaten Oldham 4-1 in the rematch at Maine Road, with Kanchelskis scoring a fantastic opener when he ran across their defence and netted with a curling left-footer from distance, and we had triumphed in another Manchester derby. Now we were manifestly better prepared and in stronger heart, putting in a terrific performance to overturn Leeds 2-0, and the vision of our first League and FA Cup double moved enticingly within reach.

Eventually Coventry did us a favour by beating Blackburn in their penultimate match and, for the second successive season, we won the title with our feet up, watching a game on TV. Coincidentally our last League outing was against our benefactors, Coventry, and although there were no goals, I shall never forget that sun-bathed Sunday afternoon at Old Trafford because it marked the emotional farewell of Bryan Robson, who was leaving to take over as player-manager of Middlesbrough. He's a tough nut but there was a tear in his eye as he received a second Premiership trophy, along with Brucie, in the centre circle, and then said ta-ra after 13 years in which he'd been the bedrock of Manchester United.

Understandably, Bryan was hugely disappointed, and probably more than a little hurt, not even to make the bench for the FA Cup Final six days later. The place was between Robbo and Sharpie; perhaps the manager reasoned that Lee was staying at Old Trafford and needed the encouragement of Wembley involvement, so Bryan had to miss out.

Our opponents in the final were Chelsea, who had beaten us at home and away in the League that season, and there was a lot of talk that they knew how to cope with us. Their manager, Glenn Hoddle, sounded particularly confident in his pre-match assessment and, fair enough, they did start brightly, with Gavin Peacock, who had supplied the winners in both Premiership encounters, smacking a powerful shot against our crossbar in an even first half which failed to produce a goal.

However, the contest was transformed by two second-half penalties awarded to us by referee David Elleray. The first one was a stonewall certainty when Denis Irwin was knocked several feet in the air by Eddie Newton. As Eric Cantona strode forward calmly to take the kick, he was approached by Dennis Wise, who offered him a £100 bet that he wouldn't score. There was barely a flicker of emotion on the Frenchman's face as he accepted the wager, then sent goalkeeper Dmitri Kharine the wrong way from the spot. It was an outrageous piece of gamesmanship by Wise, who at least had the good grace to pay up promptly after the match.

The second penalty was a bit more contentious, with Frank Sinclair being adjudged to have felled Andrei Kanchelskis as the Ukrainian sprinted into the box. Once again Eric was coolness personified, waiting for Kharine to move before slotting the ball in the opposite direction, a carbon copy of his earlier conversion. After that we were in comfortable control and there were further goals from Mark Hughes and Brian McClair, which made the scoreline somewhat harsh on Chelsea. It was never a 4-0 game on the run of play, but we did deserve our win, which put us up there alongside Spurs, Arsenal and Liverpool as the only teams to have won the coveted double during the modern era.

It was a fitting climax to a season in which we had soared to fabulous heights, but also suffered a few stutters from which we had recovered in style. As tensions built towards the end there were a few disciplinary problems, with tempestuous characters like Mark Hughes, Eric Cantona and Peter Schmeichel becoming involved. But that type of performer plays on the edge, and we never felt the situation was getting out of control. Later the manager wrote of calling a meeting with his 'bad boys' to calm matters down, but that was one little gathering to which I wasn't invited. Indeed, I wasn't even aware of it, and I think the manager did a terrific job in keeping the lid on it, despite all the media hype which, inevitably, swirled about us.

During the campaign I was more than happy with my personal form – there was particular satisfaction in our 3-0 FA Cup victory at Plough Lane after Wimbledon's notorious 'Crazy Gang' had boasted about knocking us out of our stride – and I totalled 61 senior appearances, the most in my career. As a team we lost only four out of 42 League games, with no defeats between the Chelsea reverses in September and March, and there could be not the tiniest smidgin of doubt that we were the best team in the land.

Still, there is always room for improvement, and we might have wished for that on the European front. Having admitted to that, when we bowed out to Galatasaray in the second round of the European Cup, it was only on the away-goals rule, and only after being subjected to provocation on an unprecedented scale.

Our controversial encounter with the Turks began at Old Trafford, where we just managed to preserve the club's all-time unbeaten home record in European competition. It was a close-run thing, with Eric Cantona equalising near the end, and that was after we had gone two up in the first quarter of an hour. When two Galatasaray supporters ran on to the pitch and burnt a flag, Peter Schmeichel manhandled them away. The Turkish contingent was upset by their treatment, but there is no way you can condone people invading the park. As a result we were promised a hostile reception when we travelled to Istanbul for the return leg, and they kept their word. Undoubtedly it was the most intimidating incident I ever came across in football. It made Anfield look like a tea party.

Galatasaray fans greeted us at the airport with banners informing us: 'You will die.' Another one extended the greeting: 'Welcome to hell.' What police force in its right mind would allow that to happen? People apparently consumed by frenzy were screaming insults at us in English, delivering the most bloodthirsty threats imaginable, and there was a lot more in Turkish which we didn't understand, which probably was just as well.

After detaching ourselves from that surreal scene, we were taken to a lovely hotel on the Bosporus, a stunningly luxurious place. I was last to get my bag off the bus and I trailed 20 yards behind the rest of the lads, strolling through a vast, plush lobby as I took in the palatial surroundings and thought what a fabulous pad it was. As I passed a bellboy pushing a luggage trolley, I looked at him and was going to smile, but he just ran his finger across his throat and scowled. That was the bellboy! I could hardly believe my eyes. It was genuinely shocking, and the hostility did not relent at any stage. Peter Schmeichel, the principal focus of their irrational hatred, received phone calls to his room in which hideous threats were made, and the whole business was extremely intimidating.

Because of an Achilles problem I failed a fitness test before the game, which I watched alongside Sparky, who was left out because of the rule then governing the number of foreigners each team was allowed to field. With flares going off all around the stadium, smoke hanging over the pitch, and the home supporters going berserk, we didn't feel particularly safe, even in the stand. In fact, we wondered if we'd get out in one piece. The game proved a pretty miserable experience, too, as a perfectly good strike from Lee Sharpe was disallowed for offside, and we drew 0-0, thus going out of the European Cup on away goals.

Afterwards we went down on to the pitch to reach the tunnel, where there had been a commotion in which a policeman had clubbed Eric with a shield. Robbo had tried to intervene and had got a cuffing off the police, who pushed him down the stairs. Meanwhile the hate and the vitriol continued to pour down from the terraces as the stadium seemed to jump up and down in a never-ending crescendo of noise. Just to round off our trip to Turkey our coach was bricked on the bridge over the Bosporus. It was a terrifying business which had nothing to do with sport, and can be categorised objectively as an absolute disgrace.

That was in early November, and my mind flicked back to the shameful scene some two months later in the most poignant of circumstances, when I was contemplating the death of Sir Matt Busby. What would the great man, who led his beloved Manchester United into continental football nearly 40 years earlier, have made of such degrading incidents as those we encountered in Turkey? They would have been anathema to him, he just would not have understood what was going on, and neither would any other right-minded person.

The passing of Sir Matt in January 1994 marked the end of an era for the club, and once they had come to terms with the sad news, the overriding feeling among the lads was pleasure that he had seen us bring the League title back to Old Trafford at the end of the previous season. There was something overwhelmingly right about the man who had made the modern Manchester United being present as we became champions again.

I treasure a picture of myself taken with Sir Matt on the night after the Blackburn game. I've got a bit of a shiner and the photographer's cut the top of my head off but I wouldn't part with that shot for worlds. He was an iconic figure and it was a crying shame that he didn't live to see us do the League and FA Cup double.

I'll never forget walking out to face Everton in the first game after Sir Matt had died. On an emotionally charged afternoon at Old Trafford, there was a lone piper playing; it was almost eerie, a unique experience. Fair play to the Everton fans, they behaved impeccably during the most immaculate minute's silence I have known. That silence was deafening; anywhere around the stadium, you could have heard a pin drop.

Alex Ferguson told us we had to put on a performance that would have made Sir Matt proud, and we did produce some tremendous football. Though we only won by a single goal, it should have been far more comfortable, and I'm convinced that if the grand old man was looking down, he would have been delighted with our style of play, which I like to think was a credit to Manchester United.

My own enduring memory of Sir Matt is that, even in his later years, he had his own room at Old Trafford, and that when I walked past, the door was always open. The older players tell me that when he was manager he was always accessible, and it was a policy he never changed. As I strolled past, probably on my way to the general office, he'd be in his chair, smoking his pipe, and he'd greet me in that wonderful deep voice. He wasn't well, but he still had a great dignity about him, was still a very powerful figure, and I was in awe of him. I was delighted that I met the man, and that I was in the team that brought some joy to him in the last stages of his life.

The players went to his funeral on a grey, damp, miserable Manchester day. But just as we drove past Old Trafford there appeared in the sky a shaft of bright light, which seemed to be shining directly on to the ground. It didn't seem real and at first I thought I must be imagining it. It was as if it was a blessing from above. It wasn't as if it came out of broken cloud, but out of a massive, lowering grey sky. Who knows? After all, there's a lot in this world that we don't understand.

CHAPTER TEN

WINNING SOMETHING WITH KIDS

The next couple of seasons, 1994/95 and 1995/96, produced starkly contrasting emotions at Old Trafford. The first of those campaigns was monumentally frustrating in that we might easily have won the League and FA Cup double for a second successive term, yet ended up trophyless, while the pain was heightened by a truly humbling exit from Europe. But the second, which began with much lower expectations following the departure from the club of three household names, ended on an indescribable high – despite a prophecy of doom from a certain Mr Hansen.

After celebrating the double in 1993/94, we commenced the following term in the finest of fettle, beating Blackburn in the Charity Shield, much to the delight of defender David May, who was late of Ewood Park and our only major summer signing. As the League season got into full swing, we were nicely placed, not far behind the early pacesetters, Newcastle, but the rudest of shocks was in store. Having swept the board of domestic honours, we were desperate to make our mark in Europe, and when we were drawn in the same Champions League group as Barcelona, it gave us the chance to measure ourselves against one of the world's mightiest footballing powers.

Our first encounter with the star-spangled Catalans was at Old Trafford, where we felt we were eminently confident of beating them, and everything went according to plan as Sparky put us in front after 20 minutes. But then the script began to go awry.

Alex Ferguson had dropped Steve Bruce for the game, opting instead for Paul Parker, who was detailed to shadow the Brazilian striker Romario. This had me feeling anxious from the start. There had been times in the past when the manager had demanded man-to-man marking, but Steve and I didn't like it. We felt that once we started swapping positions, we could be pulled into areas we didn't want to go. Certainly I believed passionately that following players all over the pitch caused too much upheaval, making it much more difficult to retain shape and discipline. We were far more comfortable staying as a solid back-four and trying to pass the man on.

On the night of Barcelona's visit I took my life into my hands by counter-manding the Gaffer's orders. I had a word with Parks and told him NOT to remain with Romario, but to adopt our usual method. We started out okay, but then the Brazilian came off Parks and slipped behind me; for once we weren't synchronised and he scored the equaliser. Naturally, I suppose, the manager gave me stick. On the night we got it wrong between the two of us and I hold my hand up for that. Eventually we only managed a 2-2 draw through an inspired backheel from Lee Sharpe near the end, and we were left to ponder what might have been. In hindsight, though Parks was a terrific player, maybe it would have been better to have kept Brucie in, though the evidence of the Nou Camp return, for which we were back in harness, does not suggest that it would have made a scrap of difference.

When we travelled to Spain we were handicapped sorely by the rule restricting the number of foreigners, which deprived us of Peter Schmeichel among others, and the Dane was replaced between the sticks by Gary Walsh. The Gaffer thought we could surprise Barcelona by taking the game to them, but it didn't quite pan out like that and we were hammered 4-0. In fairness it was one of the best footballing performances I've ever come across, with Romario and Stoichkov running amok. I'd even go as far as to say that Romario's was the finest display I faced in my entire career.

Just one little moment typified that, when he moved off me and turned on the ball about four or five yards away. It was like time stood still, like he was saying to me: 'Let's see what you've got.' In the blink of an eye he was past me. Ye Gods. It was one of the only times I had to admit that I couldn't live with an opponent on the night. He was sensational. I couldn't touch him; couldn't get anywhere near him. He couldn't have played like that every time, I guess, but he was in a different zone that night.

Alex Ferguson knew we were hamstrung by the daft regulations, but he told us we didn't get tight enough, that we paid them too much respect. He had called for attack, but it's a different proposition in the Nou Camp, and in retrospect I think that approach was a mistake. When you go to such places I think you have to pay due respect, proceed with a certain amount of caution. Just occasionally the adventurous approach pays off, as when United went to Benfica's Stadium of Light in 1966 and turned over the famous Eagles by five goals to one. Apparently Matt Busby had told his side to keep things tight for the first 20 minutes, but George Best ignored him, ran at the Benfica defence from the first whistle and United were three up inside a quarter of an hour. Maybe the Gaffer had that in mind, and I wouldn't knock him for his tactics because Barca had shown at Old Trafford that they could be vulnerable at the back; but it wasn't to be.

Happily, the comprehensive mauling by Barcelona did not affect our League form, and we responded with two terrific displays in a week, a 2-1 victory at Villa Park followed by the 5-0 drubbing of City, which laid a few ghosts both for ourselves and our fans. By the turn of the year Blackburn had replaced Newcastle at the top of the Premiership table, but we were continuing to bubble along nicely, there was evidence of some terrific youngsters coming through the Old Trafford system to challenge for places and keep the squad fresh, and the players faced the second half of the campaign with plenty of confidence. However, January brought two bombshells.

First, I was shocked to the core when we signed Andy Cole from Newcastle for a record £6 million, plus our promising young Irish winger Keith Gillespie. Cole was such a hero on Tyneside, where he had scored so many goals, and I was staggered that United could prise him away for any amount of money. But the Gaffer felt we needed someone who was more prolific up front, and that seemed to signal the end of Mark Hughes. Duly there was talk of Sparky leaving, but soon he was injured in the act of scoring, coincidentally against Newcastle, and any departure was put on ice. Then something happened to our other striker, which I'll come to shortly, so Mark stayed until season's end.

As for Coley, he didn't enjoy the best of starts at Old Trafford, finding it difficult to settle in, perhaps feeling a little overawed initially by the added attention that goes with being a United player. I was sitting with him one night in the Four Seasons bar in Hale, just south of Manchester, and he was not happy, seemingly doubting himself. I told him to keep pegging away and the goals would look after themselves, because all the time he was getting himself into superb positions to score; it was just that, temporarily, he was missing the chances. I was confident about his future after watching him in training, in which he'd proved he could be a top operator. Coley had very quick feet around the box; he'd knock the ball half a yard and was so quick to get his shot off. That's what stood out and made him special. The only danger was that his drought would eat away at his self-belief, as the weight of expectation at Old Trafford had overawed many strikers down the years.

But when the goals did start to flow for Andy, they arrived with a vengeance. For instance, there were five against Ipswich at Old Trafford, in what turned into an absolute debacle for George Burley's side. I was just glad, genuinely, that we didn't score ten that day. It's all very well to talk about breaking the Premiership record but in games like that I have to feel for my opponents, who are fellow professionals, after all. I've been on the wrong end of enough fives and sixes to know that it's a demoralising feeling, so the nine Ipswich conceded must have been utterly humiliating.

But even that landmark occasion recedes in significance when compared to the cataclysmic happening at Selhurst Park on the fateful evening of January 25. I am referring to Eric Cantona's surreally spectacular encounter with a foul-mouthed Crystal Palace fan, who had goaded him after he had been sent off for receiving a second yellow card. I think I was the only player who didn't run to the scene of the incident; I could only register shock and disbelief. We knew Eric had a temper but this went beyond anything we could have expected.

I was on the same side of the pitch and, after his dismissal, I was watching him walk down the touchline. I saw the confrontation and the kung-fu kick going in. It was all a bit of a confused scuffle, then I saw our kitman, Norman Davies, trying to drag Eric back. I realised the enormity of what our astonishing Frenchman had done straight away. Unarguably he had stepped way beyond the mark of what could be acceptable, even though I could understand his reaction to some extent.

By all accounts the provocation was extreme, a stream of vile abuse, but you have to learn to accept that type of thing, abhorrent though it is. Sadly, though it's completely disgusting to any reasonable person, it has become part of the game. The enormity of the consequences, to both Eric Cantona and Manchester United, were incalculable. We didn't know how the FA were going to react – it could even have been a life ban. To go into a crowd and attempt to kick a fan ... well, we were in uncharted territory.

I've never had to put up with that level of provocation, though I have seen other players pushed a long way. I recall Mark Hughes being cuffed across the top of his head when the ball went into the crowd at Swindon, and I wondered how thunderous his reaction might be. In fact, Sparky just stopped and glared hard at the guy, holding his temper in check, which was immensely commendable in the circumstances.

Eric did what he did primarily out of frustration at being sent off for retaliating against a foul by Palace's Richard Shaw. He was prone to retaliation – I saw him do it a number of times – and he was always going to be a marked man, the target of more stick than anybody else in the team, for that reason. This time he over-reacted to a colossal extent.

Nothing much was said in the dressing room afterwards. Eric was just sat there quietly, and our solicitor came in. The club tried to pre-empt punishment by suspending him for the remainder of the season, but the FA found it in their wisdom to extend the ban until October. Meanwhile sections of the media were going berserk, even advocating deportation. Obviously what he did was wrong, could not be condoned and had to be punished, but most people don't understand what it feels like to be the target of vile, mindless venom, and footballers are only human, after all. In most walks of life, no one would bat an eyelid that if a victim retaliated in similar circumstances. Surely, so-called supporters who conduct themselves so offensively should be escorted out of any ground and made to pay the price of their obscene actions.

Eric received a certain amount of sympathy from the lads because we knew he was targeted in games by players who would try to set off his short fuse. We had seen him being spat at at Leeds, being fouled horribly all over the country, and he rose above all that. But I suppose everybody has a threshold that can't be crossed. It would have been fascinating to find out exactly what was going through his mind, but I never ever heard him talk to the team about it.

Many observers believed that the nine-month ban would force him into permanent retirement, but they were proved wrong. He did his community service with local kids, which went very well because he didn't carry it out it grudgingly but enjoyed it, giving his all to the youngsters.

The FA prevented him playing in organised games behind closed doors, which seemed petty and futile. He needed to keep some match fitness, but all he could do was train with us, and we had full-scale games, with Eric lining up against the first team for the reserves. Crucially he kept involved with us, continued to socialise, and with a couple of decent holidays thrown in he managed to get through his sentence.

Much was made of his cryptic statement about sardines being thrown to seagulls. Many people found it inscrutable, but I thought the meaning was pretty obvious and couldn't see what all the fuss was about. He was saying that the press followed him because they thought they would get a story; they hounded him because they were always looking for a new line or an angle. Other people might have put it rather differently, but at least it shifted a few T-shirts. Eric was heavily into the painting and poetry and philosophy, so his thought processes were different to most people's. I never got to talk to him about any of that. We had little in common there!

What effect did the Cantona affair have on the team for the rest of the season? Well, unquestionably his absence was a heavy blow because he was a great player, but we were by no means a one-man outfit and, if the breaks had gone our way, we could easily have repeated the League and FA Cup double.

I suspect not too many people have happy memories of our eventful semi-final confrontation with Crystal Palace, but I would have more reason than most to recall it with warmth because I managed to score in both the initial tie and the replay. Mind, the first contest couldn't have been that special because I was watching a video of it recently and, with the score at 2-1 to them, I was wondering to myself who scored the equaliser. Then there was a long throw from Gary Neville, a picture came on the screen of Pally ambling up from the back, and I'm still racking my brains for the identity of the scorer. Next second the ball's on my head, then bouncing inside the far stick. What a belter!

Tragically, football was to take a back seat in discussions of that day because a lad was killed in a confrontation between United and Palace supporters. Ten minutes before the replay kicked off, the managers made a public appeal for calm, which somehow made it all the more reprehensible when violence broke out on the pitch. Roy Keane was sent off for stamping on Gareth Southgate and Darren Patterson was dismissed for retaliation in an incident which did no good at all for the image of the game. Not surprisingly, the violence overshadowed the football in the newspaper headlines but, for the record, Brucie and I both found the net with first-half headers which completed the scoring.

In the Premiership, meanwhile, United had been chipping away at what had once been a substantial Blackburn lead and it transpired that if results went our way on the final day then we would be champions for the third season running. In the event, Blackburn lost at Anfield so all we had to do was beat West Ham in our simultaneous game at Upton Park and the title would be ours, but all we could manage was a 1-1 draw.

It was so frustrating because we missed a lot of scoring opportunities. Although the brilliance of West Ham 'keeper Ludo Miklosko was a major factor, Coley, Choccy, Incey and Sparky were all off-target when well placed, so we have to put it down as a team failure. Nobody spurned the openings on purpose and we just had to accept that Miklosko had a marvellous day at the office while we were below par in front of goal. What galled me was that it was another example of West Ham having a poor season themselves, then managing to raise their game for Manchester United, just as they had at the death in 1992. Once again it seemed more important to stop us than it had been to play well in their other matches. Their joy seemed out of all proportion to an occasion which might not have been expected to hold any special significance for them. I couldn't relate to that, and neither could our manager.

Still, you can't expect any team to lie down and die for you, and certainly we didn't expect Liverpool to beat Blackburn for us, so it would have been a hell of a bonus to have won the title that year. It's worth making the point, too, that although it wasn't a glorious day for us, it was a fine one for football, because it proved the essential integrity of the game, demonstrated that the house was in order. Liverpool fans, given their rivalry with United, must have had mixed emotions about the game, but their players did a thoroughly professional job. They ensured that the opportunity was there for us, but we just fell short. We battered at the door for so long but couldn't quite open it. In the end I'd have to admit that probably Blackburn deserved to lift the crown that season anyway. They had taken a hefty lead and we gradually pegged them back when they started to show nerves on the final stretch.

Unfortunately, losing the League completely deflated us, so that we were still in shock at seeing a whole season's work go down the pan when we arrived at Wembley six days later to face Everton in the FA Cup Final. It turned out to be an awful game from our viewpoint, with Paul Rideout, who'd had a great season, scoring the only goal. Near the end one of our substitutes, a distinctly promising young fellow name of Paul Scholes, forced a terrific save from Everton goalkeeper Neville Southall, and then it was all over. It represented one of the most dismal anti-climaxes I can remember in my entire career, very much a case of 'so near yet so far.'

There followed a summer of discontent for United fans, who were still smarting at winning no trophies for the first time that decade. Three of their heroes, Paul Ince, Mark Hughes and Andrei Kanchelskis, left the club with no glamorous signings to replace them, and it's fair to say there was no shortage of observers who reckoned our manager had lost the plot.

Incey was a marvellous player at the peak of his powers when he left Old Trafford, but apparently Alex Ferguson had become irritated by his cocksure style, typified by calling himself 'The Guv'nor'. Paul was an archetypal Cockney, brash and with plenty to say, always lively around the place. That's the way he was, he couldn't help it, though there were people who thought he was getting above himself. He and the manager did have fall-outs and it seems the Gaffer felt it was becoming a problem between the two, so he accepted a big bid from Inter Milan.

The players knew that Incey was a top performer and they didn't want to see that sort of quality leave. They felt the same way about Mark Hughes, although Sparky was a few years older so perhaps his departure was not quite so unexpected. As far as Andrei Kanchelskis was concerned, I don't think there was much choice. The situation got pretty nasty with wild talk about the Russian underworld and all sorts. We were never exactly sure what was going on, but we were led to believe there was a fair amount of intimidation being exerted to get him to leave. Certainly Andrei made it clear that he wanted to go and once a player makes his mind up then there's no point in hanging on to him.

So all of a sudden there were three massively influential players leaving the team and we were told the void was going to be filled by youngsters, the likes of Nicky Butt, Paul Scholes and David Beckham. We knew they were richly gifted but we'd been expecting them to be fed into the team on a gradual basis, a process which had already begun on a smaller scale. Now suddenly they were expected to be far more integral.

As we lined up for the first game of the new season, at Villa Park, we were thinking we'd lost a huge part of our side. We were wondering how we were going to compete at the highest level, perhaps even entertaining doubts about our ability to win the title. Famously Alan Hansen came out and said it on *Match Of The Day* after Villa had beaten us 3-1. 'You'll never win anything with kids,' he told us, and after an emphatic defeat like that we had to think he might be right. Maybe it was going to be a year when we won nothing, when we started to build again. We knew the youngsters were sumptuously talented, but we doubted their experience and knowledge and knowhow to win a title. But they knuckled down, grew into their jobs as if they were born to them, and in the end it wasn't just the championship we reeled in, but a second League and FA Cup double.

By then I suppose I was one of the team's elder statesmen, and it was a pleasure to watch the new generation in action. Their coach, Eric Harrison, always used to tell us that United had this great bunch of kids, and he warned us that they would soon be after our places. Already they'd done well in the League Cup and other occasional games; nothing seemed to faze them, they were all strong characters.

Nicky Butt and Gary Neville were the first to break into the side properly, and they both had tenacity and aggression to burn. Then there was Scholesy, a great little all-round footballer with a terrific brain for the game, and he had a nasty little side to him as well, a mean competitive streak. Given his size, he had to have that, otherwise he would have been bullied out of contention.

As for David Beckham, he was pretty much in the background in the early stages, one of the last to come through. He didn't really seem to have a pronounced physical side to his game and he was loaned out to Preston, which helped to toughen him up. While at Deepdale he scored a goal or two, including one directly from a corner which, knowing Becks, would have been a deliberate effort.

I remember him coming into the club as a schoolboy, turning up at one of the cup finals and giving the impression of a cocky little so-and-so. But when he actually signed for the club, I noticed that basically he was quite a shy boy, though he had a love of fashion and cars, even at that age. Nobody was aware what he would grow into, but his talent was obvious. He was dedicated, too, spending hours on the training ground perfecting his free-kicks, crossing and passing with the likes of Scholesy. You'd see them out there all the time and I'd guess they'd taken a lead from Eric about how even the great players needed to practice.

Although we got back on track in the Premiership soon after our opening-day setback, there was to be yet more disappointment in Europe when we bowed out of the UEFA Cup in the first round to the hitherto obscure Rotor Volgograd. We lost on the away-goals rule, but the tie will be remembered for our late equaliser at Old Trafford by ... Peter Schmeichel. Afterwards we were torn between dismay at our elimination – we were acutely aware that we had done nothing in continental competition since winning the Cup Winners' Cup five seasons earlier – and taking the mick out of Peter, who always fancied himself as a striker. We were more than a little grateful to him, too, because although his clinical finish didn't keep us in the cup, at least it preserved the club's proud record of never losing a home game in Europe.

A few days later Old Trafford was engulfed by the world's football media for the return from exile of a certain Monsieur Cantona when we entertained Liverpool. United fans craved a sensational comeback, and Eric didn't disappoint them, setting up a goal for Nicky Butt in the second minute, then delivering our second-half equaliser from the penalty spot after Ryan Giggs had been hauled back. The Frenchman celebrated by jumping on the netpole at the back of the goal, a photo-friendly moment which encapsulated his joy and relief at getting back to work. It was like something from a *Boy's Own Paper* yarn, the only script available.

However, the delight at regaining our talisman was soon tempered by the fact that Newcastle were fast disappearing over the Premiership horizon. The Geordie fans, some of the most passionate anywhere in the world, were consumed with excitement and understandably so. Not only were they topping the table – and they hadn't won the title since 1927, for God's sake – but their lads were playing an intoxicating brand of attacking football under manager Kevin Keegan, with stars such as Alan Shearer, Les Ferdinand and David Ginola shining fit to light up the heavens over Tyneside.

That Ginola: what an entertainer! But put him in the framework of a team and ask him to work back, then you saw another aspect of him. The chasing and scrabbling didn't come naturally and it wasn't something he enjoyed. Could he have been a Manchester United player? In a good side, with proper balance and a strong work ethic, I think you can carry an attacking player of Ginola's sort by giving him a free role. But at Old Trafford I think he would have been far more frustrating than, say, Eric Cantona. Certainly he could not have been accommodated in his favourite wide position.

If you are going to defend as a team and attack as a team, you need your wingers to graft in tandem with your full-backs, getting back to cover. David was never that type of player, and you were never going to change what he was. He appeared to be trying to adapt at times, but it just wasn't in his make-up. Of course, as a crowd-pleaser, he could be fantastic, bringing genuine beauty to the old game, and I'd say that he symbolised that team. Kevin took a fair bit of stick over the defensive side of things but, my, those boys entertained a lot of people that year.

I talked earlier about how we didn't have any fortune at the death against West Ham in 1995, but we certainly rode our luck when we went to Newcastle in the following spring. I'd injured my back in training and by the time I woke up the next morning it had gone into spasm, so I couldn't play. Thus I was able to sit in the stand and enjoy one of the finest displays of goalkeeping I have ever witnessed. That night we owed a huge debt to Peter Schmeichel, who gave a superhuman display as they battered at our goal, especially in a first half which was almost totally one-sided. How we didn't concede I'll never know, but we came into it more in the second period and Eric volleyed a terrific winner from a Phil Neville cross. If ever there was a turning point in a season, that was it. They still had a substantial lead in the Premiership, but suddenly a one-horse race had been transformed, and Liverpool weren't out of it either. For Newcastle that night, the doubts must have begun to creep in. From our point of view it was a must-win game, and we won it.

Victory at St James' Park signalled the start of an astonishing run of six successive games in which Cantona scored, many of them the only goal. Still, though it might have looked it to some, our charge towards the finishing line wasn't a one-man effort. Certainly we would never have won that championship without Peter Schmeichel, a circumstance that became rather lost in all the media acclaim for Eric's goals. Mind, they were fabulous, and some of them he created all on his own, like the one against Spurs, when he ran at the defence from deep and beat Ian Walker with a low shot from the edge of the box. Equally sensational was the sudden volley from the inside-left slot which looped over David Seaman to beat Arsenal, who had come to Old Trafford on the back of their own six-game undefeated run. Big players rise to big occasions, and Eric was doing that twice a week during that unforgettable spring.

At one juncture Newcastle had a 12-point lead, but United cut it back inexorably as we picked up a fantastic momentum and in the end we took our third League crown in four seasons. We didn't always serve up our most fluent football but we found a way to win the games, through Eric, through Peter, through the whole team being disciplined, and through having been down that road before.

At least, some of us had, which provided an essential core of experience, but actually the new kids hadn't, and they proved themselves to be an exceptional bunch. They had been aided by watching some of the best players in the world during a key period of their development, learning avidly not only from Eric, but also from Robbo, Sparky, Schmeichel and the rest. They took their lessons aboard, they were blessed with their own talent and winning mentality, and they found whatever was needed within themselves. Truly remarkable.

Yet for all that, maybe it was a title which we shouldn't have been allowed to win. As Blackburn discovered the previous term, that final stretch is horrendously hard if you've not won it before. You're looking at games coming up and working out how many points you can expect, and before you know it your mind's playing tricks on you. You're that desperate to get over the finishing line that it's hard to do your best. Frustration and desperation can creep in ... especially if the opposing manager is helping with a few psychological effects.

The whole sporting world was amazed by Kevin Keegan's almost hysterical outburst on Sky television, when he said how much he'd love it, really love it, if Newcastle caught United, who had just overhauled his team. I bet, when he sat down to think about it, he couldn't believe he'd been drawn into it. When he was, it became apparent to everybody the kind of pressure that must have been going around at St James'. Clearly Kevin was feeling the strain, and there was our manager doubting publicly the commitment of other teams and other players when they faced Newcastle. It just got under Kevin's skin, his emotion came pouring out and he just couldn't stop himself. When we considered his immense status in the game, and all he had achieved, we were stunned that he had let the situation get to him in that way. If Alex Ferguson was looking to get a reaction, he could never have expected one as pronounced as the one he got. His words had worked a treat, and heaven only knows what the Newcastle players, who were already under intense pressure, must have made of it.

In the end we won the championship on the last day, the first time we had clinched it on the pitch for ourselves, and it was particularly significant for me that the final drama was played out at Middlesbrough. It felt hugely ironic that we were facing Robbo, who had fought so many battles in the United cause down the years. He was always going to be glad for us if we took the title, but he did us no favours and had been scrupulously professional in preparing his own team.

We needed a win to be certain of the championship, but 'Boro started brightly and had stretched us several times before David May opened the scoring against the run of play. That settled us down and we were fine after that. Coley came on as a substitute and scored a terrific goal with a little flip over his shoulder, then Giggsy smashed one in from distance to cap it all off. After that we could finally relax and enjoy the rest of the game. People said it was nice to win it on the field, and in retrospect that might be true, but at the time you'll take it any way it comes. You can't choose how you're going to become champions.

It could have all gone wrong for us on the final afternoon if Newcastle had fared better than we did, but I felt a huge calmness going into that day. It never seemed there was a possibility that we wouldn't win, and a lot of the credit for that must go to the Gaffer, who kept us pretty cool in the week leading up to it while Kevin Keegan was uptight and tense.

I think it helped, too, that Bobby Charlton used to come into our dressing room. He would say: 'Don't play the occasion, play the game,' and that's a great shout. You've got to forget what prize you're playing for and concentrate on the fundamentals of football. Bobby loved being with the players and talking to them before and after the games. He's so well respected, not just in Manchester but throughout the whole world, so it was always good to see him. It helped us, and I believe it did him a world of good as well. I'm sure he enjoyed the feeling of being close to a big match. Someone of his stature and experience was never going to get in the way or make mistakes by asking of too much of the players' time. He was an insider, and it was a privilege to have him around.

The day was topped off for me when quite a few of the 'Boro fans stayed for the presentation and they started singing my name. The Gaffer prompted me to walk forward with the trophy and I received a brilliant reception, which meant so much to me. It was a moment of forgiveness, of absolution if you like. On all my previous returns to 'Boro I had received a bit of stick from the fans, a legacy of my departure from their club. It had been particularly bad from the occupants of Ayresome Park's Holgate End, but on this particular afternoon at the Riverside, the supporters welcomed me like a returning son. It had never been in my thoughts to upset the people of Middlesbrough when I left, it was just to further my career and because of my personal problems with the manager, and I was delighted to be on good terms with the Teessiders again.

Our third Premiership triumph would have been enough to set the seal on a wonderful season, but it was not over yet. There was still the little matter of an FA Cup Final against Liverpool. In a way I was lucky to be at Wembley, because back problems had caused me to miss most of our cup run. I played in the third-round draw with Sunderland but was out of the replay, I was indisposed for the fourth-round trip to Reading when Parks shanked a goal from the right wing, I was there to help beat Manchester City in the fifth round but then absent for both the quarter-final against Southampton and the semi in which we overcame Chelsea. So you could say I let the lads get me to the final, then turned up at Wembley and picked up my medal. I couldn't forget that because they kept reminding me!

Mostly, though, I remember what everybody remembers about that final. Eric's great goal? No, Liverpool's white suits! When we saw them we wondered what the hell they were thinking about. At the time they had been dubbed 'The Spice Boys' by the tabloids because of some of their off-pitch activities, and parading round Wembley in these flashy togs seemed to underline the image. I don't think they endeared themselves to their fans, who could be excused for thinking the players had their minds on Armani rather than football.

In the game, we started quite well, but then it degenerated into a miserable stalemate, though Roy Keane gave his customary magnificent performance, smothering the creative likes of Steve McManaman and Jamie Redknapp. In both our League meetings that season Liverpool had enjoyed most of the possession, so we talked about changing our formation. The manager brought in the senior pros, like myself and Brucie, and mooted going to a 3-5-2 system and matching Liverpool man for man across the pitch. But we said we were more comfortable with our usual 4-4-2, so we stuck to it. The sides cancelled each other out for most of the match, then Eric stepped forward to win it in the style we had come to expect from him. After all the crucial goals he had scored on the title run-in, it shouldn't have surprised anybody.

What a goal it was! David Beckham delivered a corner from the right, David James slightly misjudged his punch and the ball bounced to Eric on the edge of the area. Many players would have snatched at the volley, but he had the presence of mind to take a step back and steady himself. Several Liverpool players seemed to jump out of the way as it screamed past them on its way to the back of the net.

What a story for Eric: in October he had come back from his ban, then he scored all those goals to help win the League, then he rounded off the double with that wonderful strike. I wasn't aware of it at the time but I found out later that he had been spat on by a fan as he went up for the cup. Fortunately he put that mindless vulgarity beneath him by not reacting, just wiping himself off, keeping his dignity and walking on. He had learned through the Selhurst Park incident not to retaliate, something for which he deserved colossal credit and which must have contributed to his selection as the Footballer of the Year for 1996.

Now it must have seemed to the outside world that everything in the United garden could not have been rosier, with a successful team boosted by a group of super youngsters, carrying all before them, at least on the domestic scene. But all the while there was a potentially explosive situation simmering in the background. Around this time the Gaffer's wage negotiations with the board were at a delicate stage, and he has since revealed that he contemplated walking out on the club. On the day before the final we'd got a strong whiff that something was wrong. There were all kinds of rumours, including one that he wouldn't be leading the team out at Wembley. The impression was that he felt his contribution to United's glory wasn't being reflected in the contract offers.

Did this uncertainty have any effect on the team? Well, none of us wanted to see him leave because he had brought so much success to the club and to us. Clearly it wasn't the best time to hear about the problem, but the game was too big for us to be sidetracked and we managed to put it to one side.

It was at a time when there had been an explosion in players' wages, yet managers still weren't getting paid as much. That made no sense to me when it was the gaffers who put teams together, made all the crucial decisions, sorted out the superstars and their egos; they were responsible for how their teams performed, where they finished in the table, and therefore how much money the clubs made. So I could sympathise strongly with our manager's point of view, and was pleased when his deal was sorted out. Things have changed a lot since then and I think a lot of well-paid modern managers have Alex Ferguson to thank for standing his ground.

CHAPTER ELEVEN

ERIC AND OTHER WORKMATES

A perceptive observer once said that before Eric Cantona arrived at Old Trafford, Manchester United were like a terrific Formula One car but without the right driver. Eric, God bless him, turned out to be that driver, the man who supplied the final frisson of flair and imagination that illuminated the club's pathway to renewed glory. But I feel it's important to understand that without the machinery around him, our French maestro could not have expressed himself so eloquently.

Sometimes I listen to pundits who give the impression that Eric won everything by himself. In fact, he needed nine fellow outfielders who would give their all, graft their hearts out, to provide a platform for his creativity. That was a service he had never enjoyed on a consistent basis throughout his previous career, during which he had produced flashes of inspiration without fully harnessing his incredible ability. So while I would agree that Eric was blessed with a talent supreme and that United were fortunate to find him when they did, equally I believe that he was fortunate to find United.

To be fair to Eric, whom I liked enormously, I'm positive that he appreciated the excellence of the side he stepped into after leaving Leeds for Old Trafford in November 1992. In all my time at the club, we had a supreme work ethic, something that was passed down from Alex Ferguson. Even the wingers were part of it. Okay, perhaps we had to keep nagging at Andrei Kanchelskis, but he got the message and put the effort in to get up and down the park. If you play a 4-4-2 formation with two flankmen who work hard, then you can afford what might be called a luxury player with a roaming role, someone with carte blanche to do what he wants, to open up surprise avenues of attack, to score goals out of nothing; namely Eric Cantona.

Not that Eric wasn't willing to put in the sweat, but eventually the Gaffer told him not to tackle any more because he kept getting himself into trouble! The rest of us didn't mind that he might appear dormant for periods of a game because eventually, likelier than not, he would come up with a piece of magic to get us a result. After all, there wasn't much that

Eric couldn't do with a football at his feet. He had a remarkably delicate touch and the vision to go with it, in my experience almost a freakish combination for such a big, strong athlete.

The signing of Cantona was a prime example of Alex Ferguson's genius as a manager. Howard Wilkinson, who led Leeds to the title and who clearly was no mug, appeared unable to be flexible enough to accommodate the Frenchman. At Elland Road they played in a set style, with a lot of long balls up to Lee Chapman, and I think Eric felt he was being bypassed. I can't imagine him conforming to rigid formations and tactics; that simply wasn't the type of football that he enjoyed. He became frustrated with Howard's way and that's why he ended up on the bench so often. Given his restless, demanding character, such a situation was never going to last very long. He needed a big stage on which to perform and he found it at Old Trafford.

When Eric arrived, we didn't know what to expect; he was something of a mystery man. Certainly not much was known about his chequered exploits in France. We'd heard that Sheffield Wednesday had talked about signing him, but then asked him to stay on for another week's trial, which wouldn't have appealed to him. Then Leeds took him, and he started a few games but usually came on as a substitute, earning a title medal at our expense in the process.

Thus he came as an enigma, but straight away he mucked in with the rest of the boys, fitting in socially and clearly relishing our 'team meetings', which I'll discuss in more detail a little later. He had no particular mates whom he went out with on a regular basis, he just liked being part of the group, often with his brother, Joel, who played a handful of games for Stockport County.

Eric was funny with his English. He used to play naive at times, but I'm certain he could understand more than he let on. He always knew what the story was in the dressing room, and if you thought you were talking about him without his knowledge then you were wrong. He was a shrewd one all right. Sometimes you would have to explain yourself a couple of times but usually he got the gist, and he joined in the dressing-room banter. Not being wholly fluent in the language, he wasn't one of the major chatterers or piss-takers, but he would never hold himself aloof or set himself apart in any way.

Okay, he had a big ego, but we didn't mind that. We didn't mind him strutting around, like Thierry Henry does today, providing he was producing the goods. That was all part of his singular personality, sending out signals to those around him that he had arrived. Such people have no fear, they believe so strongly that they are the best on any pitch, and their team reaps the benefit. Undoubtedly United did, as he became the catalyst for all the success which followed.

Not the least of his achievements was coming back from his astounding explosion at Selhurst Park. He could have been finished after that, and I'm sure that at one point he was ready to turn his back on Manchester United. He'd gone back to France and I didn't expect to see him at Old Trafford again. But the manager got on a plane and off he went in search of Eric. Then he sat him down in a restaurant, talked through everything, worked out how he could get through his troubles and come back to English football as an even better player.

There is one frequently-asked question about Eric Cantona: was he as devastating a force in Europe as he was in domestic competition? My view is that although he played some tremendous games for us in the Champions League, I don't think he thrived as he did in the Premiership because the continentals marked him more tightly. European coaches routinely detailed some very competent man-markers to spend the whole match closing him down, which denied him the freedom to express himself as he did in England.

In the end his departure, which was greeted as a bombshell by outsiders, didn't come as any great surprise to me. Even as he was playing his part in winning yet another title in 1996/97, he didn't look that happy in the dressing room, at least towards the end of that season. We didn't know why, and didn't realise at the time that there were problems with the club over his image rights. Apparently the negotiations dragged on and he wasn't content with how they were progressing. I believe he felt he wasn't getting paid a fair enough percentage, as his image was the biggest selling point at the club and United must have made an awful lot of money out of him. I think the whole business struck him as unfair and it upset him, so that by the spring of 1997 he didn't look the same Eric, either on the pitch or off it.

He was always a terrific professional and a fantastic trainer, so it wasn't that he was in physical decline. Ask kids like Scholes and Beckham and they'll tell you that Eric was invariably the first on the training park, then he'd stay out to hone his technique at the end of the session. The boys all watched, admired, imitated and learned from that. Soon lots of people were staying late, working on their crossing and shooting, but when we were playing two games a week, usually the manager would pull us in for fear of wearing us out.

Mind, if Eric was doing it, then probably the Gaffer would let him get on with it. That was just one of the many ways in which he was treated differently to the other players, not that any of us minded in the least. A typical example of the extra tolerance towards Eric arose at a civic reception in Manchester after we had won a trophy. Lee Sharpe turned up in an outrageously trendy suit and the manager caned him for his appearance, berating him for not showing sufficient respect for the formal occasion. But five minutes later Eric rolled in wearing a pair of trainers and not a word was said.

That told us plainly that double standards were being practised, but we accepted it as the extremely canny man-management it was, a matter of dealing with contrasting personalities in the appropriate manner. You can be the greatest coach on the planet, but if you haven't got the ability to cope with people then you're never going to be the best manager. You've got to get the best out of each individual and then mould them all into a team. Alex Ferguson always had the knack of doing that. I'm not saying he was right all the time, just more often than not.

Sharpie was young and I guess the Gaffer felt he needed to clamp down on him, while Eric could always use the excuse that he misunderstood what was going on. The lads would laugh and have a craic about it, but I'm certain that nobody resented Eric's privileged position. We thought he was unique and we accepted everything that went with him. The fact was that, despite the public perception of him as an arrogant, haughty Frenchman, basically he was a lovely bloke who could not have been easier to get on with.

For all the understandable fascination with *Le Roi*, I have tried to stress that we were no one-man show, so I'll mention individually the rest of my team-mates in that history-making line-up which brought the championship back to Old Trafford after such a deplorably lengthy absence.

Peter Schmeichel cut an unmissable figure, a big, blond, arrogant Dane who was never in the wrong – or would never admit to being in the wrong – at any time on a football pitch, an approach which played a key part in making him one of the greatest goalkeepers of all time. Away from the game he was a different person, thank heavens, a great guy and terrific company.

Peter was always a willing socialiser and a fantastic piano-player. I remember a party at his house one night when he started tickling the old ivories, playing things like *Phantom of the Opera*, and pretty well raised the roof. He's heavily into his music, with his own recording studio in his garage, and he even released a record in Denmark. I'm sure he'll tell you that it went to number one, but he might be fantasising there, even though he is an icon in his own country. For certain he wouldn't top the charts over here because he's upset too many people. Ian Wright wouldn't have bought one for a start!

Actually it's amazing to see the pair of them working together on television these days after their history of clashes during their playing days. I'm delighted they have made it up because it was all unnecessary and unsavoury at the time. I know Wrighty could start a fight in an empty room but Peter was always up for an argument, too, and it wasn't difficult to wind him up. I remember after one heavy defeat, a local radio DJ named Steve Penk phoned him live on the air, pretending to be a news reporter and asking outrageous questions. When Peter found out it was a set-up he was ready to kill someone, the steam was coming out of his ears. For some reason, though, the rest of us thought it was quite funny.

Another constant moaner on the pitch was Steve Bruce, who was like an old fishwife. I think we complemented each other as defenders, but we argued like cat and dog at times. What with Schmeichel thrown into the mix as well, the barneys could get quite volatile occasionally, but when we came off the park invariably they were forgotten. We accepted the disagreements for what they were – attempts to get the best out of each other to our mutual benefit. We understood that we all wanted to win so desperately that people couldn't keep their mouths shut. Afterwards we sat in the bath and had a laugh about it. That was particularly the case with Brucie, but it was also true of Schmeichel, Robbo, Ince and Keane, who were all ready to point the finger.

I was never like that, it just wasn't me, although if somebody singled me out then I'd have a go back. Most of the time I was too tired to say anything. I tended to be gasping for breath, and never had the energy to waste on dispensing verbals. People will always make mistakes because they're human, so I saw no point in berating someone for an error, especially someone whose ability I respected – and certainly Brucie came into that category. For me he is the best centre-half never to have played for England, a complimentary label but one which he would have swapped willingly for an international cap. In the early years Steve was labelled as an out-and-out stopper; pigeon-holed as a muck-and-bullets competitor, the type who would go where angels fear to tread, raw and rough and ready. But he's always been far more than that.

True, he wasn't blessed with pace, and maybe once a year he'd get isolated one-on-one by some speed merchant who would show him up.

Generally, though, he was an immaculate timer of tackles; whoever was running at him, he'd strike at just the right moment, invariably taking the ball and often taking the man along with it. Steve was a terrific passer, too, although not many people gave him the credit for it; they just didn't see it, failing to understand that being able to distribute the ball was a prerequisite at United. Fergie didn't want players who could do no more than stop opponents. He wanted people who could play as well; there had to be a bit of comfort on the ball.

The false image of Brucie that persisted was the main reason why he never got that elusive England cap, which was so unjust. I played alongside him for seven years, during which he taught me such a lot. In the end our partnership became like second nature and we grew into a decent unit, yet when I first joined United we were so far apart. I came from a club which defended deep instead of playing for offside, so frequently Steve would be ten yards ahead of me with his hand up in the air, like Tony Adams at Arsenal. I found it embarrassing because I wasn't on his wavelength, and we had to work for a long time on the training ground to gain an understanding.

Down the years Brucie and I have always been bracketed together in the public mind, especially after Alex Ferguson came up with our nicknames, Dolly and Daisy. I have no idea where he got them from, or even whether I was Dolly or Daisy. Difficult to know which one I prefer, really! I'd guess they came from a throwaway comment that somebody picked up on and all of a sudden a legend was born. We didn't mind, and we enjoyed the *Alas Smith and Jones* double act in the club magazine and on the end-of-season videos. It was all a good craic with one of the most genuine blokes I've ever met. He's a smashing fellow to have a drink with, honest and straightforward without any kind of edge, which does plenty to explain why he has made such fine progress as a manager.

Our right-back when we won our first Premiership was Paul Parker, a friendly, hyperactive lad who never stopped talking. We used to call him Buzby – after the character in the TV telephone advertisements – because he was always on his mobile. Even driving to games, it was as if the phone was glued to his ear, and how he hasn't boiled his brain I'll never know. He was a bit of an electronic genius too – at least, he was compared to the rest of us – and could always sort out what was wrong with a mobile. Undoubtedly Paul was the smartest dresser at the club, he was a lad who loved his gear, and he must must have spent all his wages on clothes, phones and the occasional car.

Football-wise, Parks was a superb natural defender, a little limpet who would stick to anybody, a bit like Nottingham Forest's Des Walker. Though he usually played at full-back, he could operate at centre-half, too, or do a specific marking job, though he could never have been a conventional midfielder because he wasn't the most comfortable on the ball. Though he got better in his time at Old Trafford, he could never be described as a creative player, and the joke was that we didn't want to leave him in possession too often. In the end, he struggled to throw off ankle injuries and lost his place to Gary Neville. Eventually Parks left the game and started selling cars – I could imagine his patter – and then I heard he was back in London coaching a semi-professional club. More recently I've been delighted to catch up with him in the MUTV studio, where we have both been working.

In stark contrast, our other full-back was the quiet, unobtrusive Denis Irwin. At least, he never said much in the dressing room, but get a drink down his neck and he became a different man, much chirpier and quite cutting with his wit. Not that he was nasty, but he had a dry sense of humour similar to Choccy's, and he wasn't averse to a bit of character assassination.

As for his football, that spoke volumes. What a player Denis Irwin was, at £650,000 probably the biggest bargain that Alex Ferguson ever struck. He read the game so well that he could snuff out danger before it developed, it seemed he was always in the right place. Denis was never exposed, and though he wasn't outstandingly quick, it was a rare winger who left him in his wake. In addition, he was decent in the air, a lovely passer, a beautiful crosser and a tremendous free-kick specialist who didn't get much of a look-in later on with Eric, Giggsy and Becks on the scene.

Denis was adaptable, too, moving seamlessly to the left to accommodate the arrival of Parks and working so hard to improve his 'weaker' wing that eventually he was equally adept with either peg. Put all that together and you had a fantastically high level of consistent performance. Denis wasn't the type to stand out, to hit you in the face with his excellence, but we expected him to be superb in match after match, and he didn't disappoint.

A world away in terms of personality was the self-styled 'Guv'nor', Paul Ince. A typically chatty, opinionated Cockney, he was loud and in your face – and that was just with his friends! I got to know him very well straight after joining United because we were both staying in a hotel with Danny Wallace before we sorted out houses.

Paul introduced me to the evils of gambling. He liked a bet on the horses and the greyhounds, and rather than spend all afternoon stuck in the hotel, we'd go to the bookies for a little flutter. It was nothing crazy like you read about with some people; I lost the odd £100 here and there, but it never got out of hand. I could see, though, why some footballers do get heavily involved because they have so much time on their hands and gambling offers a thrill, a real buzz.

We also spent time in the snooker clubs around Manchester. Ince was a terrific player and at one time he relished a game with Alex Ferguson. Maybe that's why the Gaffer transferred him in the end – perhaps Incey beat him too often on the old green baize!

Unquestionably Paul was the best snooker player in the club, but then he took up golf. In fairness, he wasn't bad at that after taking lessons, but you wouldn't want to play with him too much because when he hit a bad shot then he tended to snap his clubs. You might say that he didn't quite observe the traditional etiquette. He needed to win so badly but he became frustrated easily, which led to a lot of shouting and screaming.

There's no way of dressing it up, Paul was hard work on the golf course. But he was a great character, a very tough player who brought a lot to the side. It's a shame that he's not welcomed back to Old Trafford by the fans, perhaps partly because of the manager saying that he was too big for his boots, and partly because he went on to play for Liverpool. It doesn't seem right that a man who played such a mammoth part in ending the club's seemingly interminable wait for the title takes so much flak every time he returns. I wish the supporters would think it through and respond to him a little bit better, because he deserves a decent reception.

Sadly they don't like him at his first club, West Ham, either, because of the controversial way he left, being pictured in a United shirt before the deal went through. But they still love him at the Riverside, where he gave Middlesbrough several seasons of splendid service, and at Molineux, where he was even touted as a future Wolves boss. Now I must admit that I never had Paul down for management. As in the case of Roy Keane, I doubted whether he was cut out for dealing with people on a day-to-day basis. Both of them were extremely demonstrative and combative as players and you wouldn't have described either of them as a people person.

But I'm genuinely delighted to say that Paul has made a brilliant start at proving all the sceptics wrong. I'm so impressed with the way he's handled himself as a boss, first at Macclesfield, then with Milton Keynes Dons. When he accepted his first management post at Moss Rose, the Silkmen were virtually doomed to relegation from the Football League. Certainly they had one foot in the Conference. But Incey, working in harness with his experienced assistant, Ray Mathias, saved them from the drop. Having achieved what was little short of a footballing miracle, naturally enough he wanted to move on to widen his experience, and he took on the challenge of Milton Keynes Dons. Once again he has done a fantastic job, winning promotion from League Two at the first attempt, and he deserves nothing but praise for a monumental effort.

For a guy who always shot from the hip in his playing days, now he appears to have a much more balanced and rounded outlook. Not once have I heard him sounding off about what his team is going to achieve. Rather he's got on with his work quietly, no doubt inspiring his charges with the burning enthusiasm and drive that were major Ince characteristics throughout his playing career. When I think back to the young fella who joined Manchester United at about the same time as me, his current style doesn't seem in the slightest bit Paul Ince-like, but clearly he has lived and learned.

Knowing how ambitious he is, and remembering his past disappointment at the dearth of black managers in the professional game, he'll want to move on up the ladder, be somebody who makes a difference. Whatever he sets his mind on, he gives it total commitment, so I'd say that nothing was impossible for him. Paul was the first black captain of England, and maybe one day he'll be his country's first black manager.

As for the eternal question of who is going to replace Sir Alex at Old Trafford, you'd have to say that Paul is very much an outsider at the moment. He would have to get hold of a bigger club and do well at a higher level before becoming a serious possibility for the United job, but it would be unwise to write it out of the script somewhere down the line.

Wherever he goes, he will arrive with enormous respect. Once a player has walked the walk, as Paul did for so many years with a succession of top clubs, he will always have that as a starting point in management. If you've been there and done it yourself, that's half the battle in handling players. They need to know that you know what you're talking about, that you understand the situations they are in. Of course, you still have to get your tactics right, get the best out of people, maybe massage a few egos. Once I couldn't have imagined Incey carrying that off. Now, in view of his meteoric progress to date, I can only stand back in admiration and await developments.

Whatever happens, I'll always think a lot of him, and there's no denying that, back in 1995, I was deeply disappointed to see him leave Old Trafford. Yes, he always had a bit of a swagger about him. Yet ironically, if just he and I went out for a drink, when he didn't have a crowd to perform to, he was altogether different, a lovely lad who would chat and have a sensible conversation. It was just that when he was in front of a few people he had that Cockney thing, and off he went. At times I'd say he thought his approach was no more than a bit of banter, but Alex Ferguson might have viewed the situation differently.

I know they had a couple of arguments after games when the manager had wanted him to play a holding role, but Incey had ignored instructions and pushed forward, tried to do things on the ball. Speaking as an unbiased observer, I think he was more than just a hard man, even if that was his most obvious strength. He had a creative side, could run with the ball, beat people, strike a shot with either foot, pass accurately, and he wanted to use those attributes. Whatever, it's undeniable that there was friction between Paul and the Gaffer, though maybe the bottom line was merely that Paul wanted to join Inter.

Where does he stand in the pantheon of United midfielders? Well, although we're talking an absurdly high standard here, it's fair to say he was just behind Bryan Robson and Roy Keane, even though Paul was a fantastic player in his own right.

A rather less flamboyant individual was Brian McClair, my old neighbour in Wilmslow and an intelligent fellow with a fearfully sarcastic wit. Choccy wasn't a typical footballer, but a strange, deep, some might say unfathomable character who could pull people to shreds with just a few carefully chosen words. His analysis of their faults could be devastating, even cruel at times.

A perfect example of that sharpness was his reaction to the stunning news that Jim Leighton had been dropped for the 1990 FA Cup Final replay. Now Jim, Choccy and I used to car-share every day to go to training, and the two Scots were room-mates on away trips, so there was a pretty close connection between us. Hence my anguish on the goalkeeper's behalf when I learned of Alex Ferguson's ruthless decision. What did Choccy say? 'Do you think he'll still need his comps for tomorrow's game?' I could only gasp at him along the lines of 'Choccy, you sarky bastard!' Of course, I knew he didn't mean it nastily. It was just a typical piece of black humour, the type that footballers employ to make light of serious situations, to dispel the depression, and I suppose it worked for me. Obviously, Jim wasn't present at the time.

In his first season for United, before Sparky rejoined the club, Choccy scored 24 goals as a striker, the first time any Red Devil since George Best had broken the 20-mark. But in my time he was mainly a midfielder, doing a good enough job to keep Bryan Robson out for long periods in our first two victorious Premiership campaigns. Like Denis Irwin, he was an unassuming player, going about his work quietly and efficiently, though even after moving back he chipped in with his fair share of goals.

Funnily enough, for all his all-round competence and long, loyal service, Choccy was a chronically bad trainer. I had him down as worse than me, and that's saying a lot. Sometimes he would just get totally pissed off with it and kick the ball away.

When he was tearing us apart with his barbed comments, we used to retaliate by calling him 'The Manager's Son'. Clearly, we told him, he was a long-lost, illegitimate love-child of the Gaffer, it was the only explanation for him being picked all the time. He took it all in good part, knowing that he would be getting his own back, with interest. Apparently he and Gordon Strachan were quite a double act in the late 1980s, bouncing their mordant one-liners off each other. Perhaps one day we'll hear some of Choccy's gems in managerial press conferences. Currently he's coaching United's kids, but you never know.

Another character with far more to him than met the eye was Mark Hughes. When you sat down and talked to Sparky, he revealed himself to be an amenable, softly-spoken and retiring kind of guy, which came as a surprise to many people because he could be an absolute animal on the park. Talk about Jekyll and Hyde! As I mentioned before, he gave me a mauling when I faced him in my early days at Middlesbrough, provoking me like no other opponent. Mark couldn't play any other way than full-on.

Even on the training park he was downright savage, willing to draw blood from anyone, and he had us all leaping out of the way of his fearsome challenges, especially in the little keep-ball boxes. He explained that when he was at Barcelona, the other players were that good at keeping the ball that he never got it, and he used to go mad. We used to call him The Strimmer, because he'd whip your legs from under you. Another nickname was Double Ledge (as in legend) because he had two fantastic spells at United. Which is the real Mark Hughes? Somewhere in between the two extremes of Mr Nice Guy and wild man, I guess, but the important thing is that Sparky was one hell of a player.

Just as exciting, but in a different way, was our flying winger from the Ukraine, Andrei Kanchelskis, who created a buzz every time he got the ball. He put so many defenders on the back foot; they were scared of getting forward because of Andrei's extraordinary pace, knowing that if he got half a yard on them, then nobody could expect to catch him. He really was a frightening threat and, with Lee Sharpe or Ryan Giggs on the opposite flank, he offered fantastic balance.

True, sometimes he got to the dead-ball line and let the opportunity go to waste with a bad cross, which was frustrating, but it would be hard to imagine a more ideal foil for Sparky and Eric, neither of whom boasted outstanding pace. A typical scenario was Sparky holding the ball to give us time and bring Eric into play, then the Frenchman would knock a pass into space behind defenders, knowing that our wingers had the speed to capitalise. Some of our counter-attacking football was utterly breathtaking. When you add in the fact that Andrei contributed plenty of goals, then it's plain what a massive asset he was to Manchester United. Yes, we had to keep cracking the whip to make sure he worked as hard as Giggs and Sharpe, because chasing back didn't come naturally to him. But he was a strong lad, we urged him on all the time and he would listen.

To the fans, one of Andrei's attractions was that he seemed to be enjoying his football, playing with a smile, which was a pleasant change in the high-pressure days of the Premiership. To the rest of the players he seemed a nice, unassuming lad, who made every effort to mix with the boys socially, even though he didn't have a great grasp of the English language. It really surprised us the way he turned when he wanted to leave the club, becoming suddenly stroppy, petulant, difficult, none of which seemed to be a natural part of his character. Where once his approach had been all sweetness and light, now he was upset if he was left out for a game, and got the hump if he was asked to switch from right wing to left.

A lot was said about what was going on behind the scenes. We never got to the bottom of it, but he was adamant that he was going to leave. The lads tried their best to talk him round and so did the manager because we all knew he was an important player for us. His situation, as it appeared to us, didn't really add up and we got the feeling that some exterior pressure was being exerted on him. He said he couldn't get on with the Gaffer any more but there seemed to be more to it than that.

His reputation in European football had grown immeasurably, and it was obvious that there was going to be money for people to earn off the back of Andrei. We just couldn't tell what was happening in the Ukraine, but I believe there were dark influences at work. We thought he'd move to one of the big European clubs and it didn't seem to make a scrap of sense to the supporters when he ended up at Goodison Park. United got a lot of money, but Andrei Kanchelskis was a lot of footballer.

So was Lee Sharpe, who was only 17 when he made his debut for United, having been signed from Torquay, where he had played under my old Darlington gaffer, Cyril Knowles. Sharpie made an instant impact on arriving at Old Trafford, breaking into the first team at 17 as one of Fergie's Fledglings in the season before I moved to Manchester. He was another one who scared the hell out of defenders with his electrifying pace, and if David Beckham was the best deliverer of a ball from the right that I've ever seen, then certainly Sharpie was the finest from the left.

Lee was, and remains, one of life's eternal optimists, a real dreamer, and we need them. He's the type of guy whose glass is always half full, never half empty, not a bad outlook with which to face the world. How he adored all the attention lavished on professional footballers. Sharpie was a born showman who projected a pop-star image, complete with the latest suits and his own fan club, and he was a magnet for the girls. They loved his extravagant goal celebrations, swivelling his hips and giving it the Elvis bit with the corner flag.

With that sweet left foot he was such a terrific player, and it was such a pity when his career lost some of its impetus when he contracted meningitis. A distressing situation was made even worse because people were throwing rumours around town that he was involved in drugs, but I'm sure there was no substance – if you'll pardon the pun – to any of them. Just because he enjoyed the club scene, it was easy for snipers to say he had dabbled in drugs, and such stories hurt him deeply. He liked a night out, but no more than most lads of his age, and every tiny bit of tittle-tattle was blown up out of all proportion. For instance, there was the time when he and Giggsy went to Blackpool two nights before a game when they should have been resting, not a good move but youngsters are bound to kick over the traces now and then.

Lee also suffered from a serious ankle injury, and in his early twenties his body grew bulkier – no fault of his own, he was just a late physical developer. In earlier days he had been like a whippet, there was nothing of him, and that's when he had been at his most devastating. As his body grew, he was still pretty quick but he was deprived of that sensational pace that gave him an edge, and his critics made unkind comparisons. What with the ankle, and finding himself in the centre of midfield at times, he lost what made him special, and eventually United accepted £5 million from Leeds, a lot of money in 1996. In hindsight, that represented a bit of decent business by the manager, as not long after moving to Elland Road Lee suffered a cruciate ligament injury, after which he struggled to find any kind of consistent form.

I was particularly sorry to see him go because he was one of the lads I socialised with most, going on holiday with our respective girlfriends during close season, but I think everybody missed him because he was such an effervescent personality around the club. Happily, I still see Sharpie on the golf course regularly, and he keeps himself pretty busy. He does some television work and he's looking to get involved in the property business. I'm delighted to say that he remains a free spirit and an eternal optimist, a bit like Del Boy from *Only Fools And Horses*. I think they've got the same motto: 'This time next year we'll be multi-millionaires!'

Probably Ryan Giggs falls into that category already after the best part of two decades as one of Europe's finest but he had barely begun his journey towards stardom when I first laid eyes on him. Soon after I signed for United, every so often I'd get bored with hotel life and take in a youth match, and one day I watched one with the Gaffer in the directors' box. He pointed out this young schoolboy, saying he was going to be some player, a lad who was going by the name of Ryan Wilson at the time. He had the body of a pipe-cleaner, so skinny the shirt practically hung off him as he hared down the left touchline beating defenders as if they didn't exist. 'He doesn't look too bad, Gaffer,' was my considered verdict as Alex Ferguson continued to talk about him in glowing terms, though even he could have had no idea of the heights to which Ryan would ascend. After all, at a time when the club hadn't won the League title for nearly quarter of a century, who could even have dreamed that this kid would eventually collect *ten* (at the last count) championship medals and beat Bobby Charlton's all-time appearance record for Manchester United?

He turned professional during the next season and not long after that he made his full debut against Manchester City, which indicated the confidence the manager had in him. That day he was credited with a goal, though what today's Dubious Goals Panel would have made of it I don't know because there was a big deflection off Colin Hendrie. Obviously, he didn't want to claim it so it was given to Giggsy.

Soon it became clear to the world that Ryan was special and it was at this point that the manager did a fantastic job in protecting him from the media spotlight. He was touted as the new George Best and everybody wanted a piece of him, which could have been extremely destructive. But the Gaffer got Robbo's agent to help him and shield him, so that he could develop in his own time without undue hassles and distractions from the press.

Giggsy was quite a shy lad at the time and happy to be shown the way by his manager. Even as he grew up and became more confident, he retained an admirably level head, keeping the same mates that he had at school and never changing as a person throughout what must have been an incredible period in his life. Sometimes you can see the danger signs when a young footballer is feted to the heavens, but they were never there in Ryan. He was never too big for his boots, never believed what he read in the papers, never let money make him forget about his football.

As a result, he became a shining example to any kid making his way in the game. Take Wayne Rooney, for example. He's got the ability to play 750 games for Manchester United, just like Ryan, but that's provided he listens to the right advice, primarily from the manager, even though there might be times he might not like it. But if Wayne needs to talk about the situation then there's nobody better than Ryan. He had to deal with more than anyone except Gazza, at least before Becks came along, and he never put a foot wrong. I know that Gazza had more demons to contend with, but Ryan never had it easy, what with his parents splitting up, though it must be said that his mother did a magnificent job in bringing him up with his feet on the ground.

Off the park, he's a very lively character. He and Nicky Butt were always up to mischief, especially in hotels, putting pepper and salt in beds, that type of thing. It was no more than a couple of hyperactive Manchester lads indulging in some good, healthy fun, usually without stepping over the mark. Occasionally he received a dressing-down from the manager, like the night he was found partying with Sharpie when they should have been somewhere else, but you've got to expect that sort of thing occasionally from fit young lads. Even I had a bit of energy when I was that age!

His football apart, the most vivid memories I have of Ryan Giggs are as the best rapper at the club, and for his skill at Cossack dancing, which he demonstrated at a party after we had clinched the League and FA Cup double in 1994. The elasticity Ryan displayed that night at Mulligans Bar was astonishing. Maybe that's why he's had his hamstring problems down the years …

CHAPTER TWELVE

WHEN YOU'VE HAD
A FEW BEERS YOU TEND
TO OPEN UP ...

Much has been made of the debilitating effects of the so-called booze culture on British football in days gone by. Indeed, when Alex Ferguson took over from Ron Atkinson as Old Trafford boss in 1986, he remarked that Manchester United appeared to be as much a drinking club as a football club. Now the ethos has changed dramatically, so much so that alcohol is banned from the players' lounges at certain Premiership venues, including the Riverside.

Clearly, an excess of alcohol is a massive cause of misery in all walks of life, but I don't believe that footballers getting together for is drink is intrinsically wrong, provided it is done at the right time and in the right manner. In my Ayresome Park days a lot of the lads socialised together, and frequently that involved going out for a pint, a practice even more prevalent at Old Trafford when Bryan Robson was the club captain.

He would call for a 'team meeting' and that was the cue to go down the pub for the day. We would have a few drinks, put the world to rights, talk football and anything else under the sun that took our fancy. When you've had a few beers you tend to open up. Some people don't always like the truth, but it's invaluable to bring issues into the open, which is preferable to allowing them to simmer and fester under the surface.

I don't know if that policy prevails at United now, though I suspect it doesn't. These days after a match at Old Trafford there seems to be plenty of room in the players' lounge, whereas a few years back it was virtually impossible to get a spare ticket. You could hardly move in there.

It is easy to understand how the modern way has come about. Danny Murphy made the point when he left Liverpool in 2004 that one of the things which disillusioned him at Anfield was the decrease in craic between the players, perhaps because there were so many different nationalities and cultures. I think that situation has become general with the increase in overseas players in our domestic game. In the early 1990s there was a rule in force restricting the number of foreigners, so the core of our dressing room had a British mentality, which meant enjoying a pint and maybe a bacon sandwich. Today's European newcomers, on the other hand, tend not to thrive on that situation, being more aware of diets.

The way football has gone, with high finance dictating the need to get results all the time, every club is striving to grab that extra percentage of advantage which might make all the difference. The vast rewards the players are receiving has made it that much more difficult for them to have the kind of lifestyle which I enjoyed at United.

Is the new way beneficial? I think the old way was beneficial for us at the time. We loved our team meetings and they helped the team to bond. Robbo used to say if there's something eating away at you, then probably, in the normal run of events, you'll keep it to yourself because you don't want to cause conflict. But put yourself in a situation where you're not at your workplace, rather somewhere no one is forcing you to be, then you have a couple of beers and it loosens your tongue in a healthy way. Okay, you might end up in an argument, though we never had any fights or trouble – not between the players, anyway! – and problems were aired before they could grow out of proportion.

When would we do it? If we were playing on a Sunday, we'd train on a Tuesday and go straight from training to the pub, knowing that we had the Wednesday off. There was a hard-and-fast rule that there was no drinking two days before a game, and we never flouted that, though on occasions we did fall foul of the Gaffer.

During the 1993/94 championship run-in we played Liverpool on a Wednesday, beat them 1-0, and afterwards myself and three or four of the lads went into Manchester for a drink. We were facing our main title rivals, Blackburn, on the following Saturday, and we lost. Straight after that game the manager pulled in the lads who had been out – and he ALWAYS knew who was doing what, he had his spies everywhere – and went ballistic, really flew off the handle. He accused us of being paralytic, and while I admitted being out, I denied categorically that we had gone as far as he was suggesting. I pointed out that at every club I knew, players were allowed out as long as it was two nights before a game. 'That's their rules, these are my rules. You should have been at home' he stormed back. He re-wrote the rulebook when it suited him.

Bryan was the skipper, and it was his job to be social secretary as well as the team leader. I've got to say he fulfilled both functions brilliantly, and even if the team meeting was instigated by other players, they'd still get Robbo to sort out the arrangements. How long would these sessions be? Well, there was no time limit, and suffice to say that the younger lads maybe ended up in a nightclub. That's after starting at 1.30 or 2pm, so you could be talking about a 12-hour do.

Invariably, the whole team would be involved. Nobody would balk at the idea, and that was the great thing about these occasions. I'm not saying everyone would drink solidly and get drunk, but they'd all be there. For example, I can't ever remember Eric Cantona missing one. There were lots of stories about Eric being difficult, not being one of the team, but that was rubbish. He liked a night out, loved being with the lads.

Towards the time I left in 1998, it was maybe harder to get some of the younger players involved because attitudes were changing, but we still had our meetings. But even those youngsters who didn't exactly embrace the idea still turned up – they knew they would be in for a torrid time from their team-mates if they didn't. It was fine as long as they made the effort. They didn't have to get pissed, it was just a matter of being there, away from the working environment, to join in the bonding. We wanted to feel that we were all in something together, and that togetherness would help us to go the extra yard.

Outsiders need to understand that the players didn't go silly, and neither did they do it every week. Even in the 1990s, if they had gone too far then they wouldn't have lasted five minutes, such were the demands of the game.

I know our meetings might appear to cut across what Alex Ferguson said when he arrived the the club about the need to end the drinking culture, but I'd suggest that perhaps the boozing at that time was a little bit heavier than ours. For example, Paul McGrath – and what a magnificent centre-half he was – had a well-chronicled problem with drink. Bryan Robson, too, liked his beer, but he was just a freak of nature. No matter what had happened at our sessions, drink never affected him on the training park, he could train as if he had been on water the night before. Unquestionably he was the best trainer you could ever see, but I guess he was lucky in that respect, being such a fit specimen naturally. I envied him because it was always hard for me to keep up a decent level of fitness.

Bryan was the heartbeat of the side, a colossally influential leader and one of the world's greatest players. When he was in his prime, and even for some time after it, Alex Ferguson was desperate to have him in his team at every opportunity. Of course, the Gaffer knew about Robbo's fondness for a drink, and his reaction was an example of his brilliant man-management skills. Sometimes you live with things as a manager, and work round them for the overall good of the club. It wasn't just Robbo, there was also the Eric situation, with his various whims, his aberration at Crystal Palace, his other brushes with officialdom, and some of the tackles he made. None of that was easy, but what people like Bryan and Eric brought to the table was irreplaceable, so the Gaffer reacted positively and coped with it.

I know, too, that in the late 1980s and early 1990s, there was a similar approach at Arsenal, where people such as Tony Adams, Steve Bould, Paul Merson, Ray Parlour and the rest all liked a drink on their way to winning a succession of trophies. What a fascinating parallel that offers with Arsene Wenger's modern Arsenal, another smashing side but one which is it impossible to imagine holding 'team meetings' in the manner of their predecessors. Still, that hasn't stopped them achieving a notable togetherness, illustrated by the way they go into a huddle on the pitch in moments of triumph.

The prevailing continental school of thought is that sport and alcohol don't mix, and that's a philosophy that is becoming increasingly pervasive in the English game. I can see where the Europeans are coming from, but I maintain that, with a sensible approach, there is still nothing wrong with a team letting their hair down from time to time. For instance, I'd say that the fuss over the England team's exploits in the so-called dentist's chair, during a trip to Hong Kong ahead of Euro '96, was grossly over the top.

The lads had just played China in Beijing, and had been together for a lengthy period, preparing for that game and the forthcoming tournament. Ahead of them was a brief break in Hong Kong and a flight back to England, after which it was back down to serious business. Probably there was a pact that they wouldn't drink during the European Championships, but before that they had a couple of nights to themselves, to unwind and enjoy themselves. So where was the big deal in a bunch of young, fit boys getting a bit drunk during a short period of time after they had been disciplined for so long, and shortly before they would return to being equally disciplined again? Does that sound a terrible crime?

Okay, maybe some of the pictures weren't too pretty, and perhaps the notorious dentist's chair, which involved booze being poured down the occupant's throat, might not have been the best idea, but I am firmly of the opinion that they should have been left alone to have their drink. It seems that as a nation we are all too ready to shoot ourselves in the foot where England are concerned. The press appear so desperate for us to win the World Cup, yet they do their utmost to rubbish our players at every conceivable opportunity. I only hope the majority of readers are able to put the issue into context, realise that it's wrong to condemn a group of footballers on the evidence of one newspaper picture taken in off-duty hours, and understand that the lads do have to get out and let off steam at some point. My view is that we should let them get on with it.

It's not that I don't appreciate the potentially destructive power of alcohol, which has ruined countless lives and, I'm pretty certain, fuelled one of the scariest incidents I was involved in during my years as a footballer. It happened at the Midland Hotel in central Manchester, where we were spending the night before facing Liverpool at Old Trafford the following day, which was unusual at a time when we were rarely kept from our own beds before home matches.

We had dinner in the evening but, typically, I still had a yen for a snack or two and so, together with Mark Hughes and Clayton Blackmore, I set off in search of further sustenance.

To get to the shop in the Midland we had to pass through what looked like a wedding reception, and we were squeezing through the chairs at the back, as unobtrusively as possible, when I collided with a guy whose chair had been pulled right out. I apologised, he moved his chair, and we continued. It crossed my mind that it was strange that his chair was sticking out quite so far, but it scarcely registered. So we went to the shop, I bought a soft drink and my usual couple of chocolate bars, and returned to the lifts in the lobby. As we waited I was starting my drink when the guy from the reception walked past and barged into me, knocking me aside.

That was out of order and I looked at Clayton, who pulled a face and said: 'Let it go. He's probably been drinking.' By now I'd got my back to this fellow, a huge, robust individual in his early thirties, then the next minute he had barged into me again. This time I thought I couldn't ignore him again so I said: 'Is there a problem?' He said: 'Nah, nah, no problem. Is that your drink?' I said: 'Well, obviously' and he just whacked it out my hand. Now I knew we had a problem! Clayton tried to step in with the guy still insisting: 'I'm only having a laugh, just a joke, a bit of banter' but now it was stark, staring obvious that he had been drinking. Clearly he was right on the edge and I thought something was going to kick off.

That moment the lift opened and he attempted to walk in with us. I said: 'Whoah, you're not getting in there with us,' and as I went to stop him he punched me hard in the stomach. I kind of expected it and rolled as he did it, and whacked him hard right in the socket of his eye. I'm no boxer but I knew it was a good punch straight away, but the guy was enormous and I realised I had a serious problem now. So I threw my arms round him to prevent him from hitting me again and held on.

The next minute little Clayton's come flying over and dived on the fellow's neck. Tiny though the Welshman was, he was very strong, the arm-wrestling champion of Manchester United, and he was frightened of nothing. It was like a scene from some film. We were next to some display cabinets and we were reeling around, banging into them, with the fellow trying to throw Clayton off his neck and me still grabbing his arms with all my might. I was desperate to gain some control over the geezer, and stop him from doing real damage.

Meanwhile Sparky's just stood there, deadpan, watching the show. I was waiting for him to weigh in on our side, but he just looked on, as if he was nonplussed. Probably he thought we were handling it all right, though we were still clattering around the furniture. At that point the bell-boys and other hotel staff came running over to calm it down, and the guy's going: 'They just attacked me, the three of them just attacked me.'

Now Clayton took control. He said: 'We want the manager of the hotel and our own manager. This guy's crazy.' Eventually Alex Ferguson appeared and so has the fellow's wife, who said: 'This is terrible. My husband's not like this, he must have been intimidated or assaulted by these people.' For a moment, total confusion reigned, until the Gaffer stepped in. He asked what happened, we told him, and he said to the hotel manager: 'Either this fellow's out of this hotel in the next five minutes or I take the whole team out.'

Sure enough, they booted him out, and I felt great, because as he went his eye was coming up an absolute shiner, confirming my impression that it had been a good hit! Mind, I wouldn't have wanted to fight him one-on-one because he was a hulking fellow and it could have got pretty nasty, but Clayton handled himself brilliantly. Meanwhile Sparky adopted the Mr Cool approach and we gave him some stick for not joining in. He could have tripped him up or anything; that would have helped because it was all hands to the pump in there for a little while. Clayton is a lovely lad, a really funny guy and Sparky's best mate – they were practically joined at the hip – and he really had a laugh at Mark's expense. Incredibly, the incident stayed out of the press, which really surprised me as it took place in the middle of a busy hotel foyer. I always knew Sparky had a few contacts on the newspapers ...

CHAPTER THIRTEEN

PALLY'S GOT TWO!

A wind of change was blowing through Old Trafford as the 1996/97 campaign got under way. Not only were Masters Scholes, Beckham, Butt and the Nevilles making an ever more indelible impact on the first-team scene, but in the summer the Gaffer introduced five foreign newcomers, the club's biggest intake of senior players for a long time. We welcomed Karel Poborsky, Jordi Cruyff, Ronny Johnsen, Raimond van der Gouw and Ole Gunnar Solskjaer, most of whom we knew precious little about.

Karel was the exception because he had just enjoyed an outstandingly successful Euro '96 tournament and we were all excited at the prospect of his arrival. Sadly, he found it difficult to settle in England, he was in and out of the side and, ultimately, it never worked out for him at Old Trafford. It was a shame because he was a popular lad who tried his hardest to integrate around the dressing room, even though he didn't have much grasp of English. On the pitch the lads loved his effort, though maybe he was striving a bit too hard.

There was some thought that Karel might have fitted in on the right flank as the long-term replacement for Andrei Kanchelskis, while David Beckham forged a future in central midfield, but that never happened. I'm delighted, though, that he has gone on to enjoy a terrific career after leaving United, earning a century of caps for the Czech Republic. Further good news is that he has shaved back his wild crop of hair, which the manager never liked. Alex Ferguson's view was that Karel's hairstyle didn't help him become a favourite with the fans because it looked a bit comical. These days he looks positively svelte in comparison.

Jordi Cruyff, too, had played in Euro '96, though obviously his main claim to fame was as the son of the Dutch master footballer of the 1970s, the great Johan. In the end, he never settled into a single position, never claimed a regular slot with United, and moved on having made no appreciable impact.

In contrast, Ronny Johnsen, a Norwegian who had played most of his football in Turkey, was to make a real mark and pick up a European Cup winner's medal for his pains. As a midfielder who made his way back to centre-half, he was very accomplished on the ball and he was extremely quick. Ronny was one of the tightest markers I've ever seen, too, but he did suffer more than most from serial injuries.

As for Dutchman Rai van der Gouw – or 'van der Gorgeous' as he was known by the girls in the club office – he proved an ideal deputy for Peter Schmeichel, efficient, professional and a good goalkeeper in his own right.

But the new boy who stood out most vividly was the Norwegian striker Ole Gunnar Solskjaer. Here was this fresh-faced youngster who looked no different to the YTS lads on their first morning, but as soon as I saw him in training I knew what a fantastic finisher he was. He very rarely missed the target and seemed to have a natural instinct for scoring goals. Ole was a class act from day one and it wasn't long before he was making a sensational impact on the Premiership scene.

Yet for all that transfer activity, I suppose the biggest story of the summer was the one that got away – and, once again, that was England centre-forward Alan Shearer. After it had become clear that he was intent on leaving Blackburn, I sat with him at an England get-together and got the definite impression that the Rovers owner, Jack Walker, was dead set against him joining Manchester United. I'd say that Walker actually priced Alan out of a move to Old Trafford, that if he was going to cost Newcastle £15 million then United would have been asked £20 million. Ultimately the decision was down to the player and I could understand his preference for returning to the club he had watched from the terraces as a child. I'm positive, though, that he'd have won a lot more honours if he'd chosen Manchester, and that would have been fitting for a footballer of his exceptional quality.

He might have had a part in winning that August's Charity Shield for a start. As it was he made his Newcastle entrance against us, and we played them off the park, beating them 4-0 and laying down our marker for the season ahead. As holders of the double, we were confident going into the new campaign, with every reason to believe that our fabulously gifted crop of youngsters would continue to develop in their own time, but none of us were prepared for what one of those lads had in store for us in the opening League game. On a hot, sunny afternoon at Selhurst Park, a certain David Beckham catapulted himself from the status of richly promising rookie to superstar with one swing of his boot.

We were beating Wimbledon 2-0, they had given up hope of a comeback and we weren't hunting for a third, so the game was cruising routinely towards the close when it happened. David picked up the ball just inside his own half, took a couple of steps and hit it towards their goal. My first thought was: 'You cheeky sod!' Even as I watched the trajectory of the ball I was thinking: 'Nah, nah, don't be daft.' But then suddenly I saw the Wimbledon 'keeper, Neil Sullivan, back-pedalling, really starting to panic, and while the words 'surely not' were still forming in my mind, the ball sailed over his head and hit the back of the net. To say I was stunned is an understatement. I could believe neither the audacity of the lad for trying such a thing, nor the incredible technique to pull it off. I think the initial reaction of the rest of the team was that it was quite funny. We understood the astonishing execution we had witnessed, but were dumbstruck that he'd had the nerve to try.

In retrospect, that was the moment when David Beckham's life changed forever. Everybody talked about how Pele had once tried it and failed; now here was this slim teenager having a go and absolutely nailing it right down the middle of the goal just under the crossbar. It was picture-perfect. It announced to the world a precocious talent and immense self-belief to go with it. What other kid would have tried that in a Premiership game? If it hadn't come off you could imagine the manager giving him a clip round the ear afterwards, but that wasn't necessary.

David was quite shy in his immediate reaction to it. Obviously he loved it and milked the applause, but he was almost coy about it in the dressing room. The lads were all buzzing about it and I think he was a little embarrassed by all the attention.

To this day, when I think of David Beckham it's as 'the young lad.' When I knew him well he was just making his way in the game. All the hype that surrounded him and his ascendance to icon status arrived after I left the club, so I dealt with him when he remained in the realms of normality. True, the celebrity was building. He'd started to see Victoria, the hype machine was ticking over, and it was clear that he relished the good things in life. But he came over essentially as a quiet lad, even verging on the shy. He was well-mannered, the type anyone would be proud to have as a son, and his family seemed of paramount importance to him, with his parents coming to every game.

True, he had struck me as cocky when he was visiting the club a few years earlier but that could have been just down to understandable excitement. Certainly that brassy little lad wasn't the same David who came to Old Trafford full time. When he joined United as an apprentice he was a genuine, pleasant, really nice kid; no one could have picked fault with him in any way. Mind, he had a fair belief that he was going to be a professional footballer, but there was nothing untoward there. And he was right, wasn't he?

David continued to rivet the eye and capture the headlines through September and into October but then, unexpectedly, United ran into what has passed into club folklore as Black Autumn. After remaining unbeaten through our first nine League games, we were humbled 5-0 at Newcastle, embarrassed to the tune of 6-3 at Southampton and lost 2-1 at home to Chelsea, all in the space of two weeks.

At St James' Park David Ginola scored a wonder goal, Philippe Albert chipped Schmeichel with an exquisite effort and, just to rub it in, Alan Shearer got on the scoresheet. For the Geordies, obviously still smarting over losing the title the previous season, it was sweet revenge for their Charity Shield drubbing, while from our viewpoint there were similarities to the infamous 5-1 route by Manchester City seven years earlier. Once again everything that our opponents tried came off, while we created some decent chances but never put them away.

Amazing though it was that United had conceded five, the next week was even worse when we let in six down at The Dell, where an already dire situation was made even bleaker by the dismissal of Roy Keane. I was removed from the firing line at half-time when we were 3-1 behind because I was feeling pain in my knee. I'd been having problems turning sharply for some time and when I had it checked out I found I needed a cartilage operation, which sidelined me for six weeks.

Though those two results, and the Chelsea defeat that followed, came as a shock to the club's system, we didn't feel that we had been playing particularly badly and believed that we would bounce back, which we did by embarking on a sequence of 16 League games without defeat, which saw us through to March in decent fettle.

Meanwhile we were raising our eyes towards the European Cup, feeling genuinely that this could be our year, and that belief burgeoned after a terrific home performance which took us past Porto in the quarter-finals. Thus it came as an horrific letdown when we lost both legs of the semi-final to Borussia Dortmund by a single goal, and I felt especially hard done-by as both the Germans' strikes were deflected into our net by me.

I thought we played superbly in the first leg in Dortmund, where Nicky Butt shot against a post and we engineered several more opportunities, including an effort from Becks which was cleared off the line. Then, about 15 minutes from the end and with United seemingly in total control, Rene Tretschok took a punt from outside the box, it nicked my boot and spooned just beyond the reach of Rai van der Gouw, who had played impeccably as stand-in for the injured Schmeichel.

That was a blow, but still it didn't seem too crushing to be going home only one goal down, but only eight minutes into the home leg Lars Ricken struck an innocuous shot from wide on the right, it hit me and wrong-footed Schmeichel to put us two behind on aggregate. After that we laid siege to the Germans' goal, making and missing a barely believable array of chances. Their 'keeper made a succession of tremendous saves, I fluffed one sitter that I should have been able to knock in blindfolded, Eric miskicked from close range with the whole goal at his mercy. But it just wasn't meant to be and if we were still playing now I don't think we would have scored.

What irked us was that we felt we had the beating of Borussia, and they went on to overcome Juventus in the final. Ironically we had faced Juve in the early stages of the competition, and they were superb, beating us 1-0 both times. I have to admit that the defeat in Turin was the most comprehensive 1-0 hammering I've ever known. They were awesome; we couldn't put two passes together because their play was so intense, hunting every ball down throughout a traumatically one-sided first half. They tired in the second, but the damage had already been done, and they underlined their mastery at Old Trafford.

But I think we learned from the two games against them, and deserved our place in the knockout stage. I'm not saying necessarily that we would have beaten Juventus in the final, but we would have been confident of giving a better account of ourselves, so it was enormously frustrating to be deprived of that opportunity by my two vicious deflections.

Happily there was balm for our European anguish back in the Premiership, especially at Anfield, where we paid a Saturday morning call between our two jousts with the Germans. As we went into the game we were top of the table and needed to beat Liverpool to put them out of the title race, leaving Newcastle as our only real rivals. It ended up as an occasion I shall never forget, providing one of the happiest memories of my career.

United hardly ever practised set pieces, no more than once or twice a season. We just expected a good delivery because of the quality of players in the side, and we might exchange a few cursory words about who would run where when the ball came across. But suddenly, in the middle of the Borussia Dortmund games, the manager decided that we should do some work on free-kicks and corners. He said we were going to use them against Liverpool, so we spent a lot of time on near-post and far-post strategy, decoy runners and all that carry-on.

Lo and behold, the first corner we got at Liverpool, I said to Ronny Johnsen: 'You do the decoy round the back and I'll attack the middle of the goal.' Becks obliged with a picture-book corner, I managed to evade my marker, who was Mark Wright, and sent a perfect header right into a stanchion to put us 1-0 in front. Wow! We should have done this more often, I thought!

It wasn't long until John Barnes equalised, but we continued to play well and won another corner just before half-time. This time Ronny said he'd take the far post and over came another lovely dispatch from Becks. I got in front of Wright again, David James came out but got nowhere near the ball and I glanced it into an empty net. Later I saw television pictures of Alex Ferguson turning to one of our directors, Mike Edelson, and saying 'Pally's got two!' with a look of utter disbelief on his face. I'd never scored two in one match before and now it seemed doubly wonderful because it was in front of the Kop, which always hands us so much stick. In the second half David James dropped a clanger, Coley put it away and we won 3-1, playing some absolutely marvellous football. That put Liverpool out of the title picture and rubbed in our superiority to the extent that a lot of home supporters were leaving before the end of the game, not a common sight at Anfield.

But even after all that I got a bollocking from the Gaffer. Unknown to me he had done a piece on Sky television in which he'd said we hadn't been working on the set pieces, that they had been off the cuff. Obviously he didn't want Dortmund to know what we'd been up to. But then I went out for an interview and cheerfully admitted that we'd been practising all week in training! So the manager had a real go at me: 'What are you like, you? I've told 'em this and you've told 'em that. What you telling everybody for?' So that was me scoring two goals at Anfield and ending up in the doghouse.

Despite the euphoria of victory, I always found that the whole Liverpool experience got to me. The rivalry between the two clubs runs so deep that it is unhealthy, and sometimes it gets out of hand. It gripes many Liverpool supporters that, even when their team was clearly the best in the country, still United were seen as the biggest club. It made it worse for Liverpool, too, that when United weren't at their best, in the 1980s, usually they seemed to serve up a decent performance against Liverpool.

When the venom is at its height, it is truly gruesome to experience. I can't speak for the receptions Liverpool and Leeds players get at Old Trafford, but the sort of stuff we have been subjected to at Anfield and Elland Road has been nothing short of vile. The sheer, raw hatred is appalling, it should have no place in any sport. Healthy rivalry is one thing, but taunts about the Munich air disaster are utterly sickening, and I don't know how people can stoop so low.

I remember the first time Beckham, Scholes and company went to Anfield. Young fans asked them for their autographs, with which they duly obliged, only to see them ripped up in front of their faces. That was kids! Who taught them to hate like that? What do they think they're proving or showing?

I find it impossible to fathom the cause of such deeply-held and often hysterical feelings. Maybe as well as the football it is partially due to Manchester and Liverpool being rival northern cities. Many years ago they would have been vying for trade, so there's always been a tension between the two, one trying to get the better of the other, and in modern times that takes expression on the football field.

The two sets of supporters are never going to be the best of friends, and that's fine. If they want to let off steam with decent, and preferably humorous chants, then no problem. But each set of fans has a certain obligation to acknowledge the merits of the opposing club. Certainly all the Manchester United players I have known respect all that Liverpool have achieved down the years. We know that they blazed a trail across Europe with all their trophies and took English football to another level. Where's the problem in admitting that? Everybody loved watching them play at the time and they should be honoured for it.

The situation at Leeds is often as ugly as the one at Liverpool. I remember driving into Elland Road to be greeted by a guy with a six-year-old on his shoulders and both father and son were sticking up the 'V' sign at our bus, screaming bile at us. The man seemed so proud that his kid was doing that. What chance have we got of ever getting it right if people are teaching their sons in that way? It's total madness and it reflects badly both on football in particular and society in general. Educating kids to hate cannot be right.

Thank heavens, the players are far too professional to get involved in the hate thing and, in my experience, when they joined up for internationals there was never any problem with the relationships. People like John Barnes and Peter Beardsley were genuinely nice blokes and great pros.

I understand that when you go out on the pitch and you realise how desperate your own fans are for you to win, then feelings can spill over, no question. The highly charged atmosphere produces a little more edge to your game, revs you up that little bit more than usual. With all due respect, it takes time to warm up the Old Trafford crowd against the likes of Watford or Reading. You have to be scoring goals to get them going. But when you play Liverpool the buzz is already there, the crowd is electric with anticipation. On those days it is the fans who inspire the players rather than the other way around.

If things had worked out differently when I was leaving Middlesbrough, then I would have been on the other side of the Manchester-Merseyside divide, but I couldn't be happier with the outcome. If the offers from Old Trafford and Anfield had arrived at the same time, I'm pretty sure I would have chosen United anyway because the club has such a special aura. Old Trafford is where so many legends are born, it's the Theatre of Dreams, the whole package is irresistible, and nothing can change the fact.

So, in view of all that, we were tolerably pleased to leave Anfield with three points in the spring of 1997, and soon afterwards we clinched our fourth championship in five years with a couple of games to spare. Once again, we took the crown on a night when we weren't playing, as Newcastle and Liverpool both dropping points meant that we couldn't be caught. It was a tribute to the spirit and resilience of our players, as much as to their talent, that we came back so strongly from that potentially disastrous autumn, and even the departure of our talisman, Eric Cantona, after the final match did not detract from the sense of achievement.

Of course, Eric's exit left a gaping void in our attack, one which I was not alone in thinking that Alex Ferguson would ask young Paul Scholes to fill in 1997/98. But I was wrong. Though the Gaffer wasted no opportunity to praise Scholesy to the heavens, and rightly so, he did not think the time was right for him to take on the Cantona role. Instead he recruited Teddy Sheringham from Spurs as a direct replacement for the Frenchman in a deal which surprised a lot of people.

In Teddy, the Gaffer went for extra experience. Like Eric, the Londoner possessed a fantastic footballing brain and he could score goals, so I was more than content that we had acquired such a high-grade replacement for the seemingly irreplaceable. Of course, Eric's were massive boots to fill and the fans were always going to miss a cult hero synonymous with so many glorious triumphs. But even though our new man started slowly – and he wasn't helped by missing a penalty against Spurs, his former

156

employers, on his United debut – anyone who understood his subtle qualities knew that eventually he would fit the bill.

In the end he enjoyed four good seasons at Old Trafford, played a key part in winning the unprecedented treble in 1998/99 and was double player of the year in 2001. He just seemed to get better as he went on and was still performing regularly at Premiership level for West Ham when he was 40. Even then he wasn't finished, going on to turn out for Colchester in the Championship in his 43rd year, which might seem incredible given the stringent physical demands of modern football. It didn't surprise me, though, because he was such a natural athlete.

It was relevant, too, that he played with a remarkable economy of effort, his acute footballing intelligence ensuring that invariably he took up the right positions without having to sprint 60 yards to reach them. Teddy had a lovely touch on the ball, he was strong in the air, he was a fine finisher, and when he grew into the role at United he made a lot of doubting pundits eat their words.

With Teddy on board, and the efficient Norwegian international defender Henning Berg added to the squad, we progressed smoothly through the autumn, moving well clear in the race for the championship, although I did experience one perturbing personal blip. In September at the Reebok Stadium I was sent off for the only time in my United career, but I can declare honestly that it was an unjust dismissal, a fact recognised when referee Paul Durkin rescinded the red card after reviewing the incident.

There is always a bit of warm feeling when Manchester United meet Bolton – apparently it's been there ever since the FA Cup Final of 1958, when Nat Lofthouse scored a controversial goal after charging into United 'keeper Harry Gregg – and it was no exception this time. Right from the start I became involved in a bit of banter with their Scottish international striker John McGinlay, who was shouting off his mouth and handing out plenty of verbal stick. That was unusual for me because I very rarely became embroiled in a war of words on the pitch; I needed to conserve my energy rather than waste it expelling hot air. But this time he got under my skin; I think he called me fat, which amazed me because he was one of the fattest players in the Premiership. I can't recall the precise details but I can tell you the general standard of debate was pretty rarefied!

So had I been expecting trouble, then I might have anticipated it coming from McGinlay, but I was wrong. Instead it came from his fellow front-runner, Nathan Blake, who launched a terrible challenge on me and

I had to skip it or I might have been badly hurt. I was shocked by the ferocity of that challenge and the likely consequences had he caught me, but I didn't react violently. Instead, after he had had a second go at me, I did no more than kind of nudge him as I walked past. The next second he came at me from behind and shoved me. I turned round and squared up to him, but I was careful to keep my arms down at my sides. All I did was put my face out as if to say: 'Go on, then!' He accepted the invitation, not so much with a punch as a slap, but he made definite contact. I reacted by pushing into him, never raising my fists at any stage, and I thought it was a formality that Blake would be sent off. So he was but then the referee left me dumbfounded by sending me off as well.

As soon as the game was over – it finished 0-0 – our manager and chairman came to ask me why I was dismissed. They had spoken already to the referee, who told them it was for raising my fists, which I denied categorically. Happily, the Gaffer and Martin Edwards supported me and, when Paul Durkin looked at the television footage, he realised he had made a mistake so the red card was rescinded.

I had been exonerated completely and it's fair to say that not many centre-halves can point to such a good disciplinary record as mine over so many years. Maybe Tony Adams and Steve Bould at Arsenal would give their centre-forward a good, hard whacking to let him know they were around in the first couple of minutes because the feeling was that you got one foul free before the referee took a stand. But that was never the way I went out and played the game. I took the view that I'd stand my corner, but I was never a wind-up merchant. Different people deal with the verbals in different ways. Some, like Paul Ince, fire straight back from the hip, while others blank it. To me football was meant to be a physical game and if someone is trying to hurt you then you retaliate however it suits you. In my case, it was by doing my utmost to see that our team won the game.

As winter wore on we had been doing just that on a regular basis, losing only twice before Christmas, and by the time we won at Chelsea in late February we were no fewer than 13 points clear at the Premiership pinnacle, albeit with Arsenal having a game or two in hand. After that we lost only two more matches, but Arsene Wenger's team came with such a fabulous run of victories that they went past us and took the title.

The key match that spring was when they came to Old Trafford and beat us 1-0, just as we had grabbed a crucial victory at Newcastle two years earlier. After the late goal by Marc Overmars, there was no time to recover. I watched from the stand that day, being injured, and when that ball went in I discerned a feeling running round the ground that the championship was slipping away. Arsenal were on a high from that moment; fair play to them, they were unstoppable.

The absence of Keane for most of the season after hurting his knee against Leeds proved to be a colossal handicap. He had gone to kick Alf-Inge Haaland, it was a silly challenge even if it looked innocuous, and hardly seemed vigorous enough to tear a cruciate. It was obvious that Roy was seriously hurt, but there appeared to be bad feeling between the two of them and Haaland stood over the Irishman, spitting venom. That incident occurred before we faced Juventus at Old Trafford on the Wednesday, which is when we got the news that Roy was going to be out for six to eight months.

That was a crippling psychological blow, a bit like losing Eric after the Selhurst Park affair, and when we went behind to an early goal from Alessandro Del Piero our fans must have been fearing the worst. But we showed our character, playing some scintillating stuff to win 3-2, with Ryan Giggs supplying a spectacular strike from the left edge of the box and the Italians only scoring their second in the last minute. It was a hugely significant milestone for Manchester United, giving the team a whole lot of belief that, one day soon, we could be European champions. Previously we had been a long way second-best to Juventus, but now the gulf had been closed.

After that, going out to Monaco on the away-goals rule was a fearful anti-climax; once again, we had felt we had a realistic chance of going all the way. I missed both games because I was suffering from ongoing back problems, which were becoming ever-more intrusive. This time my difficulty emanated from the morning of our meeting with Chelsea at Stamford Bridge. I slipped coming out of the shower, and although I played in the game, I had to leave the action early. My back went into spasm a few hours later, and that was worrying.

Still, at that point I was happy with my form – in fact, it had been one of my most effective terms for the club – and although my next birthday would be my 33rd, I had missed only a handful of games during the season and felt I had plenty still to offer the United cause. I knew there would be more competition in the coming year because of Jaap Stam's arrival – I had already met him at The Cliff – but I wasn't afraid of that, though I suppose somewhere at the back of my head some sort of alarm bell might have been ringing.

As it turned out, the end was in sight. My last game for United at Old Trafford, or anywhere else, was the 3-0 victory over Leeds in early May. It's strange, but as I ran out that day I had an eerie feeling that I might be doing it for the last time in a United shirt. There was this irrational notion that it was my swansong, even though I had no knowledge that Middlesbrough had made a bid for my services and that it had been accepted by the United board.

Genuinely, I wasn't worried by the advent of Jaap, because I could envisage playing alongside him. I knew Wes Brown was coming through promisingly, and both Ronny Johnsen and Henning Berg were on the scene, but I felt I had controlled my back problem pretty well and remained as confident as ever in my ability to play at the top level.

It all came into the open the following midweek when I was called in by the Gaffer. He sat me down, told me Robbo wanted me at 'Boro and that an acceptable bid had been tabled. He explained that because of my back injuries, he wasn't sure he could rely on me to play regularly in the future, so United weren't able to offer me a contract extension. He was perfectly friendly, stressing that I wasn't being forced out, that I was welcome to see out the year of my existing deal, and that he would be happy if I did just that, although he couldn't guarantee me a first-team place. That in itself didn't bother me, because you never get a guarantee at United anyway. What did bother me was the spectre of going out in a way I wouldn't have wanted.

Whatever Alex Ferguson said, nothing could hide the truth that the club was prepared to let me go and, I have to say, that hurt me. After all, that season only David Beckham and Gary Neville had played more games than me, so I wasn't exactly fading away, and I pointed that out to the manager with due passion. I was mortally disappointed and made sure he knew it. But the Gaffer had made his decision and I respected that. I knew he never rested on his laurels, he always wanted to push on for the future. I realised it was going to come one day; it was just that I didn't expect it that day.

Now I had a choice, but having seen both Robbo and Brucie devastated when they were left out of cup finals, and watched Sparky's disappointment at the way his United days ended, I had always promised myself that I would not head down that route, that I would go gracefully if I felt the Gaffer was seeing me in a different light. I couldn't bear the thought of being left out of important games, I was desperate that my United career should not end in anti-climax, and the fact that an offer had

Bonny lad, aged five months.

Recognise the grin? I was eight or nine at the time.

A sunny day at the Frederick Nattrass Primary School – that's me in the middle of the back row.

I could have been a cricketing contender.

Early days at Ayresome Park.

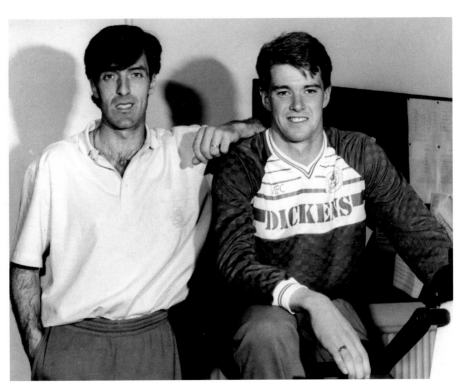

Boro buddies, Bernie Slaven and myself.

Flying high for Boro against the Magpies.

Case for the defence. Boro goalkeeper Steve Pears with the 1987/88 promotion-winning back four. From left are Gary Parkinson, Tony Mowbray, myself and Colin Cooper.

A decent start. I made my international debut alongside Tony Adams in Hungary in the spring of 1988, and we were both pretty happy after the match.

'That's enough sweeties for today.' Chewing the fat with England boss Bobby Robson in the Bisham Abbey canteen.

Having a laugh with Steve Howey (left) and Terry Venables, who treated his England players like men.

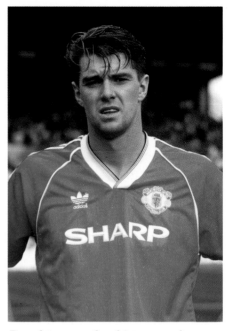

Alex Ferguson – bloody hell!'

Proud to wear the shirt, soon after joining United.

Macho men. Posing with Lee Sharpe.

Head for heights. Climbing above Gary O'Reilly in the first of United's two FA Cup meetings with Crystal Palace at Wembley in 1990.

Statement of intent. Lifting the European Cup Winners' Cup on a misty Rotterdam night in 1991 gave notice that United were well and truly back in the hunt for top honours.

The icing on the title cake. I seem tolerably pleased with myself and Messrs, Ince, Giggs, Kanchelskis and Robson are clearly impressed by my late goal against Blackburn on the night we received the long-awaited trophy in May 1993.

For all the media-hyped mystique, our French maestro was just one of the lads in the dressing room.

Roy Keane and I might have had one or two fleeting differences, but we had far more fantastic times together.

In the drink with Sparky and Robbo.

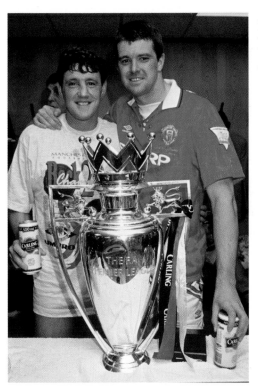

Daisy and Dolly – or should that be Dolly and Daisy? Brucie and I never knew the answer to that one.

I can't remember what we are laughing at now, but Kiddo, Incey, myself and Giggsy all saw the funny side.

Singing from the same hymnsheet. Getting happy with Schmikes after beating Liverpool at Wembley to clinch our second League and FA Cup double in 1996.

At full stretch against Alan Shearer in 1996. No defender could relax for a moment when the top scorer in Premiership history was on the prowl.

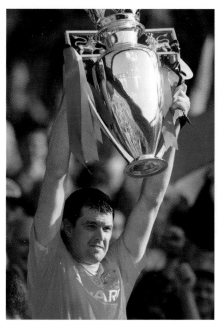

Something I never tired of doing.

Cuddling the kids, Scholesy and Butty.

Dion, Denis and I might just have taken a sip or two before this shot was taken.

A day to remember at Anfield in April 1997. Outjumping Mark Wright to rattle the Liverpool stanchion.

Taking the plaudits.

Mam and Dad and a double dose of silverware.

Obliging a snapper with young Gary Neville, Becks, Dion and Sharpie.

Going with the Flo. Taking a breather with Chelsea's Tore-Andre after returning to Boro.

The home team.

Above: A quiet moment with Mary.

Right: Lauren and Eve on our front doorstep at Yarm.

Below: The Pallys on holiday.

been snapped up illustrated my situation graphically enough.

In those circumstances, my immediate reaction was that I would speak to Robbo. So I went home, told Mary, then popped straight round to Robbo's house, where we agreed a deal there and then. After that it took a while for the businessmen to sort out the fine details, but eventually I rejoined Middlesbrough a week into pre-season.

I don't think I would have gone anywhere else. If there had been no other interest then I would have seen out the last year of my contract at Old Trafford and then hung up my boots. As it was, there was the double attraction of playing for Robbo, whom I knew and trusted, and going home to Teesside, which was a major factor both for Mary and myself. I was told that Everton had a little sniff, and if I'd moved to Everton then I wouldn't have had to move house, but I don't think Goodison Park was ever a serious option.

I felt there was a little bit of unfinished business at 'Boro, because I'd always wanted to win a trophy with them, the first in their history. They had quality players at the club, the likes of Paul Merson and Paul Gascoigne, the chairman was willing to put his hand in his pocket, and I thought there was a realistic chance of achieving my final ambition with them. You have to set yourself those kind of targets to keep yourself going, especially as you get older. The upshot was that, both personally and professionally, going back to Middlesbrough seemed like the right move for me.

CHAPTER FOURTEEN

NO GREATER PRIDE ...

I had the cherished honour of making 22 appearances for my country over the space of eight years, during which I played for four England managers whose characters and approach to the job varied dramatically. The Bobby Robson experience was fleeting and rather passed me by because I was young, pretty green and preoccupied with establishing myself in the Second Division, let alone at international level. I don't believe Graham Taylor, an exceptionally decent man, was well suited to the job in terms of his approach to playing football. Terry Venables was terrific, the ideal England boss, and it was a crying shame that factors outside the game scuppered his reign, which I believe passionately held the potential for sustained success. Finally, Glenn Hoddle was a first-rate coach full of enlightened ideas, but whose man-management skills left a lot to be desired. In view of his immense technical potential in the role, I'd put him down as a particularly crushing disappointment.

I was a latecomer to representative football, never breaking through at schoolboy, youth or under-21 level, getting my first taste when called into the full England squad in my early twenties, for a friendly against Holland in March 1988. At the time I hadn't been established too long as a Second Division regular with Middlesbrough, so I was somewhat overawed to find myself rubbing shoulders with England stars whom I had previously admired only from afar.

On the first night with the squad I could scarcely credit the company I was keeping at the dinner table. Bear in mind that I'd arrived late in the professional game, then played all my football outside the top division. Now here I was with Peter Shilton on one side of me, Glenn Hoddle on the other, and Bryan Robson was facing me. I was so intimidated by being in the presence of three of the biggest names in world football that I could feel myself shaking. I could hardly hold a knife and fork, I was that nervous.

Robbo obviously understood my position and, as the skipper, it was his job to make me feel at home, so he chatted away, did everything possible to make me feel part of the set-up. The others joined in a bit, though really

I was too much on edge to remember what anyone said. Hoddle was a huge favourite of mine at the time and it was a memorable experience to train with him. He was just awesome; nobody could get the ball off him. People tried to snap into the tackle and rob him, but they just couldn't get near him. He was on a different level.

My first cap arrived a few weeks later in another friendly, against Hungary in the famous Nep Stadium in Budapest, where the 'Magnificent Magyars', one of the finest international sides of all time, had forged their reputation in the early 1950s. I played alongside Tony Adams, with full-backs Viv Anderson and Stuart Pearce completing the back four and Bryan Robson ahead of me in midfield. Typically of Robbo, he effectively chaperoned Tony and myself, because we were both pretty raw, and I have always been grateful to him for that.

The game finished 0-0 and I spurned a golden opportunity to make a sensational impact about five minutes from the end, when Chris Waddle sent in a corner to the near post. I timed my run perfectly and should have buried it, but I headed it just wide of the post. It was a terrific opportunity and, ironically, the closest I ever came to scoring for England, but I didn't let that glaring miss spoil the occasion. All the newspaper write-ups were positive about my overall performance, Bobby Robson said he was impressed with my display but needed to look at me some more, and Brian Clough capped it when he came out with his quote about me looking a million dollars and being worth a million pounds. All in all, I could hardly feel despondent.

At this point we were approaching Euro '88, but Middlesbrough got into the Second Division play-offs, which meant I missed a succession of England friendlies and consequently lost my chance of being involved in the tournament. Some pundits reckoned Tony Adams and I might have proved the dream ticket in central defence, despite our youth, but Bobby Robson was never going to take me on the premise of one game, and I can understand why he went for more experience. Anyway, there was no way I wanted to miss the play-offs, the most important footballing challenge for me at that time, and it seemed that there would be other tournaments for me further down the line. Little did I know that this was only the first of a succession of major international competitions that would bypass me for a variety of reasons.

I didn't receive another call-up until the trip to Saudi Arabia the following November, by which time Bobby Robson was under increasing pressure from the media. I enjoyed the experience of flying by Concorde and playing at a beautiful stadium in Riyadh, but the gloss was taken off the occasion during the game when, with the score at 0-0, Tony Adams and I cantered forward for a free-kick. Somebody took it short to Peter Beardsley, the ball was cut out and Saudi scored. Next day all the papers were questioning where the two centre-halves were, but we were at the other end of the field waiting for a free-kick, so we had no chance. That's how crazy some of the criticism was, and I feel strongly that anyone who knew anything about the game would never have said such things. After the 1-1 draw, the manager was deluged in flak that was nothing short of hysterical. Recently one headlined had screamed at him: 'Go, in the name of God.' Now, because we were playing in Saudi, they hit him with: 'Go, in the name of Allah.'

I was left out of the next squad and, with Adams, Terry Butcher, Des Walker and Mark Wright on the scene, I wasn't taken to the 1990 World Cup Finals. It was disappointing but, to be honest, the England situation wasn't to the forefront of my mind around that time. 'Boro had struggled after promotion to the top flight, I'd been working hard to come to terms with the gulf in class between the First and Second Divisions, and I had some fitness concerns, so I felt I had plenty on my plate without fretting over international ambitions.

When I was selected by new England boss Graham Taylor to face Cameroon in a friendly at Wembley in February 1991, it precipitated the most embarrassing incident of my professional football life. The game had been in doubt because of severe cold weather, and I was named on the bench. I made sure I was wrapped up warmly for the pre-match kickabout, for which I wore a T-shirt, a couple of sweat-tops, a wet-top and gloves. After that I returned to the dressing room and reorganised my layers of insulation before venturing back outside to sit on the bench.

After shivering my way through most of the game, I was told to get warmed up about a quarter of an hour from the end. I ran down the track, did a few stretches and then heard the magic words: 'Get stripped, you're on.' So, with the cameras glaring at me, I pulled off half-a-dozen layers, only to discover, to my utter horror, that I had forgotten to put on my England shirt. Oh dear! Poor Graham Taylor looked at me and shook his head in disbelief. I'd rarely been used as a substitute before so I wasn't used to the routine, though I have to admit that was a lame excuse. As a result of my memory lapse, the kitman had to sprint down the tunnel and into the dressing room to get me a shirt, which meant I missed out on another five minutes of international football.

Despite that, Graham couldn't have despaired of me altogether because he picked me for the European Championships qualifier against Turkey in Izmir, which provided me with my first taste of competitive football on the international stage. The volatile atmosphere made more of an impression on me than the game itself, for which I partnered Des Walker and played my part in a 1-0 win, which was secured by a goal from Dennis Wise.

Still I was no more than a fringe member of the squad, and I missed selection for Euro '92, bouncing back into the reckoning for the World Cup qualifier against Norway in Oslo in June 1993. What a miserable occasion that turned out to be. Graham decided to change his tactics, announcing on the night before the game – so there was no chance to work on the new system – that we would play three centre-halves, with Tony Adams and Des Walker holding the middle, leaving me to man-mark Tore Andre Flo.

I was told to follow my target all over the park because Graham was worried about the big fella's aerial threat. It was a recipe for mayhem. You can't keep a balance, or maintain the overall discipline of the defence if somebody is chasing here, there and everywhere according to the whims of the opposition's centre-forward. If the manager was that worried about Flo, I feel we should have played Tony and myself in a conventional 4-4-2 formation. Terrific defender though he was, Des was the least dominant in the air, so he would have been the obvious man to leave out. It seemed sensible – just keep our shape, allow both Tony and myself to deal with aerial attacks, and we should have been secure. As it was Flo pulled me all over the shop, into places I didn't want to go, and the upshot was utter confusion, a poor team display and a severely debilitating 2-0 defeat.

I feel that was an ill-judged decision by Graham Taylor, who had entered the international arena with a reputation for direct football. That was his style and I don't think it suited the world game, even though Jackie Charlton had some success with it for the Republic of Ireland.

Graham was an intense type of guy and, sadly, when he came under pressure from the media, it got to him. Of course, a lot of that pressure was way beyond the realms of reason. It was as though he'd committed a series of murders, rather than presided over a succession of disappointing football results. The campaign to vilify him sunk to its lowest and most savage level when he was depicted infamously as a turnip on the back page of one of the tabloids. They just ripped the poor guy's character apart, and it wasn't necessary to go anything like that far.

That said, I wasn't always impressed with the way Graham, and his helpers Lawrie McMenemy and Phil Neal, handled the England team.

Certainly I never really understood Lawrie's role. Of course, I realise that a lot of his work would have been done on scouting missions, but there appeared to be no great input into the team when everyone was together.

As for Phil Neal, he had been a fantastic player for Liverpool, compiling no fewer than 16 major club honours and picking up half a century of England caps. He would always have the players' respect for what he had achieved in the game, but as a coach a lot of the lads found him far too intense.

On occasions, if you did something wrong or made a mistake, Phil would try to get you to do press-ups as a punishment. Worse, he would dispense this rudimentary form of discipline in a demeaning sort of way, as if he was trying to embarrass you in front of other people. Maybe that's a feasible approach with kids, and maybe it isn't, but there's no doubt the England players felt it was a funny way to be treating seasoned professionals. I've got to be thankful to Graham for bringing me back into the England set-up, but the fact remains that it wasn't the best time to be involved in the squad, and I didn't agree with much of what was going on.

Perhaps the key question of Graham's reign was: did he have the necessary authority for his demanding job? I think it's hard to answer in the affirmative for a manager who didn't play in the highest grade. How natural is it for someone with that pedigree to be telling top footballers how to perform in the international arena? Is it realistic for individuals who have won everything with the likes of Arsenal, Liverpool and Manchester United, by passing the ball attractively, to listen attentively to a man who embraced the long-ball game? Were they not going to wonder what in hell's name he knew about the style of football demanded at international level, where keeping the ball is so important?

I know Graham had enjoyed remarkable success in bringing Watford up through the divisions with his basic style of play, and he can point to some decent results when he took over at Aston Villa. But even when that was happening, the prevailing view, at least beyond the confines of Watford and Wimbledon, was that he was not doing the wider game the least bit of good. In fact, most people thought he was killing it.

I know it's not always the rule that top managers must have played at the top level. For instance, Arsene Wenger never set the world afire as a player, but he adapted brilliantly to dealing with high-quality footballers, and also he wanted to play the right way. People weren't happy with the way Graham wanted us to use the long ball because it seemed alien to international football.

It's a fair maxim that, the higher you go, then the more you're asking for trouble if you give the ball away. You've got to retain possession all you can. We've seen the Europeans do it for years, and we should learn from that. But Graham's arguments were all about percentages. He would say he'd fed the information into a computer, which told him if you get the ball forward much quicker then you've got more chance of scoring, while teams which go for patient build-ups don't score so many.

But the whole theory was wrong-headed. He couldn't see beyond getting the ball into areas where he could gain free-kicks, corners and long throws. The beautiful game? What a sick and sorry joke. This was terrible to watch and terrible to play. I'd come from Manchester United where it was all about passing to feet and fluid movement off the ball. Now all the talk was of getting the ball to the corners of the pitch, or into the channels for forwards to chase. Most of us had to change our fundamental thinking to embrace this method, so the manager had no chance of getting the best from us. For God's sake, we were forbidden to pass to somebody so we could get it back and make space. We had to launch it forward whenever possible. The mantra was: why involve the midfield when we can reach the front straight away? The correct answer was: because it opens space to get controlled possession in advanced areas, but that cut no ice with Graham. It was as mystifying as it was overwhelmingly frustrating, and it was always destined to come to grief in the end.

A week after the Norway debacle, we faced the United States in Boston, and suffered the humiliation of a 2-0 defeat. After that embarrassment, we were delighted at the chance to make amends against Brazil, who have set the standards for decades in world football. For a long time in the match, it looked like a David Platt goal was going to earn us a famous victory, only for the South Americans to claim a late equaliser. The three-match tour ended, as it had begun, in defeat, this time to the Germans under a closed roof in Detroit. I have never felt so bad on a football pitch; there simply wasn't enough oxygen to fill our lungs. When I went on a 20-yard run it felt like I'd just completed a marathon. It was absolute murder, and for once in my life I was pleased to pick up an injury, when I went over on an ankle towards the end of the first half, making it impossible to go out for the second. The relief was indescribable.

I find it hard to understand why national teams take players away for summer tournaments. After long domestic seasons, the exhausted footballers would garner far more benefit from resting at home, recuperating from their cumulative niggles, strains and other injuries.

Clubs, too, place a huge extra burden on their players by embarking on lucrative promotional tours, though to be fair to United, when they flew off to South Africa that summer they left Paul Ince, Lee Sharpe and myself behind to pick up our pre-season training gradually. In this case, I regretted not going and having the chance to meet Nelson Mandela, which would have been a once-in-a-lifetime experience, and also I could have caught up with an uncle in Johannesburg. When they got back the lads said South Africa was a fantastic place to visit, it was the best trip they'd ever had, so we were gutted, but I have to admit that the manager's reasoning for leaving us at home was sound.

Though some of the bigger names, like Paul Gascoigne and Tony Adams, didn't make that England trip to the States, it was of enormous importance because we were supposed to be acclimatising ourselves for the World Cup Finals the following year. Of course, it turned out to be a sadly wasted journey because we didn't qualify.

After the tour, Graham was disappointed, but tried to emphasise the positive of the Brazil game. Of course, from the moment we lost to the USA, the anti-Taylor press bandwagon really got rolling. Every day of the week there was a story begging him to quit but, to his credit, he always tried to remain upbeat in front of the players. It must have hurt him deeply, though, and I felt dreadfully sorry for him.

Mercifully the next game, a World Cup qualifier at home to Poland, brought a bit of respite, the emphatic 3-0 win affording the manager a brief breathing space. Probably that was the happiest result of my England career, and I was celebrating afterwards in the players' lounge when I felt a tap on my shoulder and turned round to be confronted by Bruce Rioch. It was the first time I'd met him since leaving Middlesbrough in such acrimonious circumstances, and it rather put me on the spot. He said 'Well played' and held out his hand, so I shook it, but then I looked away, unable to engage in a conversation. With all that had been said, I had felt pretty raw for a long time and still couldn't face the prospect of a friendly chat. Since then, though, I've kind of mellowed and have shaken his hand a few times when he has managed clubs against United, including Arsenal.

By all accounts he found it difficult at Highbury, dealing with a number of big egos. On paper he did a pretty good job there, bringing in Dennis Bergkamp and other good signings, but I don't think Ian Wright and some of the higher-profile players reacted well to his style of management. There were always stories of conflict between the manager and his footballers, and ultimately he left the club, so I would presume that player-power prevailed in the end.

After seeing off Poland so comfortably, England's hopes of progressing to the finals had leapt, but our prospects for the crucial meeting with Holland in Rotterdam were not helped by several injuries or the suspension of Paul Gascoigne. In the event we lost 2-0 but it was a game in which the outcome could have been oh-so-different, and we could easily have qualified for the World Cup tournament, if only the referee had been on the ball. I don't think there was a scrap of doubt in anyone's mind that Ronald Koeman illegally prevented a terrific goal-scoring opportunity for David Platt and certainly should have been sent off. How he stayed on the pitch I do not know. But he got away with it, and two minutes later he was down at the other end of the pitch putting Holland in front. From that moment, we were on our way out.

What most people remember about that match is the TV documentary in which Graham and Phil were going mad on the sidelines, the manager ranting that the decision had got him the sack and coming out with the immortal line: 'Do I not like orange?' That programme didn't show anybody in a good light. Taylor and Neal were never going to win friends and influence people by agreeing to it. If Graham was pilloried mercilessly beforehand, his plight became much worse afterwards, because the show called his judgement into question and he appeared as a figure of fun. It did nothing for the credibility of Graham Taylor, Phil Neal or England, and was one gigantic public-relations disaster.

Now all that remained of the poor man's reign was the next game against San Marino, officially the worst team in the world. It seemed his position couldn't possibly become any more untenable but after seven seconds in Bologna it did just that when Stuart Pearce underhit a back-pass to David Seaman and one of their lads nipped in to score one of the quickest goals in international history. After that stunning setback against the so-called whipping boys of our group it took us a wee while to get back in the game, though eventually we ran out 7-1 winners, with Ian Wright scoring four. Even that didn't save England's bacon, or Graham Taylor's, because Holland won in Poland to qualify for the finals as runners-up to Norway and shortly afterwards the FA put the manager out of his misery by giving him the sack.

When the news broke, it's fair to say that most of the players felt relief on his behalf. Though, on a professional level, I didn't think that Graham was the man for the job in the first place, I had nothing against the guy

169

personally and he didn't deserve the vitriolic character assassination he received at the hands of the tabloids. At least he was now out of the firing line and able to get on with his life again. The England job had been affecting his personality, dragging him down. He must have been punch-drunk at the mountains of vile rubbish heaped on his head and now, at last, he was free from all that.

Before leaving the subject of Graham Taylor, though, I would like to mention one aspect of his period in charge for which he deserves a bit of credit. Being on the road with England can be hard going, mind-numbingly boring. You go away for a week's training and you end up stuck in a hotel for vast swathes of time with nothing to do except play snooker. So you go out and train, come back and eat, go to your room for a rest; then it's snooker, then eat, then snooker, with maybe the occasional game of cards thrown in. Now that might sound okay to somebody working in a factory or whatever, but it's surprising how quickly it can pall and Graham recognised this. He instituted different activities, perhaps a karting trip, a visit to the theatre or even to a different restaurant, just to escape from the hotel dining room. All that struck me as pretty enlightened. It just broke things up, lessened the monotony, made people less likely to go stir crazy.

Back on the football front, once Graham had gone it wasn't long before the FA were sending Jimmy Armfield on a tour of clubs to gauge the views of managers and players on who should be the next England boss – and the virtually unanimous choice was Terry Venables. All I knew about Terry was what I'd seen on TV and read, but word of mouth was overwhelmingly favourable. I was very impressed with the way he handled himself and by the style in which his teams performed, choosing to play through the midfield instead of ceaselessly blasting long balls from one end of the pitch to the other. It was agreed that an Englishman was required, and he seemed the natural choice. True, there were people at the FA who were unsure of Terry because of his business life, but the support of so many players gave him the necessary leverage and he was appointed in January 1994.

The moment he took over, there was a more relaxed feel about the squad. The players didn't feel they were being watched all the time, as if they were schoolkids. If we joined up on a Sunday night and we weren't playing till the next weekend, he'd let us into the bar for a few drinks, or even venture to the pub down the road for a couple of beers. If anyone abused that then that was their fault and he'd come down on them like a ton of bricks. Contrary to what many people might have thought, he could be very hard at need. Most importantly, he treated us like men. We're talking here about professionals, most of them in their late twenties or early thirties. You can't treat them like first-formers, you have to recognise them as mature individuals. Terry did that and, as a result, he received far more respect than did his predecessor.

Invariably the man was great fun, a tremendous character who was always laughing and joking, someone who spread a feeling of relaxation whenever he was around. Also, of course, he was a wonderfully astute coach who talked about the game with tremendous passion and had clear ideas about how he wanted it to be played. Everybody responded to that and I find it overwhelmingly sad that it was influences outside of football which cost him his job. England were so, so close to winning Euro '96 with a team espousing classical football, playing with spirit and style, keeping the ball on the deck, enabling the match-winners and entertainers to blossom.

Bryan Robson was Terry's trusted lieutenant during this all-too-brief period of enlightenment for the English national team, and that suited me because I had a good relationship with him from our Old Trafford days together. There was also considerable input from Dave Sexton and from Don Howe, who looked after the defence. I don't think Don was a big fan of mine because I wasn't the greatest trainer. Certainly I was led to believe that he wasn't in my corner, but I wouldn't find fault with that, it was his prerogative. In this game of opinions there are always going to be people who rate you and people who don't and, fortunately for me, there were people who mattered who did have faith in me.

The fact was I just wasn't built for fitness and stamina training. As hard as I would try, it wasn't me. I pushed myself as hard as I could, and because I was so laid back as a character, maybe I appeared a bit lackadaisical, or even blase, to people who didn't really know me. I never felt I was a bad trainer. Certainly I didn't purposefully slack. I used to enjoy training, especially the five-a-sides and other short-sided games, the shooting practice, the crossing and the rest. It was only when it came to the tough stuff, the endurance work, that I struggled to cope with it. I know it sounds daft and convenient, but honestly I felt my body-frame was unsuited to it.

Still, for all his unease about my approach to training with England, I can't blame Don Howe for inspiring the 'I've Had a Pally' yellow jersey awarded to the worst trainer of the day at United. I don't know where that came from. Perhaps I should sue! I'm guessing it could be Giggsy or Keaney or Butty, so one of them can expect a writ! They introduced the yellow jersey in the season after I left, when they won the Treble. I was doing an interview with the United magazine, and they produced this picture, saying the lads wanted to present it to me as a token of their esteem. I suppose it was nice to be remembered, but it's not quite the manner I would have chosen. Now the jersey is in the club museum, next to all the famous shirts. A mate suggested that at least it was warm and affectionate, but I don't know. Did I feel insulted by it? Yes, I did! Where did they get the idea? Well, I used to moan if the warm-up was too long. I was always reminding Kiddo and the other trainers that we had a game tomorrow; and I was always somewhere near the back when we did the long runs, breathing out of my backside. Even so, I actually thought Ince and McClair were worse trainers than me, but the label kind of stuck with me. Can't think why.

In five-a-sides I always tried to play up front, or on the wing. Nobody liked playing in their own positions in practice. Schmeichel would boom: 'I'm not playing in goal, I'm going up front.' There used to be some pretty fierce contests, too, especially The Kids v The Oldies, which used to become rather ... um, competitive might be the diplomatic word!

But I digress. After being selected for a few encouraging friendlies under Terry, I was involved against the Republic of Ireland at Lansdown Road on the terrifying night when fans started rioting in the stands about half an hour into the game. All kinds of missiles, including wooden seats and benches, were being thrown from the upper tiers on to the spectators below. At that point the referee took us off, so we didn't witness how it escalated, but I believe tear gas was used to control the rioters.

Eventually the stadium officials asked if we wanted to carry on and the general consensus was to stop the game. The scenes were horrifying, and had not the slightest thing to do with sport. People could have been killed by the trouble-makers, who were purporting to be England fans. There must have been kids in the firing line and there wasn't the slightest thought for their safety. I couldn't believe that anyone could be so crazed. This was nothing to do with football, perhaps it was to do with politics; whatever, it was the worst instance of violence I ever encountered.

Tragically, hooliganism is a problem that many players of my generation are all too familiar with, having grown up with it in the 1970s. I don't think it's as bad today, although there have been flashpoints between rival gangs. It's got no part in football but, especially with

England, it seems really hard to eradicate. When it began, at about the same time as organised football in the 1800s, I get the impression it was linked directly to what happened on the field. But now yobs seem to go along with preconceived plans for violence. People actually organise scraps between rival factions on the internet beforehand, there's nothing spontaneous about it. Unbelievably many of the offenders are not traditional hooligans, but people with high-flying jobs in finance or whatever. I suppose it's how they get their thrills.

I feel sorry for some of the clubs who suffer through it. They get blamed for lack of security, yet there's little that can be done to stop people who are determined to cause trouble. It annoys me that the British get such a bad press as though we were the only ones in the world with the problem, yet frequently we learn of outrages in Italy, Spain, Holland or Germany. They have all had horrendous violence, but I don't think they've ever been punished in the same way as English fans. We've been type-cast and it's hard to shrug it off.

Some say the hooliganism is society's problem rather than football's but there's no doubt that it's become attached to football. You don't have it at cricket or rugby or other sports. Maybe that's because football grew up as a working-class sport, while cricket and rugby were more the preserve of private schools in the early days. Odd, really, because rugby is such a violent sport in itself.

As to what we should be doing about the problem in football, I believe there should be tougher punishments. If recognised trouble-makers get caught dead to rights, then they should be hit really hard. A slap on the wrist and a fine is going to achieve nothing.

After the unwelcome disruption of the Lansdown Road riot, I remained in Terry Venables' plans and felt I was settling into the side alongside Tony Adams, but during the summer of 1995 I was struggling with a rib injury which caused me to miss several games. My England ambitions took a far more serious jolt through the back problems which plagued me throughout the 1995/96 season, and which cost me any hope of a place in the much-anticipated European Championship finals on home soil. Before the tournament Terry had wanted me to make the warm-up trip to Hong Kong, but the physio advised me not to go because of the long plane journey and I had no real option but to heed their warning.

Despite not feeling properly fit, I had managed to play in the FA Cup Final but my back, which had let me down three times during the season, keeping me out for four or five weeks each time, was extremely sore.

Also I'd had a knee operation recently and I was very worried about the implications for my next contract which, as I approached my 31st birthday, was a hugely important one for me. I believe Terry Venables understood my decision to rest but probably I didn't make it clear publicly at the time that I felt I owed it to myself not to play in Euro '96 – as much as I was desperate to – to give myself a chance to make a decent recovery. I think events have shown that I was justified in my decision, as I learned to manage the injury a lot better and had another five years in the Premiership.

With England playing so well in the tournament, and reaching the semi-finals, it was agonising not to be involved, but you can't let your life be ruled by 'if onlys'. It's like my missing out on the European Cup in 1999. Who's to say, if I had played, that a shot wouldn't have ricocheted off my foot, as happened twice in 1997, and knocked United out. Of course, that doesn't disguise the fact that I was mortified never to play in a major championship at international level. I'd got very close to the Euros in '88, then we didn't qualify for the World Cup in '94, and come '96 I'd been in the team a lot so it seemed that my time might have come. Had I been fit I feel I'd have had a great chance of being in the squad, and I might even have played, so dipping out was a tough decision. It was, however, the right one.

After the tournament all the England players and staff were disappointed at the departure of Venables, especially as the decision was not based on football matters, but because the FA decided they couldn't work with the constant investigations into his business affairs. But he was the best man for the job and I feel a way should have been found for him to carry on. There was a deep and widespread belief that he possessed the combination of man-management, coaching skills and technical ability to take England forward to the World Cup in 1998. How frustrating it was that he had everything needed for that work, yet he had another existence running parallel which prevented him from fulfilling himself. I was pleased when Terry returned to the England set-up in 2006 and I felt confident that he would have a big influence once more if he could work effectively with the new chief coach at the time, Steve McClaren. Sadly, of course, it didn't work out like that.

Earlier it wasn't just the FA who made life impossible for him, but sections of the press, too. I don't think there's any way to win with the media unless you actually lift the World Cup. Even then, if you have had a few bad moments on the way, then you'll get panned. It's so infuriating when you see some people in the press, people with no idea about football, talking about what somebody like Terry should be doing. It's just a crazy situation. I suppose the public wants to read it – they must do, or it wouldn't sell – but half the writers haven't got a clue about what it takes to win a World Cup or run a football club. We can all have opinions, but to go overboard the way they do, trying their damnedest to pull people down, just doesn't seem right.

Still, life goes on, and come the following September, refreshed and with my back feeling much better, I was overjoyed to be called up by new manager Glenn Hoddle for the World Cup qualifier in Moldova, a game which marked the international debut of one David Beckham. I was thrilled by the prospect of playing under Hoddle, who had been such a sublimely talented footballer, one of the most gifted of his era. I felt it would be a privilege to work alongside such a man, and was convinced that he would have so much to offer the England team.

In that he was a terrific coach who spoke well about the game, in that his ideas were inspiring, in that I agreed with the enlightened style in which he wanted us to adopt, I was right about Glenn Hoddle. But in many other respects, I was to become woefully disillusioned about a man I had looked up to for so long.

Often it was the small things which disappointed me about the new England manager. For instance, he could be insufferably petty about enforcing little rules and regulations which might have been framed for schoolboys, and that was no way to get the best out of a group of seasoned professional sportsmen. I recall one night before a game when I was in a hotel foyer playing cards (not for money, I hasten to stress) with Stuart Pearce, Gareth Southgate and David Batty. The time was 9.45, or it might have been even earlier, when Glenn's assistant, John Gorman, came down the stairs and said: 'Right lads, up to bed.' We kind of laughed, as we thought he was joking, but he persisted that the Gaffer wanted us to turn in. He was telling a group of experienced players, including the veteran Pearce, who had a vast number of caps to his name, that they should scoot off to bed at that ridiculously early hour. It was what might have been expected of a scoutmaster on summer camp.

We were all responsible people who had prepared for big games all our lives, and knew what was right for us individually. It might have suited some lads to go to bed early, but it didn't suit us. All we wanted was a relaxing game before going up maybe an hour later. It was not as though we were doing anything untoward, drinking alcohol or stepping out of

175

line in any way. It was only a minor incident, yet it was symbolic of a small-minded, do-as-you're told regime which galled a lot of people. Unlike the informality of Venables' tenure, this had a regimental feel to it, and I don't think many players responded to that management style. As a consequence, he failed to get the best out of a lot of players in his squad.

For all that, we beat Moldova comfortably and I had high hopes of playing in the next qualifier, against Poland at Wembley the following month. But I was in for an unpleasant surprise. A couple of days before the game Hoddle pulled me aside and said: 'I'm leaving you out of this one because we're playing at home, Poland will defend deep, so we're going to be on the ball a lot. I want Southgate to play because he'll give us more on the ball.' I was kind of taken aback by that. If he wanted to play Gareth, fair enough, but to put it the way he did left me disappointed. I felt that being on the ball was a decent part of my game. Also, as he knew, at that time it wasn't ideal for me to be a substitute because of the problems with my back. If I sat on the bench, then inevitably I stiffened up and became more prone to injury. Suffice to say, I didn't think the manager had handled the situation very well. In the event, I was called into action when Gareth took a knock, and although we won, thanks to two goals from Alan Shearer, that was to prove my farewell appearance for England. I was selected for a few more squads after that but never got on the pitch again.

Other examples of Hoddle's poor man-management were evident in training sessions. Other people have made the point that such was his own awesome technique that he would demonstrate things on the practice pitch, then get upset when his players couldn't replicate his skills. I remember one time at Wembley when there were three or four of us, all centre-halves, doing a spot of keepy-up. Hoddle made us stand about ten yards apart and volley the ball to one another. Now anyone who has tried this particular exercise will know how difficult it is, even for the most gifted of players, and it was hardly surprising that balls were being shanked here, there and everywhere by all of us. He watched for a bit, then all of a sudden he snapped and made us run round the pitch as a punishment. I'd not had that kind of treatment since I was a non-League player. Basically we were being told: 'You're crap, go and do some running, that's all I can trust you with.' Quite simply, you've got to treat experienced professionals with more respect than that.

A similar lack of judgement was evident in his dealings with David Beckham at the start of the 1998 World Cup Finals. Hoddle left him out of the first game, saying that he wasn't focused. Here's a young kid playing the football of his life, a boy who had played in all the previous games and looked a key part of the team, then just before the tournament the manager absolutely destroys the player's confidence in one fell swoop. It's hard to do that with someone who has David's love of the game, but it seems that Glenn Hoddle went pretty close to it.

To be fair to David, he picked himself up to score a great free-kick when he got back in against Colombia, but I don't think relations between the two were ever the same again – and I can understand why. David had my sympathy. It was an ironic situation because much of David's game, with his range of passing and his technique for striking the ball so crisply, was inspired by Hoddle, who was one of his childhood heroes.

As for Glenn's much-mocked eccentricity, all the stuff about the faith healer Eileen Drewery and his thoughts on disabled people being punished for their sins in a previous life came after I was out of the squad. Of course, his religious beliefs are his own, and I wouldn't want to comment on them. The shame is that those beliefs appear to have encroached on his work, making a rod for his own back, although it must be understood that the press can highlight certain points and distort the facts.

Professionally speaking, I liked his philosophy and if I was judging him solely on that there would be no problem. He wanted us to play in the right way, to entertain, to attack, he was all for the beautiful game. But all that fell by the wayside because he was unable to get the best out of his players.

In the end I was startled at the manner of Hoddle's departure, but I wasn't surprised that they took the job away from him. Obviously he would have lasted longer if his controversial remarks had not been made, but having unnecessarily lost the relationship with somebody like Beckham, who was becoming the biggest star in English football, then it was unlikely that he was going to survive in the long term.

In the period leading up to his departure, Hoddle was crucified in the press, like so many of his predecessors, and I do feel it's time that over-the-top sensationalism was replaced by more balanced coverage. Traditional quality newspapers, what we used to know as broadsheets, are more acceptable, offering a more reasoned insight into the workings of the football scene than the more lurid tabloids, which often fill their pages with malicious gossip. I find it totally reprehensible that they should lampoon, say, David James as a donkey after he's made a mistake. The guy's got kids, for God's sake; it's they who have to go to school and face the consequences of irresponsible journalism, while the writers are moving on to their next target. They have no respect for people's feelings.

I don't think we do enough to protect people from this sort of intrusion and hysterical treatment. I wouldn't allow people to stick a camera in someone's face on the street; it's a gross invasion of privacy, as is camping outside people's houses when they're in the news. I know it's difficult but some laws should be in place, some moves should be made. I feel for individuals like David Beckham, who can't walk outside their door and have their own space. It must drive them mad. Fortunately it never happened to me, because I don't know how I would have dealt with it. Certainly I can understand it if people snap occasionally.

I shudder when I think of what Wayne Rooney will have to put up with in the years ahead. The tabloids will be digging constantly, ready to put any tiny mistake he might make under the most intense of public microscopes. It's wrong, sometimes it's downright inhuman, and the time has come for legislation to curb such behaviour from the so-called guardians of our freedom. I won't be holding my breath, though, and I'd guess that any England team that doesn't win a major trophy will continue to be pilloried mercilessly.

But even that sort of treatment, which I'm happy to say was never visited on my head, can't besmirch the essential honour of playing for your country. It's a truly amazing feeling to be selected as the best in England at what you do. When I made my debut I was overjoyed. It ran through my mind that only four years earlier I had been playing non-League football, and now here I was at the top level. I have known no greater sensation of pride than when I was standing in line with the lads and the national anthem was playing. I felt proud for my parents, knowing how proud they were of me; I felt proud for my girlfriend, for the rest of my family and for my friends. My children arrived after I had effectively finished playing football, so my keenest regret is that my girls, Lauren and Eve, didn't see me playing for Middlesbrough, Manchester United and England. I'll be able to show them the videos, and they can read this book, but how I would have loved them to sample those glorious days at first hand.

CHAPTER FIFTEEN

BACK TO MY ROOTS

When I returned to Middlesbrough in the summer of 1998, my reception was decidedly mixed. Some of the supporters welcomed me as an Ayresome Park old boy who had proved himself at the top level with Manchester United and who could be expected to have plenty to offer the 'Boro cause. But others looked at my age, remembered that I'd had problems with my back and concluded that I was not the soundest of investments.

Unfortunately, when people get an idea in their heads that you're injury-prone, it can be difficult to shift it, even though I could point to the fact that I had missed only a handful of games for United in 1997/98. As recently as 2004, years after my retirement, I was asked at a question-and-answer session if it was true that I'd had a special bed fitted in the United bus to cope with my bad back. Absolute nonsense! There *was* a bed on the bus, but I never used it. Without fail, I'd be sitting in the card school all the way home from games, but once such a misleading story has been put about, then lots of people take it as gospel-truth that I was in a desperate way. Eventually I was saddled with an image as some kind of handicapped footballer, which was a chronic distortion of the facts.

When I walked back into Middlesbrough, I found a very different animal to the one I had left nine years earlier. In my absence they had moved from Ayresome Park to plush new surroundings at the Riverside; they had been promoted to the new Premiership, then relegated, promoted, relegated and, in 1997/98, promoted yet again; and now they were able to spend big money on buying players of world renown, the likes of Fabrizio Ravanelli, Juninho and Emerson. With Robbo at the helm and the two magnificently gifted Pauls, Gascoigne and Merson, on the staff, I believed 'Boro were all geared up, at last, for a serious tilt at some major trophies.

For me, one of the most significant factors was the presence of Robbo. It can be a strange situation when you've been a player alongside someone. You've enjoyed good times together as friends and team-mates, then all of a sudden you have your mate as your boss. But you just have to be professional, accept the changed circumstances and get on with the job. In

Bryan's case, I viewed it as a definite positive that I was working for such an inspirational character and one for whom I had the utmost respect.

Had he changed since his Old Trafford days? I don't think people can change, essentially. Their true character is always going to come out. Oh, Bryan had to disassociate himself a wee bit from the dressing room, but I wouldn't say he was a lot different. Together with his coaches Viv Anderson and Gordon McQueen, both former United men, he fostered camaraderie among the players at the same time as commanding a lot of respect.

Obviously he had learned a great deal from Alex Ferguson, but he wasn't a slavish clone of the mega-successful Scot and, despite having spent a fabulously productive lifetime in football, he had nothing like Fergie's vast management experience to call upon. When he was skipper of United, Robbo had been like a manager on the pitch, spotting problems and sorting them out in the heat of the action, and now he continued to do that by joining in the five-a-sides at training.

His greatness as a footballer was the main strut of his status. Players had such a huge respect for what Bryan had achieved, and that helped him to get his ideas across. They knew he was the ultimate leader of a football team and so many lads of my age and younger were in awe of this figure who was the best around when they were growing up. Certainly when I first came to United I was in awe of him, despite having met him at England get-togethers, where I had found him to be a down-to-earth guy. He underlined that impression by welcoming me to Old Trafford with the sort of question I could deal with: 'Do you fancy a pint?' Maybe there was a bit of extra affinity between us because we are both north-easterners, though I'm not sure about that, because he's a Mackem and I'm a Smoggie!*

As Bryan readied 'Boro for the 1998/99 campaign, it seemed that he had the whole of a talented squad pulling in the same direction, only for our progress to be jolted rudely by Paul Merson, who came out with allegations about drinking and gambling at the club before leaving to join Aston Villa. It's well documented that Merse had terrible personal problems at that time, but we were all immensely disappointed by what he did. Certainly I feel it was an absolute cop-out for him to throw such wild accusations in the face of a club which was doing its utmost to help him, and his behaviour stuck in a lot of people's throats. There was no more a drinking culture at Middlesbrough than there was at Manchester United or any other club. As for the gambling, that was down to himself.

* For the uninitiated, a Mackem hails from the Durham area, while a Smoggie comes from Middlesbrough.

Nobody forced him to gamble. Maybe he was misinterpreted, as often happens, but certainly it was a label the club could have done without, especially only three games into a new season.

Still, Robbo rallied his troops and we played a lot of decent football that term, including a memorable display at Old Trafford just before Christmas when we inflicted on United what proved to be their last defeat of the season in any competition. On a day when Alex Ferguson was absent due to a family bereavement, leaving Jim Ryan in charge of his team, 'Boro took an astonishing 3-0 lead before United pulled it back to 3-2 with 20 minutes left. That gave them plenty of time to chase an equaliser and it looked like they'd get it when our goalkeeper, Mark Schwarzer, played the ball to me and Coley robbed me. He was one on one with the 'keeper, and I expected him to score, but Mark saved the day and my blushes. That was a massive result for 'Boro and the scenes in our dressing room were fantastic, it was almost as if we'd won the FA Cup. I remember a reporter asking me what it felt like to win at Old Trafford, and I pointed out that I was not exactly a stranger to that feeling!

However, one member of the side had a price to pay for that memorable victory. Before the game, the irrepressible Slaven had pledged that, if we won, he would bare his backside in the window of a leading Middlesbrough store. Typically, he proved himself a man of his word. Fortunately I wasn't there at the time, but I saw the pictures, and there was no doubt about it. I'm happy to report that he kept his jockeys on, but there were ample glimpses of Bernie's backside, and it wasn't a pretty sight. Still, it might have been worse, he might have shown his face. Only kidding, Bern!

Back in the real world, United's defeat left them off the pace at the top of the Premiership, and I could never have dreamed that they would go through the rest of the season undefeated. That said, they were still passing and moving brilliantly when they were three down, and it gave me a taste of what visitors to Old Trafford had been suffering over the years. In some of the games we had hardly needed a defence at times. Visitors just came and tried to shut up shop, so I could just sit there and admire what our midfield and attack were doing. But it was hard work being on the receiving end of United's dominance, and now, having clung on with 'Boro, I could appreciate that fully.

The result to one side, I relished going back to Old Trafford, and still do to this day. I always get a warm reception, especially from the manager, who invariably invites me into his office for a coffee and a chat. Whether that will continue when Fergie leaves eventually remains to be seen. If his replacement was Brucie or Keaney or Incey that would be fine, and there's always Sparky. Even though he's now at Manchester City he is held in such great esteem at Old Trafford that I still wouldn't rule him out of becoming United's manager at some time in the future. But more of that later.

It's just such a great club to be associated with. When I arrive on match day, all the security men and stewards ask me how I'm doing, nothing's too much trouble for them, there's a great feel to it. People tell me I'm part of the history of the club, and that I'll never be forgotten. That's very nice, even though it's hard to imagine myself in those terms.

I had a chance to savour the Old Trafford hospitality again only a couple of weeks after our famous victory when 'Boro faced United in the third round of the FA Cup. When Andy Townsend put us 1-0 up just after half-time, we were wondering if lightning could possibly strike twice. Any team that achieves a positive result in one of football's fortresses takes on a belief that they can do it again, but United hit back ferociously to run out worthy 3-1 winners.

Middlesbrough went on to finish the season in a highly respectable ninth place in the Premiership, a fine effort for a newly-promoted club. I was pretty content with my personal contribution, having managed consistently decent form and missed only a handful of games through back trouble. Now I shared Robbo's conviction and determination that the club could go from strength to strength.

If 1998/99 wasn't a bad season at the Riverside, then in what category can my former club's campaign be placed? Manchester United won the Treble, and I have to admit I was casting an envious eye in their direction. When I was at Old Trafford, having won the Premiership a few times, for some seasons the European Cup became our new Holy Grail. We'd had a couple of near misses and there had been a belief building that we could go all the way because we felt we were getting better all the time. This was the culmination of all that, and it must have been utterly incredible to have been a part of it. It was just one fairytale after another, as little things went United's way at key moments. For instance, there was the FA Cup semi-final replay against Arsenal in which Roy was sent off, Peter saved a penalty and Giggsy scored one of the most breathtaking goals in the competition's history. Then there were the chances missed by Internazionale in the quarter-final of the European Cup, and the amazing comeback from two down to win 3-2 in the semi-final against Juventus in Turin. It was as though the Treble was written in the stars.

I wouldn't have been human if I hadn't wished I was involved, but I couldn't have been happier for the club, the lads and especially the manager. I know he wouldn't have felt his United career was complete if he hadn't won the European Cup. It was an uncanny feeling watching my ex-team-mates playing in that final, and I felt so wretched for Keane and Scholes, who were suspended on the night. They'd given so much to the side, and must have been devastated to miss out on the biggest occasion of all. I know I would have been. I was lucky enough never to miss a final at professional level, but I remember being out of a cricket final at school, and I was gutted, so I can't even begin to imagine what must have been going on inside the heads of Roy and Paul. I know they got their medals but it would have eaten away at them that they weren't part of a European Cup-winning team.

A lot of people reckoned that United were lucky to beat Bayern Munich because their goals arrived so late, but that's rot. They had made a habit of scoring in the dying stages of matches, and that was part of the team's ethos. Anyway, I thought United played the better football and they were the only side that looked like they wanted to take the game by the scruff of the neck. I know Bayern hit the woodwork twice, but I felt they were the more cautious team throughout.

Mind, it looked as though the Germans had got their tactics right, soaking up pressure, letting United have a lot of the ball as long as they didn't muster anything with it. Then towards the end they started catching United on the break, but as they missed those chances to go two up and thus finish the game, I had a sneaking feeling that it would be wrong to write off my old mates. Of course, no one could have expected two goals in stoppage time. United would have been delighted just to get to extra time through Teddy Sheringham; the thought then would have been to take it on from there with the fresh legs of Ole and Teddy up front. I'm sure those two would have been a key influence in extra time, but who needs extra time if you can come up with a grandstand finish like United's? I've been involved in plenty of stirring fightbacks down the years, but even I was stunned by Ole's winner at the end.

In fact, everybody seemed to be in shock except David May, who had spent the entire game on the bench, then threw himself into the jollies with total abandon, emerging at the apex of the pyramid of celebrating players when the pictures were being taken. Some people might have been amazed by the substitute's extrovert antics, but his old team-mates at Blackburn wouldn't have been among them.

Soon after David joined United, I met up with some Blackburn lads in the England squad and they asked after him. I told them he was quiet, kept himself to himself, and they wouldn't believe me. At Ewood Park, they assured me, he never shut up, he was always up to some trick or another. After his first year at Old Trafford, when maybe he'd been a tad overawed by the place, he settled down and we found out exactly what the Blackburn boys had been talking about. He was my room-mate for my last couple of years and he was totally hyperactive, always full of fun, and it was typical of him that he dived across the whole team in Barcelona to get his ugly mug in the picture.

Sadly, injury wrecked David's career but I think most United fans had a soft spot for him, and they loved using his name to bait Alan Shearer at the FA Cup Final against Newcastle: 'David May, superstar, got more medals than Shee-ee-rar!' But David wasn't just a funny lad, he had quite a bit about him as a player, too, which is why Alex Ferguson played him so much in 1995/96 and allowed Steve Bruce to leave at the end of that season.

Meanwhile, back at the Riverside we entered 1999/2000 with high hopes of genuine progress, especially with my old betting buddy Paul Ince and the German star Christian Ziege added to the side and Juninho returning to the club on loan. Unfortunately, it didn't happen and Robbo started to get stick from the fans. We finished 12th, which was disappointing in itself after making the top half in the previous season, and in all honesty we weren't playing great football. Ince did the terrific job expected of him, Ziege played tremendously well at times but suffered from injuries, but I'm afraid we didn't play to the strengths of the little Brazilian, opting instead for a more direct approach which meant he was bypassed too frequently.

The cause wasn't helped, either, by the distressingly sad circumstance that Paul Gascoigne's life was threatening to fall apart as he fought both alcoholism and depression. I had first bumped into Gazza at an England 'B' team gathering at Brighton in the late 1980s, soon after he had left Newcastle for Tottenham, and already he was showing signs of struggling to cope with the pressure of his fame. He talked frequently about the cameras following him around, how he couldn't hack it, and how he was looking for better ways of dealing with the ceaseless intrusion.

At the time most people, myself included, were unaware of the tragedies he had known in his childhood, events which had obviously left a deep psychological mark, and he was generally viewed as a bit daft and very funny, the team clown who could always make people laugh. It was only as we went further down the road with him that we realised his inability to balance his life. He would do crazy things for no apparent reason, like committing the regrettable foul which ended his involvement in the 1991 FA Cup Final and placed his entire career in jeopardy, and outraging practically the whole of Italy by belching into a live TV microphone during his spell with Lazio.

Closer to home, there was the day he hijacked the brand new team bus at Middlesbrough, bought by the club at great expense after the players had moaned long and hard about our rickety old vehicle. It had just been delivered when the driver brought it to our training headquarters at Rockcliff and went inside for a coffee. When he stepped back outside the bus wasn't there – Gazza had decided to take it for a warm-up. The training facility is in the grounds of a big old country estate, with a long road leading to it, and just by the entrance there is an enormous boulder, placed there expressly to prevent people from cutting the corner. Of course, Gazza didn't allow for that when he went out in the bus and he tore a huge rip in the side of our gleaming new charabanc. Even that didn't stop him in his tracks, though, and he drove it through the nearby village and back to the training ground in its severely damaged condition.

Robbo has seen plenty in his time, and he allowed his players every reasonable latitude, but he took a dim view of this, fining Paul two weeks wages as well as making him pay for the damage. It was an incident that typified Gazza. He did it for a laugh, because it was fun at the time, but he failed totally to grasp the enormity of his actions. That particular escapade had nothing to do with drinking. It happened merely because, as Bobby Robson put it so aptly, the lad could be as daft as a brush.

That was nearly the end of the road for Gazza at 'Boro. He was suffering from injuries, he was drinking and his career was going nowhere. He went on to brief spells at Everton and Burnley before pitching up in China, which turned out to be a huge mistake and did him no favours at all.

Yet I maintain that there's never been a scrap of malice in Gazza, never the slightest intent to harm people. It was just that in trying to make everybody laugh he was prone to overstep the mark. Ask anybody who played with Gazza, and they'll all say how much they loved him. Basically he was a good guy, as genuine as he was funny, and the other players took him at face value. Certainly you could never meet a more generous fella, he'd do anything for anybody, try and accommodate everyone; but ultimately he found it difficult to handle the fact that people constantly wanted a piece of him, hounded him endlessly for stories. He had nothing like a normal life, and the way he lived came close to destroying him.

Perhaps his lowest point arrived after 'Boro had been to Dublin on a team-bonding excursion and he had socialised just a little too freely, getting himself into a terrible state. Just after we returned to England he took himself to a railway station down south and, as he has since revealed, seriously contemplated throwing himself under a train. Happily, after admitting his problems with drink, and confronting demons in other areas of his life, he has undergone rehabilitation treatment which I hope will help him plan a more stable future.

That said, I do fear for Gazza. It's imperative that he gets the right help to turn aside from his old ways. At one time, making a vigorous effort to be positive with his life, he said he wanted to get into management and coaching. Looking in from the outside, I had to wonder if he was cut out to be a boss, but he was genuine in wanting to be taken seriously. Duly he was given an opportunity by Kettering Town but, sad to report, he lasted only 39 days. The fact is that he needed qualifications which would have taken him two years to acquire, and it was always going to be a big ask for Gazza to find that much commitment and concentration. Attention-span is a big issue with him, because he wants to be doing something stimulating every waking moment, and life just isn't like that.

The Paul Gascoigne situation took an even more worrying twist in February 2008 when he entered an institution after being detained under the Mental Health Act. At that point so many people were saying that they weren't surprised, but everyone in football whose path he has crossed – including myself, and all his other team-mates at different levels – were left to wonder if they could have done anything more to help him before his problems escalated so distressingly. It is desperately harrowing to contemplate the ups and downs he has experienced with his health and his mental state, and now we have to hope that he has the right people around him to help him get better. Of course, he's got to help himself, too, and I hope and pray that he can find the strength within himself to do that. Certainly everybody who has come across him will wish him all the best for a complete recovery. Ominously, however, their concern heightened when he was detained again in June.

As a player, of course, he was an absolute genius, and it was such a shame that he suffered his debilitating cruciate injury, because that did take a little bit of something away from him. Afterwards he still produced some marvellous performances, but never quite reached his former level on a consistent basis. Paul was a magic manipulator of a football, he could go past people and they could do nothing to prevent him. He had no great pace, yet if you tried to stop him he'd dance away from you, just drop a shoulder and send you in the wrong direction.

In 1988 Alex Ferguson went away on holiday believing that he'd secured Gazza from Newcastle and the question will always be asked: just as the Gaffer harnessed the previously ungovernable talent of Eric Cantona, might he have extracted greater things from Gazza if he had signed him for Manchester United? It's hard to say, because Terry Venables at Spurs was a terrific man-manager and he found it difficult.

I think Gazza presented a wider range of problems than Eric – alcohol, insecurity, dark issues from his childhood. He was a far more complicated character than the Frenchman, who was complex enough but who didn't go in for the outlandish stunts that blighted Paul's career. Eric might crack, as he did at Palace, but that was just a recognisable aspect of human nature. Gazza was totally unpredictable, utterly off the wall, so that no one knew what to expect, and I believe he would have presented a far more daunting challenge for the United manager, even than Cantona. Of course, had Alex Ferguson succeeded in getting a grip on the Geordie genius then the mind boggles at what they might have achieved together. As it is, Gazza will go down as probably the best player of his generation. Even after his cruciate operation, he produced memorable performances at Lazio and Rangers before he was dogged by further injuries.

After rupturing a cruciate, your body tries to compensate for the fact that you've had such a serious injury, but the road back to fitness is long and harrowing. At first you have no stretch in the knee; you've got to work, work, work on that, and degrees of improvement are so small it can be almost impossible to notice. It's a mammoth test of patience and Paul Gascoigne's recovery from that goes to prove that he had more staying power than many people gave him credit for.

I consider myself lucky that I never suffered a major injury, falling prey merely to steady wear and tear which built up over the years. In 1999/2000 I was still managing to play more games than I missed, but my back was painful much of the time and I needed a knee operation at the end of the season, so the signs were not good. Sure enough in my third year at the Riverside I played only nine times because my back went completely in November, when I suffered a major prolapse. I trained on a Friday ahead of a home game with Leicester, and my back felt very sore afterwards, then deteriorated further at home that evening. By the time I woke on Saturday morning the back was in spasm. I couldn't even get in a car to go to the ground and had to ring in to say I was bedridden. It was worse than it had ever been before and, frighteningly, I had lost all feeling in three of my toes.

While I was deciding what course of action to take, Terry Venables arrived at the club and he was brilliant, telling me: 'Whatever it takes, whoever you want to go and see, anywhere in the world, just tell us and we'll sort it for you.' So I went to a specialist, who told me the longer the pressure remained on the nerve, the more damage it was going to do. He called for an operation, they took away part of a disc and, thank God, the feeling returned to my toes. But still I couldn't run properly, my efforts at training were a complete failure and I had to face the awful truth that my days of making a living as a professional footballer were drawing to a close.

While my condition had been worsening, we had made a chronically poor start to 2000/01, winning only two of our first 17 Premiership games as we slumped to the foot of the table and duly the screw tightened on Bryan Robson. There were plenty of excellent players but we weren't performing as a team and in December Robbo made the supremely unselfish decision of calling in Terry Venables to produce some fresh ideas. In theory Middlesbrough were being run by a Robson-Venables partnership, but although they did operate in tandem, in practice Terry took over as the guy in charge of training and tactics.

The public perception was that Robbo had been humiliated, which was why his stance was such a courageous one. A lot of people care about nothing but self-preservation, but although Robbo knew he was putting his own future on the line if he asked Terry to come in, he placed the interests of the club before his own. That's the type of fellow he has always been, both as a player and a manager. He admitted that he had become bogged down, he felt an obligation to chairman Steve Gibson and so he sent for the man he believed could save the day. As I expected, having worked under Terry for England, he did a superb job of bringing the best out of the lads and ultimately led Middlesbrough clear of relegation.

But he wasn't looking for a long-term commitment, and not long after Venables' departure, Robbo suffered the fate that befalls most football bosses in the end – he was sacked. After seven years of faithful service, it was a poignant exit by one of the bravest and most inspirational characters the modern game has known, and it would be scandalous if he were to be judged as a failure.

It's all too easy to forget just how much Bryan Robson achieved at Middlesbrough. He took them to three cup finals, when they had never reached one in their history before, and he was horribly unlucky not to lift at least one trophy; he presided over the First Division championship triumph of 1995, and although they went down two seasons later, he led them back up in 1998; and he brought in world-famous footballers such as Ravanelli and Juninho, engendering untold excitement for the fans.

Sure, it all went a bit stale for him in the end, but he was brave enough to recognise that and take the necessary steps to rectify it. I was always confident he would bounce back as a manager, but in his next job, at Bradford City, he was never given a fair chance, being marooned without money after a chairman had resigned. After that he took stock for a while before returning with West Bromwich Albion, where he faced another mountainous task and where there were no easy answers. Still, despite taking over an ailing team at the wrong end of the Premiership in November 2004, he presided over a near-miraculous escape from relegation on the last day of the season and deserved colossal credit for that. Unfortunately there was a shortage of cash for new players and there were other problems at the club which made his job exceedingly difficult, and soon after Albion were demoted a year later he left the Hawthorns a sadder but wiser man. Being the fighter he is, Bryan learned from his trials and bounced back as boss of Sheffield United, only to pay the price for expectations at Bramall Lane of an instant return to the top flight. He wasn't given much time, he was working on a shoestring and it didn't happen for him. After so much tribulation, it makes me wonder whether he will want to throw his hat into the management ring again, especially as he was being lined up for a global ambassadorial role for Manchester United, the club where he is rightly revered for his magnificent service as a player.

Returning to my own situation, shortly before his dismissal at the Riverside, Robbo pulled me in and told me Middlesbrough couldn't give me another contract but the offer was there to come back and train in pre-season, so we could re-assess the position depending on my fitness. In the circumstances I couldn't ask for any more than that, and accepted readily, but a couple of weeks later Robbo was sacked.

Steve McClaren came in and just before the pre-season training recommenced he rang to say they were trying to bring down the average age of the squad, so he wouldn't be needing me. I didn't have a problem with that. I'm sure I would have struggled to meet the physical demands because the last year had been very difficult. When I had played in games then I had suffered for it, the pain and length of time needed to recover taking away much of the enjoyment. I was taking anti-inflammatory tablets all the time, which I knew couldn't be healthy in the long run, and it was clear to me that my body had had enough.

I suppose it was painful to face such a stark truth, but what irked me most was that some fans appeared to believe that I'd only come back to 'Boro to finish off my career in comfort. That was hard to take because that wasn't the way it was meant to be. I had seen that sort of thing happening in my first spell at the club; I had been contemptuous of it then, and I didn't want to be party to anything like it now my own time was up. I was mortally disappointed not to play more games in my second stint, and I had truly believed that I would last a lot longer.

Even at that stage, I received a couple of offers from Premiership clubs, but now I knew in my heart that I'd hit the buffers. My specialist underlined it for me when he said: 'You're 36, you've had operations on your back and on your knees. Do you really need to be pushing your body through hell any more?' There was only one sane answer I could make.

It had been terrifying when I had lost feeling in my toes because I knew that damaged nerves don't always heal, and that people less lucky than I have ended up as cripples in similar circumstances. I still suffer aches and pains, but by and large I've been fortunate and can live a normal life. I can play a bit of football, as I did in 2004 and 2005, taking part in *The Match*, which was screened on Sky Television; I play golf and tennis, but I have to be careful and always mind my back. Unquestionably my condition is down to a lifetime of sport. I've been a fast bowler, basketball player, hurdler, high-jumper, long-jumper and footballer, all activities which had a heavy impact on the back. It was bound to catch up with me in the end.

Enforced retirement affects different people in different ways, but I think I coped with it pretty well. By then my first daughter, Lauren, had been born; now I had the chance to spend time with her, to see her grow up, and reflecting on that helped me to accept the position. I liken retiring from the game to leaving school. You feel as though you're outside of the environment you have known for so long. You know there's a whole big world out there and now you've got to come to terms with it. As a footballer you've been wrapped in cotton wool, with every little detail being taken care of for you. Then all of a sudden you have to confront the stark realities of life, knowing you must fend for yourself. Not that I'm complaining; after all, not many people can put off growing up until they are 36!

CHAPTER SIXTEEN

IT TAKES ALL SORTS ...

Two decades in professional football have brought me into contact with plenty of remarkable men who I look on as friends for life. In previous chapters I have relished revisiting memories of Bryan Robson, Steve Bruce, Alex Ferguson, Bernie Slaven, Tony Mowbray and the rest, for all of whom I have endless respect and affection. Now I'd like to talk about a few more of the characters who have influenced me positively and for whom I'll always have a soft spot, then I'll finish by mentioning one wretched individual for whom I have no time whatsoever.

Though I'll never forgive him for setting me up in that SAS helicopter – and I swear I'll get my own back one of these days – I'd like to start with Brian Kidd. When Fergie's assistant, Archie Knox, left United to join Glasgow Rangers in 1991 a lot of the lads were hoping that Kiddo would get his job, and they were delighted when he did. Everyone at the club knew Brian, partly because he was steeped in Old Trafford history – having scored against Benfica as United had won the European Cup on his 19th birthday in 1968 – but also because he had been working alongside Eric Harrison with the youth side. Thus when he moved up to first-team level, the respect was already there; we knew he was a good guy to be around.

Kiddo was known for his sharp sense of humour – which I was to experience to my cost – and, even more importantly, for being a players' man first and last. His creed was that coaches could do the most brilliant job in the world, but in the end football was all about the players, and it was they who really mattered.

Brian impressed me so much with his desire to embrace every aspect of his work, and he was so dedicated to improving his performance that he travelled the world to watch how they coached in Brazil, Argentina, Spain, Italy, just about anywhere he felt he could learn something new. He returned to Old Trafford armed with immense knowledge about diets, conditioning exercises, new routines, and as a result our training became both more scientific and more enjoyable.

The main tenet of Brian's enlightened approach was that there was no point in running a player until he dropped, as they did, for example, during my time at Middlesbrough. Bruce Rioch would have us running over sand dunes, beaches, hills, mountains; you name it and we had to run over it. Now Brian took training to another level, and as he made himself into a better coach, so Manchester United became a better team.

To talk of that improvement is not to knock Archie, who was from the old school. But we liked the way Kiddo would explain everything he asked us to do. If he was going to make us sweat our bollocks off with a really hard session then he would tell us exactly what benefit we would garner from it. Everything was tailored to what our bodies needed for the job we were paid to do – after all, no one runs up dunes on a football pitch. Mind, Brian was no soft touch. He made us work hard, for example with high-intensity runs over 400 metres or 600 metres, but the traditional ethos of flogging people until they couldn't put one leg in front of the other went out of the window. I worked with plenty of coaches in my time, and he was the best, without any doubt.

Alongside all that, Kiddo was always having a laugh and the lads loved him. I can still recall my mortification when he stitched me up at a function when I was at the microphone, asking me to put out a call for someone called Mike Hunt. The words were out of my mouth before I realised what I was saying. You might say I was embarrassed, but the rest of the team thought it was hilarious.

I think everyone at United was saddened when the relationship between Brian and the Gaffer became strained after Brian left the club because the pair of them had always been terrific together, their contrasting personalities dovetailing perfectly for the good of the team. Though it did come as a surprise when Kiddo departed to become boss of Blackburn, not long after I had rejoined Middlesbrough, I could understand that he wanted to try his hand as a Premiership boss. I suppose he had to take the opportunity, otherwise he would have been wondering for the rest of his life whether he could have met that particular challenge.

But alarm bells were ringing in my head. Brian was a great one for the banter with the players, and I found myself pondering his prospects. Could he separate himself from the footballers enough to carry the ultimate authority? Was he ruthless enough? Did he have the capacity to be downright brutal at times? Alex Ferguson had it (still has), no question, but Brian? I don't know. To be honest, he must have worried about that himself. In the event it didn't work out for him at Ewood Park, and soon he had moved on, which made a lot of people wonder: would it have been better if he had stayed at Manchester United?

We were all grateful for what he had given us, and I'm sure that the Gaffer appreciated deeply what Kiddo had brought to his team. Percentages count so much in modern football. If you can get just a tiny edge on other sides then it can make all the difference, and Brian's training techniques most certainly did give us an edge. I'm glad to say that time has proved to be a great healer and the frost between them has thawed. All the lads are delighted that they appear to have put past differences behind them and that now they are happy to remember the good times, of which there were so many. I think I can speak for everyone who played under Kiddo during his spell at United in saying that they all felt enormous warmth for the man and that he was hugely instrumental in bringing the team to the peak of its potential. Alex Ferguson, too, is held in boundless esteem and affection, so we are all pleased that peace has been restored.

I understand that there had also been a temporary falling out when Kiddo's predecessor, Archie Knox, had opted to leave Old Trafford at a time when the Gaffer was still in the process of constructing his first title-winning United combination. Archie and the manager had been good friends for a long time, so it's easy to appreciate why the Gaffer should be upset, but the players could see the other side of the coin, too. If the rumours were true, Archie's move to Ibrox meant an enormous upgrade in lifestyle, and while money is not the be-all and end-all of football, it is a significant factor, particularly when you have reached middle-age.

As a player, especially a youngster with time on your side, the situation is rather different. It might surprise outsiders, but every footballer I've worked alongside at Old Trafford could have got a far better deal by playing elsewhere. Certainly many clubs were paying far more than United until 1993, when Roy Keane blew the wage structure out of the window. After that the board had to face paying top whack if they wanted top players, they couldn't keep lid on it any longer.

Ironically Archie gave me the nickname of 'Cash' when I arrived at Old Trafford, because of my record fee. Like Kiddo, he could be very funny, but I thought it depended which side of the bed he'd got out of in the morning. Sometimes he'd come in and I had the feeling that he'd tripped over the dog. Unfortunately, if he was in a foul mood then you knew you were in for a stinking time at training. Nothing was going to be good enough for Archie in those circumstances. There were even occasions when he would tell us that an entire session had been crap and that we had to get ourselves back in to work in the afternoon. I'm not saying that he wasn't right, but it didn't feel like it at the time.

Jim McGregor, who was United's physiotherapist when I arrived at Old Trafford, could be described as a more easy-going individual. Jim liked a drink and, provided you dropped him a bottle of whisky now and then, he wouldn't let the Gaffer know if you'd turned up late for treatment or special training. I found that out straight away when I was placed on a weights regime to build me up. I had to be in half an hour before the rest of the players, and Jim had to be there, too, to supervise my efforts. I guess it won't please the manager too much if he reads this, but I wasn't above offering a spot of bribery and Jim wasn't above accepting it. It wasn't that he was lazy, just that he had loads on his plate sorting out his treatment programmes for the day and could do without spending time in the gym with me.

Alex Ferguson was convinced I wasn't punching my weight, because I was only 13 stone wet through, not much for a fella of 6ft 4in. I was far too skinny, the problem being that I never ate a balanced diet, often not being bothered with proper meals but filling up on junk foods. Fortunately I beefed out naturally as I grew a bit older and I was 15 stone by the time I left United. I always put that down to going on a few team meetings – you could say I was drinking for the good of the club!

Not that I was ever a real boozer, of course, although I didn't do my reputation much good at one of my first supporters' functions. I was standing at the bar with some other players when the Gaffer came over to ask us what we wanted. I was new and thought I'd better make it look as though I wasn't a big beer drinker so I said I'd have a Malibu and Coke. The lads broke up and Robbo in particular would never let me forget it. The image of a big hairy-assed centre-half asking for a Malibu and Coke was just too much for them. As for the Gaffer, his jaw dropped and he told me in no uncertain terms: 'We don't drink shorts here. They're bad for you. I'll get you half a lager.' All of which was pretty ironic because I'd been on halves of lager before he walked over.

Getting back to Jimmy, in the end Alex Ferguson let him go and I never quite understood why. I missed him, though, because he was part of the card school, and whatever story you had, then Jim had a better one. He was fun to be around and a really good physio trusted implicitly by all the players.

Replacing such a popular figure was always going to be difficult, but United did the trick by appointing Dave Fevre, who joined us from Wigan, the Rugby League club. He had a lot to prove to the players but it wasn't long before he won our trust. Dave came in with a lot of new rehabilitation ideas, his diagnoses were invariably excellent and he was very clear about explaining the conditions. Certainly he was a huge help to me as my back became an increasingly worrying problem. For instance, he pointed me away from chiropractors, believing they would do more harm than good. I realise that not everyone feels that way, but his advice worked for me as my back pain eased. Eventually he left Old Trafford for Blackburn, and I'm sure he is doing a fantastic job at Ewood Park.

Two more behind-the-scenes bastions of successive Manchester United teams have been kitmen Norman Davies, whose death in June 2008 saddened so many people at Old Trafford, and Albert Morgan. Both of them were funny, down-to-earth local guys who joined in the craic with the lads and were totally reliable. When I arrived it was as though Norman had been doing the job forever; he was part of the furniture. He never left anything to chance, all our kit was never less than immaculate and he catered faultlessly for all our little whims, such as sorting out our favourite shinpads. Norman was so popular that when he reached retirement age the lads said they would pay his wages if he could stay on, but that was against club policy so he had to go. For a lot of years afterwards, until his final illness took its toll, he continued to turn up for games, and often you'd find him in the manager's office, exchanging yarns. The pair of them always had a close relationship, and I recall the Gaffer winding Norman up over the Eric Cantona sending-off at Selhurst Park, reckoning it was all the kitman's fault for not getting the Frenchman out of the way in time. He had so many friends at the club – players, management and other staff alike – that it's fair to say a little piece of Old Trafford will never be quite the same again.

Prior to Norman's exit in the mid 1990s, Albert had spent a year as his assistant, so he had learned everyone's little quirks and was ready to take over. Since then he has proved just as impeccable an operator as his predecessor, and all the players love him. Crucially, both men have proved themselves to be utterly discreet. They have been privy to all the goings-on in the dressing room during the Ferguson era and if they wanted to sell their stories I'm sure they could make a fortune.

I have already mentioned many of the lads I have played with during my career, but there are a few I'd like to revisit, starting with Dion Dublin. When we were at United together, we lived on the outskirts of neighbouring towns, me in Wilmslow and Dion in Alderley Edge, so the two couples saw quite a bit of one another. They still do, actually – Mary and I have enjoyed some smashing holidays in Marbella with Dion and Louise – and the girls cost Dion and myself a fortune with the time they spend on the phone to each other.

As a United man he was abominably unlucky to suffer serious injury just when he had broken into the side, and just as things were starting to take off for the club. He's a strong character, though, refusing to despair and remaining positive as he fought his way back to fitness, ultimately excelling for Coventry, Aston Villa and Leicester and earning four England caps.

On the rehabilitation trail Dion took his mind off his troubles by knuckling down to learn the saxophone. These days he's an extremely accomplished player and music plays a massive part in his life. I felt that was a really great thing to do – well, I guess it wasn't so great in the early days when he wasn't so proficient and I had to listen to some of his screeching! I would never have had the patience to stick with it like Dion did. In fact, I proved that when Sharpie and myself bought electric guitars. I gave up after two lessons, I just couldn't hack it. I wanted to be able to play blistering solos straight away, and when I realised how much practice was involved I packed it in. Daft, really, spending £500 and only playing it twice. It's still for sale, if anybody's interested.

An altogether quieter fellow than the likes of Lee and Dion is Paul Scholes, though he could be a bit like Denis Irwin in that once he had a drink he could become noticeably cutting. When the team was celebrating, Scholesy would gang up with Nicky Butt and Ryan Giggs and they were three rascals, like the Three Manchester Musketeers, but that was strictly within the team environment.

Paul has rarely, if ever, offered glimpses of his true self for public consumption. He's never enjoyed the publicity merry-go-round, it's not often he gives interviews, and I'm happy to say that most people in the media respect his craving for privacy. You don't see journalists chasing him or complaining about him not doing his bit, and for such a talented player to get away with it for so long is amazing. Certainly footballers in the past who have not talked much to the press have taken stick for it. We have been told how they owe it to the fans and the public to speak out and say what they feel, but in Paul's case people have recognised that he's genuinely shy and reserved.

Scholesy is a great kid – and what a player! I had expected him to take Eric's role when the Frenchman departed, but then we bought Teddy. After Teddy left the manager put Scholesy in that role behind the front runner and he spoke of his dislike for it, which surprised me because I thought it was perfect for him. As an asthma sufferer he hasn't got the greatest of all-round fitness levels, and this would have relieved him of most of his defensive duties. But he wanted to be in centre of midfield so passionately that there was even talk of a fleeting bust-up with Fergie over it, which would have been out of character for Paul.

All the same, there is a granite-tough streak to the lad. He can be a tenacious little so-and-so at need, an absolute terrier, and though there's not much of him he punches far more than his weight. I recall Scholesy and Butty playing central midfield against Chelsea when we beat them 5-3 in the FA Cup in my last season, and Dennis Wise was trying to wind the pair of them up. Wise put himself about, energetically shall we say, but our two just kept steaming into him all day long. Dennis was still at it when United faced Millwall at the Millennium in the 2004 FA Cup Final. He was full of all his old tricks, such as pinching opponents while helping them up in the hope of provoking his victims into a violent reaction, which might earn a red card. But that didn't faze Paul in the slightest. He just stood his ground, played his football and picked up his winner's medal, as usual.

I was sorry when I heard he had retired from international football, because he still had plenty to offer on the international scene. I understand his reasoning, though, because he's got a young family and doesn't want to be away from them more than he has to be. Whatever, it should be great news for Manchester United because he's had hernia problems in the past and now he should get the chance of more rest. Meanwhile the loss to the national side is incalculable. I'd say Scholesy's technique is unequalled by any other Englishman on the current scene, his shooting, passing and vision are all out of this world.

One goal which sticks in my mind is his 25-yard scorcher at Riverside when United were closing in on yet another championship in the spring of 2000. The ball came across him at an awkward angle, but he hit it so perfectly true, just pinging it into the top corner so that Mark Schwarzer didn't have a prayer of reaching it. The 'Boro boys could hardly believe what he'd done, but I was used to watching him hit balls so sweetly in training. It's all in his timing, which is sublime.

Crucially, too, Paul has the footballing brain to go with all his technical assets. He can spot and deliver an unlikely pass, often an awkward reverse ball, quicker and with more precision than seems possible. I can see why first Eriksson and then Steve McClaren urged him to change his mind about playing for England because that sort of service would be priceless to strikers like Michael Owen, Wayne Rooney or Jermain Defoe, but I'd be surprised if he came back. He thought long and hard before making his decision, and I'd say he was not for turning, even if the latest England coach, Fabio Capello, made the same request.

Two other lads of Scholesy's generation, Gary and Phil Neville, have also made a colossal contribution to the Old Trafford cause, but they haven't always got the credit they have deserved, taking frequent unfair stick from press and non-United fans alike. When they were coming through as boys they were known at the club as 'sport billies', being good at everything – I think both had a chance of becoming professional cricketers – and they appeared so absorbed by sport that they didn't realise there was a whole other world out there. Maybe Phil was a little more easy-going than Gary, but they were both remarkably intense, wanting to get on with their football to the exclusion of everything else. When we had our team meetings they would come out with the rest of us but they wouldn't have a drink, being very reserved and unsure about getting into that kind of area.

More recently they have loosened up considerably, come out of their shells as they have matured, though Gary remains, by nature, the voice of reason. One thing that hasn't changed about him is the consistency of his play, and it beats me why more people don't appreciate what he brings to the table. Maybe there was one season at United when he made a series of high-profile mistakes and many critics, choosing to forget what had gone before, absolutely crucified him. But the lad's got 80-odd international caps at the time of writing, every England manager has picked him regularly, and that alone should tell us something.

It was obvious to me when he was playing for the youth team that he was an exceptional natural defender with a gift for organising those around him. Everybody had him down as a future United skipper, though his chance might have receded because Roy Keane kept the job for such a long time, then later the talk was of Rio Ferdinand. Personally, I always thought Gary would be an ideal choice and was delighted when he was appointed, knowing that he would let nobody down. Of course, what he didn't bargain for was the injury, suffered in the spring of 2007, which kept him on the sidelines for more than a year. It's been incredibly frustrating for him, especially as he is in his thirties now and the finishing line for his career is in sight. Obviously his time for further achievements is limited, but it would be wrong to write him off because he's always been a formidable fighter.

I know Gary's put a lot of people's backs up as the spokesman for England players on controversial issues, but you have to remember he's just that – the spokesman, putting across the collective view. I'm sure his team-mates are delighted to have a representative who will speak up for himself and for them, and I don't understand why that should be seen as ungracious. Sometimes the things he says are taken out of context and blown up, like his so-called aversion to Scousers, which I think has embarrassed him. The chants follow him whenever United play Liverpool but it's not something he fosters deliberately and I know that he doesn't want to be a symbol of continued ill feeling between the two sets of supporters.

I guess Gary is never going to be loved at Anfield, nor be a favourite at many grounds around the country, but I do detect a gradual mellowing towards him as people begin to appreciate what he has brought to the England set-up over so many years.

As for Phil, he committed an error against Romania in the European Championships and has never been allowed to forget it. He rose through the United ranks as a fine all-round footballer, only to be hindered severely by glandular fever during 1996/97 when he was still at a formative stage of his career. That knocked the stuffing out of him more than anyone realised and it took a long time to regain his former standard. I don't know whether it was a physical thing, or whether it affected his confidence, but for quite a while he took backward steps, becoming a bit-part player instead of the principal we all expected him to be.

Then there was the phase where he was switched into central midfield with sensational success. I'll never forget the game against Arsenal in December 2002 when he overshadowed Patrick Vieira, absolutely battered him out of contention and stole the show against one of the world's best players. But somehow, with all the strenuous competition for places at Old Trafford, he never managed to make the role his own and in 2004/05, despite having signed a new five-year deal, he barely got a sniff of regular action. It was puzzling, especially when newcomers such as Eric Djemba-Djemba and Kleberson found it so difficult to adjust to the pressures of the Premiership, but the Gaffer has never been frightened of making difficult decisions and usually he is proved right in the end. Whatever, Phil Neville was a magnificent servant to Manchester United and since joining Everton in search of regular first-team football he has been a tremendous success, becoming captain of a fine, well-balanced side. It was a brave decision to leave a club where he had known so much success from an early age, but he has proved to be right. A lot of players depart Old Trafford and then fail to re-create the personal standard they achieved for United, but that's an accusation which can't be levelled at the younger Neville brother. His reputation is still very much intact, he has become a key player in an emerging force which has genuine aspirations of joining the Premiership's elite group, and I am sure he enjoys working under David Moyes, who has done such a marvellous job at Goodison Park.

Above all, Phil has always been a model professional, and the same can be said for one of my earliest footballing comrades, Colin Cooper, who started in Middlesbrough reserves around the same time as myself. At first he was the sweeper in a back five, a smooth and reliable player who read the game fantastically well. Later Rioch wanted to play four across the back, and though he was right-sided Coops was slotted in at left-back, where he adapted superbly. He played a few games in midfield, too, and made a name for himself with a few spectacular goals, belted in from distance.

Unfortunately, in the late 1980s he suffered stress fractures in his foot. The condition was extremely painful but he struggled on with injections for a while before being forced on to the sidelines. As a result he was missing for a time and might have lost a bit of confidence, which was why he was sold to Millwall, for whom he played at centre-half. Later he moved to Nottingham Forest, regained all his earlier poise and received a well-deserved call-up for England.

Back in our early days together, off the pitch Coops cut a bit of a dash with his streaky blond hair and he was a target for the girls, who used to hang around him, swooning and looking for autographs. After a while I got fed up with pretty girls approaching me only to ask for Coops' number!

I was delighted when he went back to 'Boro shortly after me and we renewed our old friendship, invariably rooming together. As ever, he was totally dedicated to his work and was in the habit of going to the gym after training just to keep himself toned. Me, I used to sit in the bath and soak away the pain.

Coops lost his two-year-old son, Finlay, in an accident at home in January 2002, a tragedy which touched everybody who knew him.

Finally in this chapter, because it takes all sorts to make a world, and because I feel people should know exactly what he's all about, I'm going to talk about one of the game's most celebrated extroverts, Tommy Docherty. I sat with him on the top table at a dinner in one of the Old Trafford function suites only a week or so after I had joined United, and he was very friendly. He told me what a great move I had made, and we discussed the inevitable pressure I would be under because of my record transfer fee. He warned me there would be a lot of people looking for me to fail, waiting their chance to stick a knife in my back. I thought this was terrific advice, and I was grateful that he had taken the time to help a youngster who faced such a gigantic challenge in making his way at the top level.

A week later, we were hammered 5-1 by Manchester City, and who supplied the quotes for a massive newspaper spread ripping me to shreds? None other than Tommy Docherty, the very same fellow who had put an avuncular arm around my shoulder only a few nights earlier. I could hardly believe what I was reading. This was the guy who had told me about the assassins who were queueing up to ambush me – and it was he who was plunging the biggest knife of all between my shoulder blades at the first opportunity.

I have never been so disappointed in anybody. When I met him I had no preconceptions about him, though I knew he had been sacked by United and wondered whether there was any residual bitterness, even though it had happened a long time ago. Immediately he won me over with his sound common-sense, but then he hit me with that cruellest of sucker punches. I know I was an easy target at the time, and he wasn't the only one to have a go, but his attack seemed the most despicable to me, given the circumstances. It wasn't as though I was setting myself up as the finished article. Despite the size of my fee, I knew I was no more than a rookie, and what I didn't need was to be cut down by someone I thought I could trust.

It didn't end there, either. At the time Docherty was working for a local radio station, and he went to town regularly with his criticism of myself and others, notably Paul Ince. I never listened to it, but it kept coming back to me second hand, and some of the other players brought it up at a meeting. I believe it was way over the top, an absolutely scandalous way for a former United manager to behave, and we all decided we wouldn't have anything to do with the station after that. There would be no interviews, we wouldn't speak to Docherty or anyone connected with the programme. The whole of the team had been getting flak, though Incey and I came in for the worst of it and we were delighted that the rest of the players showed such solidarity. There was support from the manager, too, who described his fellow Scot as a sad, bitter old man, and even had him banned from the ground for a while.

Before the Docherty episode I had always been fairly trusting with the media, though I had learned a lesson or two at Middlesbrough. I find it sad that footballers have to be so cautious because of all the abuse, and sometimes the downright lies, which get bandied about. There is nothing wrong with constructive criticism, anyone should be prepared to take that, but people who throw mud just to sell newspapers or to boost a radio show's ratings have no place in sport.

Astonishingly Tommy Docherty's vilification of me continued for something like eight out of the nine years I was at Old Trafford. Apparently he had nailed his colours firmly to the mast and he wasn't going to change them. He refused to accept that I was good enough to play for Manchester United, and that was an opinion he was entitled to hold, but it seemed that his stance went beyond that. It was as though the issue had become personal, and I suppose it's possible that he blamed me for causing the radio ban.

His attitude was summed up when I received my PFA award in 1992. He was a guest speaker at the presentation ceremony, and as I walked out of the banqueting hall afterwards, still clutching the trophy, he was stood near the door with four or five other guys. Every one of them came up to me and shook my by the hand, but he just stood there motionless.

A few years after that I noticed him as I arrived at a restaurant. He was there having a meal and I tried to catch his eye. I wasn't going to make a scene, but I wanted to look him in the eye to see if he had anything to say to my face, but he never did.

Much later still, after I had retired, I was attending a function in Dublin with Johnny Giles, Norman Whiteside, Lee Sharpe and Bryan Robson. I didn't know that Docherty was going to be there and I wasn't happy when I found he was to be on the same table as me because I still couldn't stand the sight of the guy. I had a word with the organisers, who made sure I wasn't sat next to him, but when I was at the bar before the meal a photographer asked us all to get together for a picture. I knew exactly what Docherty would so and, sure enough, he came over and shook Sharpie's hand, then offered his hand to me.

I just couldn't bring myself to take it, so I just said: 'Don't think so, Tom.' He said something about letting bygones be bygones, adding that I had proved him wrong and that it was time to forget about it. But it still rankled too deeply with me. I get on well with almost everybody, and certainly I have never rejected an olive branch before. If somebody doesn't like you as a footballer, then fine, I can accept that, but he had made it poisonously personal.

That night on the stage he waxed on about United, mentioned the fact that I was there, and admitted that he'd made a mistake in his assessment of me. He said that I had proved him wrong with all the years I had served at Old Trafford and all the trophies I had helped to win. But an apology like that in front of 500 people in Dublin didn't make any impact on me. I don't think I deserved his sort of treatment from somebody in the game. I think I'd earned a bit more respect than that. For all that, it is not in my nature to be bitter, and there is no way I will let one rotten apple spoil my overwhelmingly positive memories of my life in the game.

CHAPTER SEVENTEEN

BURNING ISSUES

As football becomes ever more firmly established as a national obsession, there is no shortage of burning issues to exercise the minds of supporters, players and administrators alike, and perhaps the hottest one of all is the commercialisation of the sport most of us have loved all our lives.

Clearly money is the game's god now, and there is a danger to the interests of the average fan as the top clubs vie to push ahead of one another. Certainly, given the celebrity status of modern players and the wages they are on, and the astronomical financial stakes involved for the likes of Manchester United, Arsenal and Chelsea, I don't think it's legitimate to call football the working-class game any more. Well, to be strictly accurate, most footballers still hail from working-class backgrounds, but it's not the same for many of those who pay so heavily to watch the action.

Just as every manager is striving for that extra few per-cent from his players, so commercial departments at Old Trafford, Highbury and Stamford Bridge are searching for an extra per-centage from their club's name, or to put it the modern way, their brand. It seems to be an unstoppable spiral, with ticket prices rising so high that many fans with everyday jobs can no longer afford to go to all the games, especially when the enormous cost of travel is taken into account. But those same fans do want Wayne Rooney, Cristiano Ronaldo and whoever the next superstar might turn out to be, and the only way that can happen is if the club makes more and more money to pay their wages. That is why one of the mottos of the United commercial department concerns 'turning fans into customers', which demonstrates vividly what a distance we have travelled from what a football club used to be, and I have to sympathise with those who see it as a worrying trend.

It's a situation totally removed from the climate of even 20 years ago, and the new corporate mentality was highlighted unforgettably by Roy Keane's famous tirade about the prawn sandwich brigade. I have to agree with him that, even a few years ago when I was at Old Trafford, we had the feeling that we had to entertain the crowd before they got behind us, unless it was a big European game, or a local derby, or perhaps a visit from Arsenal. When lesser teams came to call, there were occasions when there was a deathly hush in the stadium, and we found that highly frustrating. That said, when the atmosphere is fully charged then there's no greater crowd than United's. It's just such a shame that that priceless buzz is so much rarer these days, though modern all-seating requirements have something to do with that.

Meanwhile Roman Abramovich continues to spend, spend, spend at Chelsea, Liverpool became embroiled in a seemingly interminable ownership saga involving two businessmen from the USA and a consortium from Dubai, West Ham were acquired by a very rich man from Iceland, Americans took the reins at Aston Villa and Derby County, Manchester City became the property of a controversial politician from Thailand, Portsmouth are owned by a Franco-Russian and Fulham by Mohamed Al-Fayed, and there has been further talk of tycoons from all over the world taking over various other leading British clubs. Where is it all going to end? Professional football in this country has been around for more than 130 years and we've always known exactly where we've stood. But now people who don't have any knowledge or feeling for our traditions are moving in. Billionaires appear to be using long-established clubs in a game of one-upmanship. I'm afraid we could be in danger of losing the identity of English football, maybe its very soul.

Without being the slightest bit xenophobic, I think that bringing in so much foreign investment is dangerous. Look at the betting and fixing scandals which have been linked to the game; they have all emanated from the Far East. Are we going to end up with that over here? The fair-play aspect of our game, the fact that we know it's not bent, is crucial. We have always been known for our honesty, and if we lose that reputation then what have we got left? If fraud becomes rampant, so that fans can't believe in the integrity of what they are paying to watch, then the whole shooting match becomes a worthless sham.

It would appear that we are moving inexorably towards a European Super League, and when it finally arrives I fear that our remaining clubs will suffer terribly. A lot of them will go part-time and then there won't be any widespread public focus on them as there has been for so long. I grew up with a four-division league, and there was deep interest in everything that went with it. As the format is diluted, that fascination, some might call it obsession, will inevitably recede, and as the rich get immeasurably richer, then probably the poor will fade away and die.

That would be a calamity, and I hope the players take a vigorous stance against it. We have stuck together in the past, campaigning heroically in the middle years of the 20th century against unfair domination by the clubs regarding footballers' pay and the horrendously one-sided retain-and-transfer system. More recently the PFA have stood up to be counted when the authorities sought to cut the union's money, much of which goes to help players in the lower leagues, lads who don't make anything like the cash to be found in the Premiership. Undoubtedly there are big battles ahead, and professional footballers owe it to the game to fight them with the utmost vigour.

I see the PFA as a crucial force for good in these tempestuous times, not only regarding issues which hog the headlines, but also in dealing with countless everyday problems. For instance, a lot of players don't make it beyond the trainee stage, and have to plan for a future outside the game. The union does its utmost to help in the necessary re-education process by sending those lads on courses and pointing them in whatever direction suits their individual needs. Then there are people who have left the game but are still struggling with injuries, perhaps needing operations, many of which are part-financed by the PFA. The household names don't benefit from that sort of money, and they don't want to. They're quite happy that it filters its way down to those in financial need.

On a wider issue, I'm afraid there will be fewer and fewer opportunities for English kids in our professional game, because of all the players coming in from overseas. I didn't used to like the foreigners rule, which so hampered United in my heyday, forcing us to leave out two of our top men every time we played in Europe. But looking at the current situation, there might be a place for some sort of restrictive legislation of the sort proposed by UEFA. To get a handle on the alternative, we only have to look at the Scots. Their game has been so comprehensively invaded by incomers that they have not been able to bring on many of their own youngsters for a long time now. As a result the Scotland international team is very poor, although I must admit that there was significant improvement under Walter Smith, then Alex McLeish, and I sincerely hope the trend continues under new incumbent George Burley. But whereas every side in England used to boast a good Scottish player, that isn't the case any more because they are simply not being produced. Do we want the same thing to happen to us? Do we want England to become one of the minnows in international tournaments? Would we be content to watch Premiership matches in which the only Englishmen on the field were the referee and his assistants? Is that not monstrously unfair on our own talent, which needs to be nurtured intelligently if it is ever to emerge? Those are uncomfortable questions, but answers must be found, and found quickly, if an acceptable balance is to be struck before it is too late.

Another feature of the changing scene is the modern conflict of interests between managers worried about crowded fixture lists and clubs arranging pre-season tours to distant places in order to swell the coffers. Take Manchester United as an example. At the start of one recent campaign Sir Alex Ferguson's playing resources were stretched, with tired players returning from international tournaments and resting at home while the club travelled to the USA. However, there were complaints in the States about the strength of the side, and soon he was sending Paul Scholes and Mikael Silvestre across the Atlantic as reinforcements, presumably to keep the sponsors happy.

So on the one hand we digested what seemed to be incontrovertible evidence of over-commitment, then on the other we heard of the club looking forward to their next summer jaunt, to Asia. I think the fans were entitled to ask: 'What's the difference?' Of course, United wanted to go to Asia to generate commercial interest from a massive market, but it could hardly have been good for the team. Undoubtedly long-haul travel is extremely exacting for the players, most of whom wouldn't particularly enjoy going away for two weeks at that point. So there you have it, an insoluble problem: tours generate cash and prick global interest in your 'brand', but it knackers your footballers. Something's got to suffer and I think money's always going to talk, so extravagant summer expeditions are likely to become the norm rather than the exception.

So far all the matters I have raised in this chapter could be placed under the rough heading of 'political', but there are some purely football-related issues I feel the need to address, too. For instance, it irritates me beyond belief that the powers-that-be keep tinkering with the laws of the game. The latest interpretation of the offside rule, in particular, can be nothing less than farcical, with clever forwards such as Ruud van Nistelrooy and Thierry Henry taking it to the very limits. If someone cracks in a goal from 30 yards then I wouldn't want to see it ruled out because someone was standing marginally offside. But there are times when referees claim forwards aren't interfering with play when palpably they are, because they are distracting defenders. I know it's a grey area and I can understand the authorities wanting to make their product more entertaining, but it's selling anyway so what's the problem? If it ain't broke, don't fix it!

Another bone of contention is the professional foul. When a defender attempts to make a legitimate challenge as the last man, and commits a foul by being a split-second late, then I cannot see it as a sending-off offence. There's got to be more understanding of what players are trying to do. Given the pace of the modern game, it's ever harder to time tackles properly because the attackers are so quick. As a result it's become a common occurrence for a defender to be an inch out in his calculations, inevitably he is sent off for a professional foul and the balance of the game is ruined. Where's the sense or the justice in that? My definition of a professional foul is when someone grabs hold of a forward's shirt and pulls him back, or deliberately handles when a ball is going over his head. In those situations then the defender should be red-carded instantly because what he's done is against the spirit of the game. Similarly I am not condoning the violent tackle, but a tiny misjudgement which results in a trip? It's not a heinous crime in my eyes.

Apart from the lack of natural justice in the current regulations, I feel they make life impossible for the officials, the majority of whom deserve tremendous sympathy. Oh I know there are the referees who think they are bigger than the game, see themselves as stars of the show, and always want to be making the big decision which will shine the spotlight on them. Such people I find pathetic, but there are an awful lot of excellent officials and they are doing an extraordinarily difficult job. I know because, working as a pundit, I can watch an incident two or three times and still have no idea whether it's a penalty; but the guy in black gets one look in a split-second of live action, and he's got to be dead right or he's going to be caned for it.

That leads me naturally to one of the most contentious footballing issues of the age, namely the use of modern technology to help referees come to a fair decision. I know some people swear that it would decrease the official's relevance, but I don't buy into that for one moment. The technology exists and we should introduce it now, at the very least to determine whether or not the ball has crossed the line. Surely no one could argue with that after witnessing the injustice of the 'goal' by Tottenham's Pedro Mendes being disallowed at Old Trafford despite the cameras proving categorically that United goalkeeper Roy Carroll had pulled the ball back from way over the line.

Some people ask what would happen if, after such an incident, the ball switches to the other end and a goal is scored there. The answer is simple. The second goal doesn't count because, if a correct decision had been given in the first place, then it would never have been scored. Another argument employed against the use of technology is that it would interrupt the flow of a game, but there is no reason why it should. If the referee is uncertain about an incident, then he signals to a colleague who has access to the screen. Meanwhile the game goes on as if nothing had happened, stopping only if the referee hears through his earpiece that an injustice has occurred. In effect, the crucial decision has been made by a man on the sidelines blessed with every means to get it right, and I believe that would remove a significant degree of pressure from the fellow in the middle.

Any slight delay in, say, a goal being given might upset the fans on occasions – although it might add to the excitement, too – but if there are hard, clear facts for evidence then they would have to accept it. Surely, if the pictures show that a ball has definitely crossed a line then it puts a stop to controversy rather than causes it. I can't imagine anything easier or fairer, and I can't understand why there is any resistance to the idea.

We're talking here about the winning and losing of championships and cup finals, so let's be sure we've got it right. I'm positive that the players would support the introduction of technology, because there's nothing worse than feeling cheated over a goal that hasn't been given. I don't see why the cameras couldn't be used to rule on offsides, either, and diving could be reduced if the culprits knew the eye of the camera was on them.

That's got a few of my thoughts on the modern game in general off my chest, now I'd like to reflect briefly on the prospects for both Manchester United and England in the summer of 2008. Though it might sound like a contradiction of my earlier comments about foreign ownership, I have seen nothing to alarm me at Old Trafford since the Glazers' arrival in 2005. They stressed they were not out to tamper with the running of the club, or the way it has always been perceived, and so far it appears to me that they have been as good as their word.

Ticket prices have gone up a bit, but when you look around the rest of the Premiership I think they're quite balanced – I can't actually say they are fair at any club, because ordinary working people just can't afford to pay today's prices. In United's case, the new owners promised to back the manager in the transfer market, which is a crucial commitment and one they have honoured. I know some people are worried about the vast debt incurred by the purchase of the club, but that's an area where we can only await developments. The big crossroads will be reached when the Gaffer finally retires, and the Glazers will face the challenge of bringing in another manager who can build teams like Sir Alex has done over the last two decades. Overall, though, what we have seen of the new owners so far doesn't give me too much to be concerned about.

On the field, meanwhile, the new Manchester United team is maturing nicely. Some critics were writing off the manager as too old for the job, but I feel he has demonstrated conclusively that he retains the hunger and drive to create a successful new era at Old Trafford, witness his ninth Premiership triumph in 2006/07, followed by his tenth League crown and second European Cup a year later. His players have always had to match his own astonishing appetite for success and the latest crop, even though they are earning such vast amounts of money, appear to have that all-important hunger to a high degree. Even in the rare interludes when the trophies have been fewer, the desire has never faltered in lads who have been there a long time, the likes of Scholes, Giggs and Neville, and now it's rubbed off on young newcomers like Rooney and Ronaldo.

It's obvious to me that they have a clear sense of what it takes to be a championship-winning combination. I suppose it's harder than ever before in the current climate because of the Abramovich millions, but they are playing wonderful, free-flowing, attacking football, and they are a joy to watch. True, there have been some buys that haven't worked out, but I believe that now United's squad is stronger than anyone's, even if it remains a tough battle over the next few years to match Chelsea in terms of spending power.

For me, one key acquisition was the Serbian central defender, Nemanja Vidic. He took a bit of time to settle, but he's solid and aggressive, and has emerged as an ideal partner for Rio Ferdinand, who seems to have matured, put his off-the-pitch problems behind him, and become more consistent. The more they play together the better they look, and their understanding has been compared to the one I used to enjoy with Steve Bruce. Just like Stevie, Vidic is a throw-himself-through-a-brick-wall type of player, while Rio is easier on the eye, a smooth and classy reader of the game. Admittedly the Englishman can look a little lackadaisical and can be robbed of possession at times, a jibe that used to be thrown at me occasionally, but overall they are an effective pairing and my satisfaction with them mirrors my happiness with the way the whole team is progressing.

As for Ronaldo, he's got to be the best footballer in the world as I write this in the summer of 2008. In the past he has come very close in various polls, but has lost out to the likes of Kaka, AC Milan's brilliant Brazilian, and Argentinian Lionel Messi of Barcelona, but next time around I think he should be way ahead of them. I know he has had his critics, but when you look at his phenomenal goal record alongside a pretty well comprehensive catalogue of assets – speed, flair, shooting power, heading ability, work rate – it all adds up to something very special.

Some have argued that to ascend that final mountain top, to be recognised as the world's most complete player, Cristiano has to come up with outstanding performances in the biggest of games. He took a lot of flak for not producing the very best of himself in the 2007 Champions League semi-final defeat in Milan and subsequently when United lost the FA Cup final to Chelsea. But I believe that's a harsh assessment and I take issue with it. True, he wasn't at his jaw-dropping best in either of those games, but on both occasions he was part of an indifferent team performance and I don't see why all the blame should be heaped on his shoulders.

Certainly he was one of the biggest reasons for United's continued competitiveness in 2007/08, taking the pressure off the likes of Wayne Rooney and Carlos Tevez, giving them time and space in which to work their own magic. Cristiano Ronaldo is a wonderful footballer and I think people are being extremely picky if they start highlighting his quiet games. When he's flying, which is pretty often, he is absolutely breathtaking. For me, there is nobody like him anywhere on the planet.

That made it all the more unsettling for United fans ahead of Euro 2008 when speculation became rife that he was keen on a move to Real Madrid. At the time of writing I didn't know the outcome of that, but the fact that the player didn't clearly lay the matter to rest created enough doubt for me to feel that, from the viewpoint of United wanting to hang on to the extravagantly talented Portuguese, all might not be well. I think the overtures by Real made an impact on Cristiano, but I hope he didn't go. I hope that he looked at what Sir Alex Ferguson and Manchester United had done for him in the five years since his arrival, that he respected their input and decided to stay. But ultimately if a player wants to leave, and makes that known, then it is devilishly hard to keep him.

It's not as if Ronaldo's had an unhappy time at Old Trafford, or that the club is not moving forward. He's been playing for a team that could become one of the best ever, and he's been an integral part of it. To lose him at this stage would be a huge dent in United's plans for the coming seasons. For the best player in the world to accept a transfer to the Bernabeu would portray Real as the bigger club, which wouldn't sit well at Old Trafford. It was a tricky situation which Sir Alex could have done without as he plotted his course for the next campaign.

Still, any team is about more than one man, and I have been mightily impressed by Sir Alex's quartet of expensive acquisitions in the summer of 2007. Anderson, Nani, Carlos Tevez and Owen Hargreaves have all, in their different ways, brought plenty to the Old Trafford party. I must admit, though, that it is the young Brazilian midfielder who has really fired my imagination. Most people in England didn't know much about Anderson when he arrived from Porto, but after he had settled down, and that didn't take long, some of his performances have raised plenty of eyebrows. He's only just out of his teens, but what a player he might turn out to be. He's tough, he's got endless energy, he's got flair and he's not afraid to try different things. I think he's a fantastic prospect and there is no limit to what he might achieve with Manchester United.

The other young man who arrived at the same time, the winger Nani, is taking a little longer to find his feet and in his first English season we have seen him move from one end of the footballing spectrum to the other, and back again. One moment he will do something that takes your breath away, then the next you'll be tearing your hair at his decision-making. But that's just his youth. About his exceptional ability there is not the slightest question. He's an amazingly talented kid who has put in some terrific displays which bely his tender years, and if at other times you see that little bit of naivety which goes with immaturity, it is nothing to worry about in the long term.

Despite his controversial bout of ball-juggling during the 4-0 FA Cup victory over Arsenal, what Nani doesn't do as a rule is showboat in the manner Ronaldo did when he started at United. I'm sure the Arsenal incident was a one-off and that is just as well because every player in the English leagues knows that if you're going to pull that kind of stunt then you're going to be smacked. Somebody's going to hurt you. I know the manager had a word with him about it afterwards, and I'm sure his team-mates did, too. I know the fans love it, and football is supposed to be an entertainment, but it's wrong to take the rise out of fellow professionals. Mind, it was ridiculous that the FA should have turned a blind eye when the Arsenal defender, William Gallas, took a blatant kick at Nani. Our current disciplinary procedure is crazy, an absolute mockery of natural justice, when Gallas can get away with that while another player might be banned for several matches for lightly caressing an opponent's cheek.

Returning to the young wingman, I'm confident he will learn his lesson as he gets older, and when Ryan Giggs eventually hangs up his boots, there is the mouth-watering prospect of Ronaldo and his fellow

Portuguese operating down United's flanks (Real Madrid permitting!). That will go a long way towards ensuring that the club maintains its tradition for thrilling football – happy days, indeed, for the fans.

There there is Carlos Tevez, another young fella who has still not reached his prime and another exceptional performer. Clearly Sir Alex looked at the vast influence of Tevez as West Ham escaped relegation in 2006/07, when he virtually kept them up on his own. I suppose you can't quite say that because he was part of a team, but the difference he was making to the Hammers reminded me irresistibly of the effect Eric Cantona had on United, especially in 1995/96, when he scored in so many 1-0 victories towards the end of the season. Tevez has so much confidence with the ball at his feet, and he's immensely tough, both physically and mentally. As for his work-rate, it's little short of prodigious as he scurries around the pitch, closing down opponents and harrying centre-halves to distraction.

He's been a superb addition to United's strength, and the same can be said of the experienced England international Owen Hargreaves, a fabulous athlete with boundless energy and plenty of pace. He relishes the sort of hard graft that a lot of top players don't like and does a marvellous job of protecting the back four, which is particularly important in European competition. Of course, with so many truly wonderful players at his disposal, it must be a constant headache for the manager to keep them all happy. For instance, when you've got a quartet of central midfielders like Paul Scholes, Michael Carrick, Anderson and Hargreaves, who do you pick for the big matches? Scholesy and Carrick are the two best passers, but the others bring their own distinctive qualities, too, and then there is Darren Fletcher to consider. I have to feel sympathy for the lad, being in the midst of so many high-quality rivals for a place. He's never done anything wrong and it must be highly frustrating for him. He needs time on the pitch to show what he can do and he's bound to wonder whether he is ever going to get equal opportunities with the rest. As someone who has captained his country and already has the taste of playing in big games for United, he is faced with a dilemma. Does he sit at Old Trafford and take his turn with the others, or does he leave to find regular football elsewhere.

If it were me – and I'm not being specific about Darren here, merely using his position in 2007/08 as a convenient example – I would be looking to go if I wasn't getting my quota of games. I would find it unfulfilling to sit on the sidelines and play only once or twice a month out of a fixture list of perhaps ten games. I know Ole Gunnar Solskjaer did it, and it worked for him, but it requires a certain type of mentality which I would say is rare among professional footballers.

But whatever questions faced various individuals, for Manchester United 2007/08 was yet another golden season during which they, along with Arsenal, played the best and most attractive football in the Premier League. They provided fabulous entertainment to regularly ignite the Old Trafford crowd, offering plenty of goals and excitement and the most thrilling players, while their defence was the tightest in the division. Also they dealt brilliantly with all the pressure and expectation heaped upon them. Winning the League in 2006/07 had massaged expectations hugely, but they dealt with the situation superbly during an extremely tense run-in. Both United and Chelsea lost ground at vital times and in the end United prevailed by two points, but because they had scored so many goals, and conceded so few, they had the edge on the Stamford Bridge side anyway. In my book they would have deserved the title even if they had finished level on points with Chelsea. Certainly I wasn't in agreement with Avram Grant's contention that there should be a play-off if the points were level. That would have been a nonsense to me, with one team having scored so many more goals than the other.

As for the climax of the Champions League, that was even more nerve-shredding than the title race. I wasn't in Moscow, having returned from a trip to Singapore at 6.30 on the morning of the final against Chelsea, but I spent the rest of the day working in the MUTV studios, and at times I was striving not to fall asleep. There was no danger of that once the action started, though.

It was a great game, exciting and open, which was a tonic after some disappointing finals over the years. United had the better of the first half and could have been three up, but Chelsea equalised with a flukey goal just before the break when the ball flicked off Rio Ferdinand's back into the path of Frank Lampard and Edwin van der Sar slipped. That gave Grant's team impetus for the second period, in which they were the better side. But I thought United edged extra time and I felt it was rude of the Chelsea manager to claim afterwards that his team had dominated the game. That was a ludicrous proposition.

Regarding the shoot-out, nobody in the game relishes settling the destination of a major prize by penalties, and nobody likes to watch a tremendous leader such as John Terry missing the vital kick. But that fate had to befall somebody and in the end United deserved to win. I think they were due a little bit of luck in Europe in view of what has happened on previous occasions and they got it when Terry missed the penalty. Also they merited their massive reward for the beautiful football they had served up all season, and there's also the fact that they didn't lose a match throughout the whole Champions League campaign.

I watched all the Moscow action from the MUTV studio along with David May and presenter Mandy Henry. Maysie couldn't look towards the end, he turned his back. When van der Sar made the decisive save from Nicolas Anelka I leapt into the air and Maysie went ballistic, charging round the studio. He was that excited, if he had been in Moscow I reckon he might have made it on to the celebration pictures, just as he did in 1999.

For Sir Alex it represented a phenomenal achievement, and as ever he had showed himself to be the master of tense situations as both competitions had approached their climax. He always throws a couple of hand grenades into the mix, by commenting on the opposition, or certain players, or a referee, just to stir things up. He protects his own players loyally and he expresses trust in them, which is exactly what any footballer wants to hear, especially at times of pressure. He's been down that route many times, knows what's expected, knows all about how to handle a tight finish. He held his nerve and positively thrived on the cut and thrust of it all. There are always people who doubt him, who reckon he's coming to the end, but he always manages to leave them with egg on their faces. He ended up getting all the accolades yet again, and he earned them. He's showing not the slightest sign of losing his hunger for success. He's still got that mischievous glint in his eye which bodes ill for his opponents. There's no doubt that he's still up for the challenge and is ready to take the pressure that comes with it.

Working alongside the terrific young players at Old Trafford, who make up what I believe to be United's best ever squad, must keep him feeling young. The wonderful thing is that the team is nowhere near its full maturity yet. If he can keep those lads together – and that's not easy, as demonstrated by the Ronaldo affair – then we should see the best of them in three or four years time. It could be awesome.

Of course, we're bound to wonder just how long Sir Alex can go on, but I'm never surprised when he bounces back and we can be sure of one thing: when he does go out eventually, he'll be doing his damnedest to make sure it's on a high.

Who will be his successor? You pays your money and you takes your choice. I think his current number-two, Carlos Queiroz, must be in with a big shout because he has played his part in recent United successes, he knows the players well and he's very familiar with all aspects of the club.

Two more who will be mentioned are Roy Keane and Paul Ince, both of whom have made tremendous starts to their managerial careers, but are unlikely to be judged as ready to take over at Old Trafford just yet. Still, Roy is already in the Premier League and Paul was being linked with a top-flight job in the summer of 2008, so they are both in a position to build up a case and it will be fascinating to watch them working to improve their credentials over the next two or three years. Certainly they are both winners who rejoice in universal respect within the game because of what they've already achieved and, depending on the timescale, I wouldn't bet against either one.

Then there is Steve Bruce, who did enormously well at Wigan to ensure that they remained in the Premier League after taking over in November 2007 when they looked to be in danger of relegation. Near the end of the season he received a glowing accolade from Sir Alex, who called him the best young manager around, and I'd say he would be one of the principal names to come under consideration when a change is made. Unquestionably his efforts in his first six months at the JJB have put him right in the mix.

Finally I must mention Mark Hughes. I have to admit I was surprised by Sparky's move from Ewood Park to Eastlands in June 2008, bearing in mind the fierce rivalry between the two Manchester clubs and the fact that he looked to be one of the most likely and well-qualified of Sir Alex's potential successors. Of course, I can understand the lure of a club that's clearly looking to make a huge impact on the Premier League, given the amount of money the City chairman is likely to put at Mark's disposal. That appeared to be the biggest reason why he chose to leave Blackburn, where there is not the cash available that there used to be in Jack Walker's time as owner.

Mark did fabulously at Ewood Park on a comparative shoestring, but obviously his sights are set even higher. He wants to get to the top as quickly as possible and the City job offers him the vehicle to try and do just that. Now he will be able to compete for the best players in the world, and that's the carrot that has tempted him. Some people believe the switch might shut the door on the Welshman ever replacing Sir Alex, but given the fact that he is held in such esteem at Old Trafford, where he remains a true legend, I wouldn't write off his chances.

I think everyone has been impressed by the way he has handled himself at pitch-side and in his dealings with the press. He has been assured, he has spoken well and his teams have reflected the competitive attitude he always took on to the pitch as a player. That was something other players always saw in Sparky and they tried to emulate him. He likes to see people putting in the graft and there is no doubt that he will be a very demanding boss. He was always physically tough with a very strong mentality and would never be bullied. Transport that to a team ethic and you have a side that is difficult to beat.

Mark Hughes is one of the brightest young bosses in the game and he has every chance of achieving his lofty ambitions. He rejoices in the respect of players, because there is nothing that he hasn't done on the pitch. He speaks from his own experience playing with and against the best in the world during his stints with three giant clubs, Manchester United, Barcelona and Bayern Munich. So although the odds against him taking over at Old Trafford one day might have lengthened, I'd say the book is far from closed.

And so to England, and first I'd like to comment on the farcical manner in which the FA handled the exit of Sven-Goran Eriksson. Though I have never believed that football managers should be judged by their private lives, it was hard to shed a tear when he departed. A glimpse of Sven on the side of the pitch was enough to understand that he didn't instil a lot of passion into his sides. I heard players say that he never handed out rollickings in the dressing room, yet there's times when football teams need the hard word. Certainly it's expected in England, where it's part of the game's culture, but I don't think it was in the Swede's character to be confrontational.

When he went I can't say I was surprised, whether he jumped or was pushed. Maybe he should have gone earlier, at the time of the 'fake sheikh' affair in Dubai, which many believed would be the last straw. Since then the situation has become mortifying for both the FA and Sven himself. It's just so embarrassing – firstly because he never took England as far as he should have done given the exceptional group of players at his disposal, and secondly because he was still being paid massive sums of money after he had gone.

As to his successor, Steve McClaren, the press picked up on the fact that he wasn't first or second choice, then he found life very tough in his first few games in charge. To be fair, anyone would find the job difficult because the media makes any criticism so personal, and some of the coverage after the early defeat by Croatia was way over the top. But was he the right man? Well, one moment we were hearing what a great coach he was, but the next we were told that he fell out with players at

Middlesbrough and that it was his eventual successor at the Riverside, Gareth Southgate, who had pulled the dressing room together. It made me wonder whether, without the input of Southgate in his days as a player, they would have reached the final of the UEFA Cup and the semi-final of the FA Cup in 2005/06. Of course, that begged another question: without that success with 'Boro, would Steve's profile have been high enough to get him the England job, even though he had already worked for the FA as Sven's assistant? It's all ifs and buts, but whatever the truth, I wished Steve McClaren well and hoped that he could be the first man since Sir Alf Ramsey to bring home silverware for England.

But sadly, oh so sadly, it didn't work out for Steve. I was in the pub with some mates watching England's crucial final Euro 2008 qualifier against Croatia at Wembley, and as soon as the manager's umbrella went up I knew there was only one possible outcome. I said to the lads that I could imagine the next day's headlines, and one of them actually came up with 'Wally with the brolly'. Remarkable really, perhaps he should have a top job in newspapers. But the pictures we were viewing of Steve under that blue-and-red FA-issue brolly made me shudder. I could understand why he needed some shelter to keep his notes clear, but I think it was a grave mistake. If you're the England manager, and things aren't going too well, then you ought to be a bit more media-savvy than that. Once the result went against him he was always going to be pilloried, but the brolly business made it a whole lot crueller than it might have been.

The bottom line was that we'd been given a tremendous chance to get through to the European Championship finals and we had failed dismally. Ironically the most compelling condemnation had come from Steve's own mouth a little earlier when he had said: 'Judge me by whether or not we qualify.' Well, we *didn't* qualify and he *was* judged accordingly. Once you make a statement like that, and your team has the chances and the breaks that England did get towards the end of the campaign, you're in trouble.

I don't think he failed because he was fatally implicated in the Eriksson regime, as some critics have suggested. I think he was his own man who tried to have his own ideas at Middlesbrough, and I think he would have attempted to implement those ideas with England. Let's give the man his due and emphasise that within the game he has a reputation for being a tremendous coach. I certainly wouldn't argue with that. But I would question whether he had the full confidence of the players and whether he managed to get the best out of the terrific resources he had.

Being completely honest, though I have nothing against Steve

McClaren, he would not have been my choice for the job. He has many attributes, but I don't think he has that stimulating vibe which Terry Venables creates, and I can't see that he carries that little bit of fear in the way that Sir Alex Ferguson does. In the end it might not have been easy for him to command respect, and if you haven't got that then you haven't got an earthly. Right from the start I feel some of the ground was cut away from under Steve's feet because the FA had tried to get in other people ahead of him. That made a mockery of the whole situation and put him under pressure straight away. Then when his side didn't perform there was only one outcome.

Now we have Fabio Capello in charge of our team, and I have to say I was deeply disappointed that we couldn't make an English appointment. If we were to win anything under Capello I feel very strongly that his nationality would detract from the achievement. Let me stress that this is in no way a racist rant and that my opinion has nothing to do with xenophobia in any form. I merely believe that if England are entering World Cups and European Championships, then they should be contested by the English, both on and off the pitch. I don't want to see our campaign masterminded by an Italian or a Frenchman or a Spaniard or whatever. I don't want to hear that England won the World Cup but we had to be told what to do by an Italian. That would take away from the achievement; it just wouldn't rest easy with me.

Having got that out of the way, I have nothing against Capello himself. He has been a terrific manager, his CV is virtually second to none and history tells us that he knows how to put together winning teams. He's got something about him, too, a certain charisma, a personal strength that brooks little argument. Indeed, if some of the interviews with people who have played under him are anything to go by, then it seems he has intimidated a lot of footballers in his time. Clearly he's not afraid to upset individuals, he's not cowed by any sort of reputation, and a few of his early moves in charge of England bear testament to that.

Now I hope he gets the right reaction from his players. If he goes in too heavy-handed he might alienate a few. Provided he gets the balance right there is nothing wrong with a bit of discipline, letting people know he is the boss, because ultimately it is his job that is on the line. In terms of winning, he might be exactly what the England team has been needing for a long time.

As I have outlined, however, I think there should be more to it than that, but I realise it's not good enough for me simply to say that I don't want to employ a foreigner as England manager. I must come up with a viable alternative, and although there will be those who accuse me of going back in time, I have no hesitation in nominating Terry Venables. Okay, he's in his sixties, but let me get the age thing out of the way immediately. Sir Alex Ferguson, who is older than Terry and still making a fair fist of running Manchester United, has made the point that the ideal age for an international manager is 60 and over, so there is no problem there. The fact is that Terry Venables would know exactly what he was doing and would quickly earn the respect of the current generation of footballers. I'm sure if you asked all the England players from my era who was the best England manager, then 99 per-cent of them would plump for Terry, and I don't think the game has changed so much in the few years which have passed since then. I have given my views on him at length in an earlier chapter, so here I will merely say that he treats his charges like men and offers an ideal workplace in which to thrive. If I were Wayne Rooney or Steven Gerrard or Rio Ferdinand, that would do for me.

CHAPTER EIGHTEEN

WHAT NEXT?

When it finally hit me that I would no longer be making my living as a professional footballer, a deeply perplexing question catapulted itself to the front of my mind – what happens next?

All I knew at that moment of truth was that getting back into the game was not really a possibility. As the inevitability of retirement had loomed ever larger, I had made the decision to take a year out to consider my options. Obviously football was one of them, but even though there had been times when I felt I might take my coaching badge, it was never more than a fleeting thought. To be a manager or coach at the highest level demands a vast amount of commitment, with lots of travelling and other time spent away from home. Having just acquired a young family, I just didn't have the desire to do that.

Even as a player I used to hate going away on a Friday night and staying in a hotel. I was all for home comforts, kipping in my own bed with my own familiar things around me. But some of my team-mates, the ones with kids, would be saying: 'What a blessing to get away from home and have a decent night's sleep.' I used to think they were exaggerating, but now I've got two daughters I realise that your life's not your own after you start a family. How some of the lads coped I do not know. Take Roy Keane, for example, with five children. At any given time you can bet that one of them's up in the middle of the night, raising the roof. Now I'm sure that most players' wives will take the responsibility of seeing to them, especially near a game, but you still get disturbed by all the screaming and shouting. I only played a few games after we had Lauren, my eldest, but that brief taste was enough for me.

I know I'm a lucky man, being able to retire from my main employment at the age of 36. I've got plenty of friends with mortgages who won't look to have any more kids simply because they can't afford them, and I do appreciate all the fine things that have come along with a life at the top level of football, most of all the ability to give the very best of my time to my children. But although I would never deny what a wonderful privilege it was to find myself in that situation, when I laid aside my boots I still had a lot of years ahead of me (at least, I hoped so!) and I couldn't spend my whole time doing the dishes and cutting the grass.

Clearly a new challenge was needed and, not for the first time in my life, I got lucky. Within a day of announcing my retirement, I answered the phone and it was Sky Television, asking me to do some pieces for them. A couple of days later I was approached by the local TV station, then I received commissions from 'Boro TV (destined to cease operating in 2005) and the BBC. They all wanted to pay me for talking about football, which struck me as the perfect way of staying involved in the game.

I particularly enjoy being a panellist on *Football Interactive,* a feature introduced by the BBC on Saturday afternoons. Together with presenters such as Ray Stubbs and fellow 'experts' such as Lee Dixon, Garth Crooks, Gavin Peacock and Carlton Palmer, I'm required to watch all that day's live Premiership games on a bank of TV screens and give my views on them, as well as holding forth on any current issues. I guess it's the sort of thing a lot of fans would like to do, the equivalent of chewing the fat with their mates at the pub (without the beer, I hasten to add), but it can be more difficult than it looks. You have to concentrate very hard the whole time, because you'd look pretty stupid if you missed something in front of millions of people.

It's great fun to trade opinions, and the occasional good-natured insult, with the likes of Lee, a born-and-bred Manchester City fan and an arch-rival over the years as United and Arsenal have vied for the big prizes. Working for the BBC has also meant bumping into old chums like Peter Schmeichel, whom I hadn't seen since I left Old Trafford in 1998. He hadn't changed, still had plenty to say for himself, and I still got on well with him. He was a big, arrogant sod on the football pitch, but off it he was always brilliant company and I couldn't have been happier at linking up with him again, though it wasn't too long before he left the corporation as a regular. These days he still makes the occasional appearance, while concentrating on being a TV football presenter back home in Denmark. Meanwhile, for my own part, I have no aspirations to be the next Alan Hansen. For the moment, at least, I'm happy enough with the role they've given me.

Appearing on the quiz show *A Question Of Sport* is marvellous fun, too. I think the version that goes out publicly is entertaining enough, but some of the craic we have off the air is downright hilarious. Sue Barker holds it all together magnificently. I grew up watching David Coleman in charge, and it was difficult to imagine anyone else stepping into his shoes, but Sue brings her own special style to it. She adds a touch of glamour to the proceedings, bless her, and she's always ready for a laugh, proving an ideal foil for Ally McCoist, who was a brilliant resident team captain until he left the show to help Walter Smith at Rangers.

As for Ally, he could have been a stand-up comedian. He played the crowd really well, always bringing them into it, and his asides and quips were razor-sharp. He was always up to something, forever dumping the rest of us in trouble, and there were an awful lot of out-takes. In one show there was a piece of video footage about a cycle race in the Olympics, which featured a big crash with cyclists going down all over the place. We had to answer five questions on it and the last one was: what colour was the Korean cyclist's helmet? Matt Dawson, who is pretty quick on the uptake, said: 'You can't ask me a question like that!' and Ally went: 'Sue, I'm surprised at you after all these years, I never realised you were that kind of girl!' Matt then came out with: 'Was it purple?' The banter and the craic was sparkling.

Eventually Sue calmed everybody down and when the other team did their piece of footage, their first question was about a Brazilian. I said: 'You can't start discussing Brazilians after you've been talking about a helmet' and then it was all off again, with Mr McCoist fizzing one-liners at everybody. Over the years Ally had scintillating rapport with various colleagues, especially John Parrott who has also now moved on, but he's always been the star for me. There have been none wittier, it just came naturally to him, and like all the best funny men, he could take a joke at his own expense.

As much as I love doing the show, there's no way I would fancy myself as a team captain one day because I haven't got that wicked brand of wit necessary to carry it off. I've seen other people try and take on the role and not live up to captains of the past. I wouldn't even pretend that I could do it, I'm just happy to be invited to join in from time to time. Mind you, it helps if they get my name right. When I was roped in as the mystery personality, Ray Wilkins recognised me easily enough, but he identified me as Gary McAllister. So many people do that, for goodness sake! I don't know whether the other Gary is ever called Pallister, but I'm sick of being referred to as Gary McAllister, nice chap though he undoubtedly is.

That just about brings the life and times of the real Gary Pallister up to date. I am extremely content, both at work – by 2008 I was dividing my time between the BBC and MUTV, United's own station – and at home. With my partner Mary, who I met in 1990, and our two little girls, eight-year-old Lauren and Eve, who is five, I am happily settled in the north-east, where I was born and brought up. Even when I was in Manchester I used to get back whenever I had the chance, and I always intended to return to Teesside permanently when I retired from the game.

Not that we weren't happy in Wilmslow, which is a lovely town on the doorstep of a fantastic city. We had a wonderful social life there, finding lots of great restaurants and everything else we could have wanted. But both Mary and myself have got close family in the north-east, and that's where it feels like home. Now we live just outside the pretty little market town of Yarm, near Middlesbrough, in a house which we planned and had built to our own requirements. I'd seen a Georgian place that I liked in Hale, just to the south of Manchester, so I stole the idea from there.

Middlesbrough's taken a lot of stick over the years for being an eyesore, and some of the lads at United even called it 'Miserableborough'. That was always a bit harsh, but it was easy to see how the negative image was conjured up because the drive to Ayresome Park in the old days was dominated by a backdrop of the ICI buildings, all unsightly smokestacks and massive cooling towers. Yet what the critics often failed to appreciate was that within five minutes they could be in beautiful countryside, which is where we are now.

In fairness, the area's taken a lot of unwarranted criticism over the years, with stories of some players refusing to go there and others leaving at the earliest opportunity, but I believe it's been a classic case of 'give a dog a bad name'. Whatever, we love it and, certainly for now while the girls are growing up, we wouldn't be anywhere else. As for the long-term future, we'll have to wait and see.

IMPRESSIONS OF PALLY

STEVE BRUCE

I got on well with Pally from the moment he walked in the door at Old Trafford as a record £2.3 million signing. At the time, I knew little about him beyond the fact that he had picked up rave reviews for his displays with Middlesbrough and England, but before long we were mates.

Maybe it helped that we were both from the north-east, which was a decent starting point. One thing I am sure of is that our enduring friendship off the pitch was a massive help to our partnership on it. You just can't beat playing alongside a mate you can really trust, and he certainly fell into that category.

Whatever he was doing, Pally was, and remains, a supremely unruffled character. Nothing ever fazed him, no matter how hectic the situation. He and I were opposites, but I think we complemented each other pretty well. I was the up-and-at-'em type, while he was overwhelmingly laid back. That didn't mean he didn't care – far from it, he had a huge amount of personal pride – but he just couldn't see the point in losing his cool.

On top of that fantastic composure, of course, Pally possessed enormous talent. He had terrific balance, he was a natural ball-player and he was exceptionally quick. Nobody could run away from the big fella.

Meanwhile I was as slow as a carthorse, and was never blessed with his grace on the ball, but our respective attributes must have been pretty well suited, and we played together week-in and week-out for six or seven years at the top level. One season United played 62 games and we didn't miss one. Everybody else had a rest, and we were crying out for a breather, but there was no chance of that for Pally and me.

There was no chance, either, for us to forget the fact that Alex Ferguson had labelled us 'Dolly and Daisy.' It was a back-handed tribute if I ever heard one, and probably no more than a throwaway line. But it stuck, because once Sir Alex makes a statement it tends not to be forgotten. I suppose they weren't the nicknames we would have chosen for ourselves, and we never found out which was supposed to be which, but it gave everybody a good laugh.

Ironically, considering the success that awaited him, Gary experienced a traumatic United debut against Norwich when my old club beat us at

Old Trafford, and some individuals might have crumbled. But he handled it impeccably, and that's what playing for United is all about: coping with the awesome size of the club and the constant pressure that goes with it.

A lot of very fine footballers fall by the wayside because they can't do that. They simply can't stand the intensity, and it's true that the goldfish-bowl existence can be very demanding, with every mistake being monitored and highlighted mercilessly. Pally took some stick for that opening game, but then he showed his strength of character by finishing the season as United's player of the year, which spoke volumes.

How would I describe him away from football? One big, lazy, easy-going … are you getting the message? Of course, he was famed for his sweet tooth, and I can vouch for the fact that he'd nick your kids' sweets if he was desperate enough!

He wasn't averse to a drink, either, and I have a vivid image of him at his first United Christmas party, getting a little mellow, shall we say, on Malibu and pineapple. His choice of drink was the funniest part, and a few eyebrows were raised at this fearsome great centre-half drinking Malibu and pineapple, but he took all the joshing in good part. Really, he couldn't care less.

In more recent years, I have stood back in amazement at Pally's new career on TV. I never thought it would be possible because he always shied away from that side of things when he was a player. But he brings a different and refreshing slant to football punditry; he speaks well and people like to listen to his opinions.

When he first went on the air he was a bag of nerves, but he takes it all in his stride now, and he is impressive on *A Question Of Sport*, too. In fact, he's become a bit of a media mogul, which helps to pay his bills and his green fees.

He and I had great times together during our years in Manchester and we're still good mates today. People in football tend to have plenty of acquaintances but not that many truly close friends. I'm happy to say that I count Pally as one of my closest.

BRYAN ROBSON

It's fair to say that Pally was a pretty relaxed character. In fact, if he was any more laid back then he'd fall asleep. He always loved to sit back, watch TV, play computer games and let the world go by – a lovely lad without an ounce of malice in him.

You might say it's unusual for someone as chilled out as the big fella to be such an out-and-out winner at the highest level, and I've known only a couple of other people who fell into the same category. Both Gary Lineker and Paul McGrath often appeared as if they couldn't care less in training but, just like Pally, they could go out on the pitch when it really mattered and turn on their terrific talent.

When he arrived at Old Trafford in 1989, I didn't know much about him beyond the fact that he'd had a year in the top division with Middlesbrough and that he'd played for England. Gradually, as I worked with him on a regular basis, it became obvious that he was blessed with colossal natural ability, but that he needed to be a bit stronger physically.

Almost immediately he was put on a weights programme, but the coaching staff always had to keep a close eye on him to make sure he was doing it. A bit like Paul McGrath, he was not the best of trainers, but his sheer quality always shone through.

Gary Pallister was a tremendous all-round footballing centre-half. He was fantastic in the air and, for a big lad, he was extremely quick. When he built up his muscles a bit, for quite a few years he was the finest central defender in the Premiership. Unfortunately some of the England coaches didn't fancy him as much as their counterparts at United, and I could never understand why.

Later in his career he suffered with his back, which is why I was able to take him to Middlesbrough for what I thought was the really good price of £2 million in 1998. It's a shame that his condition meant that he had to pack in the game when he did, because with all his talent he could have played on at centre-half until he was 39 or 40.

As a manager I knew I was taking a little bit of a gamble, but it worked well enough for a while as we held our own in the Premiership for a couple of seasons. I needed Pally to replace Nigel Pearson, who'd had to retire earlier than he would have liked with a knee injury, and he proved to be a positive influence on the whole squad.

Yet for all his superb contributions on the pitch, some of my most lasting memories of Pally are away from the action. I'll never forget him at his first club Christmas party after joining United. He wasn't a really big drinker, but he'd been mixing a lot with Clayton Blackmore and Mark Hughes, who both liked a pint, and that day he was a bit the worse for wear. We had to swill him down and revive him a little to make sure he wasn't going to fall asleep at the party in front of all the wives and girlfriends.

This was at a time when Sir Alex was being very strict with his players, which was a really good thing. The general move was away from the British tradition of boozing, more towards the continental custom of being careful with what footballers ate and drank. The manager turned the situation around and the results are there for all to see.

In a way, I suppose Pally represented a bit of a challenge to that policy. On one of his first England trips I roomed with him, and it was quite amusing. I went in and put my stuff in the wardrobe, but he wasn't interested in that. He just threw his bag into the corner and lay down for a rest. Then he pulled out a big carrier bag and tipped out the contents between his bed and mine. There was this big pile of sweets and crisps and chocolate bars and he said: 'Robbo, whenever you want anything, just help yourself.'

Pally was a marvellous footballer and a smashing team-mate. I wish him nothing but the best.

LEE SHARPE

Though it's more than a decade since Gary and I were at Old Trafford together, I still knock around with him; we often have a game of golf, and I think he's funny, a really lovely guy. We have totally different personalities – he's an exceedingly chilled out character, while I'm a bit more active – but we get on really well and have a terrific laugh.

That laid-back nature of his was of colossal value to United's defence, his coolness and composure always evident in the heat of battle, no matter how hectic the action around him.

He never panicked or tried to kick anyone up in the air. He was always a footballer first and foremost, comfortable on the ball, very rarely giving it away and reading the game brilliantly. He was very quick, too, beating most centre-forwards to the ball without having to get into top gear, so that it wasn't often that we saw him at full tilt.

Pally had a wonderful relationship with Steve Bruce, both on and off the pitch, and their understanding meant that we midfielders could push forward without worrying too much about what was going on behind us, one of the most powerful reasons why we won so many titles and cups.

He could hold his own with nippy, skilful attackers or with big, aggressive dominators such as John Fashanu. He was the best central defender in the land, without a shadow of a doubt, and I could never understand why he didn't play more frequently for England.

Back in our playing days, at one point we both bought electric guitars and we were going to have a competition to see who would learn to play first. In the end, neither of us won because we both gave up after only a couple of lessons, which was a shame. Learning any musical instrument is a slow, painstaking process, and I'm afraid neither of us had the necessary patience.

Often we used to go on holiday together – Gary and Mary, myself and my girlfriend at the time – which made sense because Gary and Mary weren't keen on flying. At one point, they'd only book a holiday if they knew we were going, because once they'd made an agreement with us they didn't like to let us down.

On some of those trips, particularly to Portugal, we would meet a few other footballers and occasionally we might while away most of the night with a few drinks. Invariably we put the others to shame, because while they tended to end up under the table, Gary and I were usually out on the golf course the next morning, bright as buttons.

Both of us used to enjoy the Manchester United team meetings, too, referred to by Pally earlier in the book. They contributed a lot to team spirit – at least, that was our story! We all socialised as friends and became so close that we were always ready to run that extra yard to help our mates. The camaraderie was absolutely fantastic.

If someone called a team meeting, then everybody went to it, from skipper Bryan Robson all the way down to young lads like myself and some of the reserves.

Pally threw himself into that scene with unbridled enthusiasm. Once he'd been at United for a couple of seasons, he was seen as one of the older hands with the responsibility of looking after we impressionable youngsters. I must say he took those social responsibilities extremely seriously. Even if he had to stay up all night, he'd do it without the trace of a complaint, setting the perfect example to us all …

TERRY VENABLES

I selected Gary Pallister eight times for England, and I wish I could have picked him more often, but he suffered from back problems which limited his availability for internationals.

He was such a natural footballer, an impeccable all-round defender. In the air he was as impressive as anyone in the land, his use of the ball was extremely neat and tidy for such a big guy, and he was quick.

I played Gary alongside Tony Adams, which surprised some people because they were both tall lads. Most coaches like to use a smaller, quicker fellow around the big one, but they both read the game so beautifully and played so intelligently that there was never the slightest problem.

Tony was an outstanding performer, but I wouldn't have been afraid to play Gary alongside his clubmate, Steve Bruce, who was very unfortunate never to win a cap somewhere along the line. In fact, I did actually choose Steve for a place on the bench in one of the Umbro International Trophy games in the summer of 1995, but he decided to have an operation he was needing – or maybe his manager made that decision! – and he missed out, which was a shame.

As a character, Gary was a delight to be around. He has a terrific sense of humour and can be a very funny guy.

When our paths crossed again at Middlesbrough I counted myself as unlucky that his back ruled him out of the picture, because he would have been invaluable in our fight to get out of relegation trouble.

Still, it was always good to have him around the place because he was such a respected player and such tremendous company. I wish him nothing but the best for the future.

TONY MOWBRAY

When Pally first arrived at Ayresome park he was a classic beanpole. As you can tell from glancing at the old photographs, he was spindly, to put it kindly. There was no real co-ordination to his movements, he hadn't really grown into his body, he was like a young colt – but the raw talent was obvious for all to see.

As time went on he improved in all respects; and more and more he believed in himself, in his heading ability and in his ball skills. Then, when the pace and power developed, he really was some centre-half.

It was a pleasure to play alongside him and I think we complemented each other, particularly in our personalities. While he was on the quiet side to start with, I tended to be more forceful with a loud voice, and as I was a little bit older I had some knowledge and experience that might have been of some use to him.

Understandably, to begin with Pally wasn't quite sure of his place in the club pecking order. Once you move into any football dressing room, with all the banter and mickey-taking, you either sink or swim. He latched on to it very quickly and became an exceedingly strong personality in our dressing room as the years went by and his confidence continued to grow.

He developed a terrific friendship with Bernie Slaven, and I like to think with myself, too, as well as other players who were around, such as Colin Cooper, Gary Parkinson, Gary Hamilton, Stuart Ripley and the rest. It was a truly exciting time at Middlesbrough for a young team which was taking the club back from the brink of financial disaster.

It's always difficult to tell how far any individual might go in the game, no matter how gifted he might be, but after one performance Pally gave for 'Boro against Wimbledon I had no doubts about him. He was facing the fearsome John Fashanu, written up in the press as a beast of a man, but that day Pally out-jumped him, out-ran him, out-muscled him, out-thought him and out-skilled him. Everything he had was better than Fashanu, and I knew then that he could go all the way.

If you reach the stage where you have all those attributes as a footballer, you can only stop yourself from reaching the summit by becoming sidetracked by other things in life. Pally proved he had the drive and the application to make it, and I think joining Manchester United helped him to achieve his full potential because of the quality of the manager and the players around him at Old Trafford.

One telling memory I have of our days together at Middlesbrough is his reaction when we both received our sponsored cars. I got a sparkling black XRiii, which was the smart car at that time, and Pally got a little Citroen. Oh, he wasn't happy about that!

Now I think that maybe one of the reasons he went on to achieve so much was that he wanted to show people who doubted him just how wrong they were. Everybody needs a driving force in life and maybe the image of that white Citroen stuck in his mind, so that he concentrated that little bit harder when his next international came round, or he was playing in a cup final, or scoring the goal to cement another championship.

Whatever, he went on to a fantastic career, and no one could have deserved it more.

BERNIE SLAVEN

It's strange to think about it now, but Pally and I didn't hit it off straight away. When I first arrived at Middlesbrough, he was just starting at the club, too, and he was just a raw young lad who wasn't very talkative. On our first coach trip together, travelling away to Grimsby, I looked across at him, neither of us said much and I thought: 'I don't like this guy.'

A few week later he went to Darlington on loan and I thought: 'Thank God I've seen the back of him!' But when he came back to Ayresome Park, gradually I got to know him properly and we became the best of mates.

He turned out to be a pretty placid character, almost always very cool and calm. It takes a lot to stir him up, though when something does trigger him and he loses his rag, then he loses it big time.

I thought it was going to happen once with Bruce Rioch when, after a cup game in which we hadn't been brilliant, the manager went to Pally and told him: 'You've got your head in the clouds, son. If you want a fight, let's go outside.' Just for a second I thought it was going to happen and I was right behind Pally shaking my head, going 'No, no.' I knew that if he went outside then I'd have to go with him, and I didn't fancy it! Happily it wasn't necessary.

Rioch was a great motivator, good for me as an individual, but Pally needed a different type of treatment. I came from Glasgow where the basic idea was that if you trained hard then you played well. But Pally killed that theory for me. He didn't have to train, he just went out and played. I think he'd admit that he was the world's worst trainer – well, he ought to anyway – but amazingly, when the game started, he was the top man.

At Middlesbrough he lined up alongside Tony Mowbray, and a lot of people would have it that Tony was the better player. Well, it's true that Mowbray was marvellous, but he was a different type altogether.

Pally was composed, with lovely control on the ball. His distribution was excellent, he could beat a man, he was a tremendous defender who could head the ball superbly, and he was very quick, too. I used to run with him in training, and while he couldn't get near me on the long runs, on the short ones I needed to jump in a car to keep up with him.

Tony complemented him perfectly, as did Steve Bruce at Manchester United. Despite being such a big fella, Pally was never the bravest and he needed to play with someone who was the opposite. There were some situations where he wouldn't put his head in, while Mowbray and Bruce would stick theirs into places where Pally wouldn't even risk his boot.

He was always more the classical footballer, something like Alan Hansen, and I always reckoned he was destined for bigger and better things.

When he did move on to Manchester, though, it wasn't easy at first. When he made his United debut against Norwich at Old Trafford he invited my father and myself down to watch, I suppose because he was used to our company and felt that would help to calm his nerves.

Before the game he drove to Old Trafford and we followed in my car, so I saw him arrive at the ground, where hardly anybody recognised him even though there were loads of fans milling around.

As it turned out he had a bad first game, costing the team a goal, and on my way out a couple of United fans shouted at me: 'Slaven, you can take your mate back to Teesside.'

Wouldn't I have loved to have met those guys again a few years later after Pally had helped to win so many trophies! Everybody needs time to adjust to a new club, and when he did he was magnificent, one of the finest centre-halves I've ever seen.

GARY PALLISTER
CLUB STATISTICS (16 SEASONS)

1985/86

MIDDLESBROUGH
21st in Division 2
Manager: Willie Maddren
League: 28 games, 0 goals
FA Cup: 1 game, 0 goals
League Cup: 1 game, 0 goals
Total: 30 games, 0 goals

LEAGUE

	Appearances	Goals
Peter Beagrie	21 (4)	1
Mitchell Cook	3 (3)	0
Colin Cooper	9 (2)	0
Steve Corden	1	0
David Currie	21 (5)	4
Gary Gill	9	0
Gary Hamilton	33	4
Tim Heard	25	2
Alan Kernaghan	2 (4)	0
Phil Kite	2	0
Brian Laws	42	2
Tony McAndrew	34	2
Charlie McManus	2	0
Tony Mowbray	35	4
Irving Nattrass	19	0
Donal O'Riordan	41	2
Gary Pallister	28	0
Steve Pears	38	0
Stuart Ripley	7 (1)	0
Alan Roberts	1	0
Gary Rowell	27	10
Bernie Slaven	32	8
Archie Stephens	26 (2)	4
Lee Turnbull	1 (1)	0
Paul Ward	3	0

1985/86

DARLINGTON
on loan
13th in Division 3
Manager: Cyril Knowles
League: 7 games, 0 goals
Total: 7 games, 0 goals

LEAGUE

	Appearances	Goals
Carl Airey	31 (3)	12
Graeme Aldred	11 (5)	0
Mike Astbury	14	0
Fred Barber	32	0
Steve Carney	10 (2)	0
Mitchell Cook	3	1
John Douglas	3	0
Chris Evans	33	0
Mark Forster	1	0
John Green	30	1
Garry Haire	3 (3)	0
John Huntley	5 (1)	0
Philip Lloyd	29	0
Gary MacDonald	35 (1)	16
David McLean	37 (1)	9
Gary Morgan	41	1
Clive Nattress	1	0
Gary Pallister	7	0
Malcolm Poskett	18 (3)	4
Alan Roberts	38	4
Peter Robinson	29	1
Mike Sanderson	1	0
Ricky Sbragia	6	0
Phil Shute	2	0
Steve Tupling	38 (2)	4
Paul Ward	35	2
David Woodcock	13 (10)	2

1986/87

MIDDLESBROUGH
2nd in Division 3
Manager: Bruce Rioch
League: 44 games, 1 goal
FA Cup: 3 games, 0 goals
League Cup: 3 games, 0 goals
Total: 50 games 1 goal

	LEAGUE	
	Appearances	Goals
Colin Cooper	46	0
Ron Coyle	1 (2)	0
Gary Gill	33 (3)	2
Gary Hamilton	41 (2)	7
David Hodgson	2	0
Alan Kernaghan	10 (3)	0
Paul Kerr	20	0
Brian Laws	26	8
Tony Mowbray	46	7
Gary Pallister	44	1
Gary Parkinson	46	0
Steve Pears	46	0
Paul Proudlock	2 (1)	1
Stuart Ripley	43 (1)	4
Gary Rowell	0	0
Bernie Slaven	46	17
Steve Spriggs	3	0
Archie Stephens	44	16
Lee Turnbull	7 (7)	4

1987/88

MIDDLESBROUGH
3rd in Division 2
Manager: Bruce Rioch
League: 44 games, 3 goals
League play-offs: 4 games, 0 goals
FA Cup: 5 games, 1 goal
League Cup: 4 games, 0 goals
Total: 57 games, 4 goals

LEAGUE

	Appearances	Goals
Mark Burke	8 (8)	0
Colin Cooper	43	2
Gary Gill	2 (1)	0
Dean Glover	36 (2)	4
Gary Hamilton	40 (1)	6
Alan Kernaghan	24 (11)	6
Paul Kerr	43 (1)	5
Brian Laws	24 (5)	1
Tony Mowbray	44	3
Gary Pallister	44	3
Gary Parkinson	35 (3)	0
Steve Pears	43	0
Kevin Poole	1	0
Pat Proudlock	0 (1)	0
Stuart Ripley	40 (3)	8
Trevor Senior	5 (1)	2
Bernie Slaven	44	21
Archie Stephens	8 (3)	2

1988/89

MIDDLESBROUGH

18th in Division 1
Manager: Bruce Rioch
League: 37 games, 1 goal
FA Cup: 1 game, 0 goals
League Cup: 2 games, 0 goals
Total: 40 games, 1 goal

LEAGUE

	Appearances	Goals
Mark Barham	3 (1)	0
Mark Brennan	25	3
Mark Burke	21 (8)	5
Colin Cooper	35	2
Peter Davenport	23 (1)	4
Gary Gill	6 (2)	0
Dean Glover	8 (4)	1
Gary Hamilton	35 (1)	4
Alan Kernaghan	5 (18)	0
Paul Kerr	18 (2)	1
Nicky Mohan	5 (1)	0
Tony Mowbray	37	3
Gary Pallister	37	1
Gary Parkinson	36	2
Steve Pears	26	0
Kevin Poole	12	0
Mark Proctor	10	0
Pat Proudlock	0 (1)	0
Stuart Ripley	36	3
Trevor Senior	4	0
Bernie Slaven	36 (1)	15

1989/90

MIDDLESBROUGH
21st in Division 2
Manager: Bruce Rioch/Colin Todd
League: 3 apps, 0 goals
Total: 3 apps, 0 goals

LEAGUE

	Appearances	Goals
Ian Baird	19	5
Mark Brennan	36 (4)	3
Mark Burke	3 (9)	1
Simon Coleman	33 (3)	1
Alan Comfort	15	2
Colin Cooper	18 (3)	2
Peter Davenport	30 (5)	3
Gary Gill	1	0
Alan Kernaghan	34 (3)	4
Paul Kerr	13 (4)	1
Owen McGee	12 (1)	0
Nicky Mohan	21 (1)	0
Tony Mowbray	28	2
Gary Pallister	3	0
Gary Parkinson	40 (1)	2
Steve Pears	25	0
Jimmy Phillips	12	0
Kevin Poole	21	0
Mark Proctor	45	4
Trevor Putney	25	0
Stuart Ripley	26 (13)	1
Bernie Slaven	46	21

1989/90

MANCHESTER UNITED
13th in Division 1
Manager Alex Ferguson
League: 35 games, 3 goals
FA Cup: 8 games, 0 goals
League Cup: 3 games, 0 goals
Total: 46 games, 3 goals

LEAGUE

	Appearances	Goals
Viv Anderson	14 (2)	0
Russell Beardsmore	8 (13)	2
Clayton Blackmore	19 (9)	2
Mark Bosnich	1	0
Derek Brazil	0 (1)	0
Steve Bruce	34	3
Mal Donaghy	13 (1)	0
Mike Duxbury	12 (7)	0
Colin Gibson	5 (1)	1
Deiniol Graham	0 (1)	0
Mark Hughes	36 (1)	13
Paul Ince	25 (1)	0
Jim Leighton	35	0
Brian McClair	37	5
Giuliano Maiorana	0 (1)	0
Lee Martin	28 (4)	0
Ralph Milne	0 (1)	0
Gary Pallister	35	3
Mike Phelan	38	1
Mark Robins	10 (7)	7
Bryan Robson	20	2
Les Sealey	2	0
Lee Sharpe	13 (5)	1
Danny Wallace	23 (3)	3
Neil Webb	10 (1)	2

1990/91

MANCHESTER UNITED
6th in Division 1
Manager: Alex Ferguson
League: 36 games 0 goals
FA Cup: 3 games, 0 goals
League Cup: 9 games, 0 goals
Europe: 9 games, 1 goal
Charity Shield: 1 game, 0 goals
Total: 58 games, 1 goal

LEAGUE

	Appearances	Goals
Viv Anderson	1	0
Russell Beardsmore	5 (7)	0
Clayton Blackmore	35	4
Mark Bosnich	2	0
Steve Bruce	31	13
Mal Donaghy	17 (8)	0
Darren Ferguson	2 (3)	0
Ryan Giggs	1 (1)	1
Mark Hughes	29 (2)	10
Paul Ince	31	3
Denis Irwin	33 (1)	0
Andrei Kanchelskis	1	0
Brian McClair	34 (2)	13
Lee Martin	7 (7)	0
Gary Pallister	36	0
Mike Phelan	30 (3)	1
Mark Robins	7 (12)	4
Bryan Robson	15 (2)	1
Les Sealey	31	0
Lee Sharpe	20 (3)	2
Danny Wallace	13 (6)	3
Gary Walsh	5	0
Neil Webb	31 (1)	3
Neil Whitworth	1	0
Paul Wratten	0 (2)	0

1991/92

MANCHESTER UNITED
2nd in Division 1
Manager: Alex Ferguson
League: 37 (3) games, 1 goal
FA Cup: 3 games, 0 goals
League Cup: 8 games, 0 goals
Europe: 3 (1) games, 0 goals
Super Cup: 1 game, 0 goals
Total: 52 (4) games, 1 goal

PFA Footballer of the Year for 1992

LEAGUE

	Appearances	Goals
Clayton Blackmore	19 (14)	3
Steve Bruce	37	5
Mal Donaghy	16 (4)	0
Darren Ferguson	2 (2)	0
Ryan Giggs	32 (6)	4
Mark Hughes	38 (1)	11
Paul Ince	31 (2)	3
Denis Irwin	37 (1)	4
Andrei Kanchelskis	28 (6)	5
Brian McClair	41 (1)	18
Lee Martin	0 (1)	0
Gary Pallister	37 (3)	1
Paul Parker	24 (2)	0
Mike Phelan	14 (4)	0
Mark Robins	1 (1)	0
Bryan Robson	26 (1)	4
Peter Schmeichel	40	0
Lee Sharpe	8 (6)	1
Gary Walsh	2	0
Neil Webb	29 (2)	3

1992/93

MANCHESTER UNITED
1st in Premier League
Manager: Alex Ferguson
League: 42 games, 1 goal
FA Cup: 3 games, 0 goals
League Cup: 3 games, 0 goals
Europe: 2 games, 0 goals
Total: 50 games, 1 goal

LEAGUE

	Appearances	Goals
Clayton Blackmore	12 (2)	0
Steve Bruce	42	5
Nicky Butt	0 (1)	0
Eric Cantona	21 (1)	1
Dion Dublin	3 (4)	1
Darren Ferguson	15	0
Ryan Giggs	40 (1)	9
Mark Hughes	41	15
Paul Ince	41	6
Denis Irwin	40	5
Andrei Kanchelskis	14 (13)	3
Brian McClair	41 (1)	9
Gary Pallister	42	1
Paul Parker	31	1
Mike Phelan	5 (6)	0
Bryan Robson	5 (9)	1
Peter Schmeichel	42	0
Lee Sharpe	27	1
Danny Wallace	0 (2)	0
Neil Webb	0 (1)	0

1993/94

MANCHESTER UNITED
1st in Premiership
Manager: Alex Ferguson
League: 41 games, 1 goal
FA Cup: 7 games, 0 goals
League Cup: 9 games, 0 goals
Europe: 3 games, 0 goals
Charity Shield: 1 game, 0 goals
Total: 61 games, 1 goal

LEAGUE

	Appearances	Goals
Steve Bruce	41	3
Nicky Butt	0 (1)	0
Eric Cantona	34	18
Dion Dublin	1 (4)	1
Darren Ferguson	1 (2)	0
Ryan Giggs	32 (6)	13
Mark Hughes	36	12
Paul Ince	39	8
Denis Irwin	42	2
Andrei Kanchelskis	28 (3)	6
Roy Keane	34 (3)	5
Brian McClair	12 (14)	1
Colin McKee	1	0
Lee Martin	1	0
Gary Neville	1	0
Gary Pallister	41	1
Paul Parker	39 (1)	0
Mike Phelan	1 (1)	0
Bryan Robson	10 (5)	1
Peter Schmeichel	40	0
Lee Sharpe	26 (4)	9
Ben Thornley	0 (1)	0
Gary Walsh	2 (1)	0

1994/95

MANCHESTER UNITED
2nd in Premiership
Manager: Alex Ferguson
League: 42 games, 2 goals
FA Cup: 7 games, 2 goals
League Cup: 2 games, 0 goals
Europe: 6 games, 0 goals
Charity Shield: 1 game, 0 goals
Total: 58 games, 4 goals

LEAGUE

	Appearances	Goals
David Beckham	2 (2)	0
Steve Bruce	35	2
Nicky Butt	11 (11)	1
Eric Cantona	21	12
Andy Cole	17 (1)	12
Simon Davies	3 (2)	0
Ryan Giggs	29	1
Keith Gillespie	3 (6)	1
Mark Hughes	33 (1)	8
Paul Ince	36	5
Denis Irwin	40	2
Andrei Kanchelskis	25 (5)	14
Roy Keane	23 (2)	2
Brian McClair	35 (5)	5
David May	15 (4)	2
Gary Neville	16 (2)	0
Phil Neville	1 (1)	0
Gary Pallister	42	2
Paul Parker	1 (1)	0
Kevin Pilkington	0 (1)	0
Peter Schmeichel	32	0
Paul Scholes	6 (11)	5
Lee Sharpe	26 (2)	3
Gary Walsh	10	0

1995/96

MANCHESTER UNITED
1st in Premiership
Manager: Alex Ferguson
League: 21 games, 1 goal
FA Cup: 3 games, 0 goals
League Cup: 2 games, 0 goals
Europe: 2 games, 0 goals
Total: 28 games, 1 goal

LEAGUE

	Appearances	Goals
David Beckham	26 (7)	7
Eric Cantona	30	14
Andy Cole	32 (2)	11
Terry Cooke	1 (3)	0
Simon Davies	1 (5)	0
Steve Bruce	30	1
Nicky Butt	31 (1)	2
Ryan Giggs	30 (3)	11
Denis Irwin	31	1
Roy Keane	29	6
Brian McClair	12 (10)	3
David May	11 (5)	1
Gary Neville	30 (1)	0
Phil Neville	21 (3)	0
John O'Kane	0 (1)	0
Gary Pallister	21	1
Paul Parker	5 (1)	0
Kevin Pilkington	2 (1)	0
William Prunier	2	0
Peter Schmeichel	36	0
Paul Scholes	16 (10)	10
Lee Sharpe	21 (10)	4
Ben Thornley	0 (1)	0

1996/97

MANCHESTER UNITED
1st in Premiership
Manager: Alex Ferguson
League: 27 games, 3 goals
FA Cup: 1 game, 0 goals
Europe: 8 games, 0 goals
Charity Shield: 1 game, 0 goals
Total: 37 games, 3 goals

LEAGUE

	Appearances	Goals
David Beckham	33 (3)	8
Nicky Butt	24 (2)	5
Eric Cantona	36	11
Chris Casper	0 (2)	0
Michael Clegg	3 (1)	0
Andy Cole	10 (10)	6
Jordi Cruyff	11 (5)	3
Ryan Giggs	25 (1)	3
Denis Irwin	29 (2)	1
Ronny Johnsen	26 (5)	0
Roy Keane	21	2
Brian McClair	4 (15)	0
David May	28 (1)	3
Gary Neville	30 (1)	1
Phil Neville	15 (3)	0
John O'Kane	1	0
Gary Pallister	27	3
Karel Poborsky	15 (7)	3
Peter Schmeichel	36	0
Paul Scholes	16 (8)	3
Ole Gunnar Solskjaer	25 (8)	18
Ben Thornley	1 (1)	0
Raimond van der Gouw	2	0

1997/98

MANCHESTER UNITED
2nd in Premiership
Manager: Alex Ferguson
League: 33 games, 0 goals
FA Cup: 3 games, 0 goals
Europe: 6 games, 0 goals
Charity Shield: 1 game, 0 goals
Total: 43 games, 0 goals

LEAGUE

	Appearances	Goals
David Beckham	34 (3)	9
Henning Berg	23 (4)	1
Wesley Brown	1 (1)	0
Nicky Butt	31 (2)	3
Andy Cole	31 (2)	15
Michael Clegg	1 (2)	0
John Curtis	3 (5)	0
Jordi Cruyff	3 (2)	0
Ryan Giggs	28 (1)	8
Danny Higginbotham	0 (1)	0
Denis Irwin	23 (2)	2
Ronny Johnsen	18 (4)	2
Roy Keane	9	2
Brian McClair	2 (11)	0
David May	7 (2)	0
Phil Mulryne	1	0
Gary Neville	34	0
Phil Neville	24 (6)	1
Erik Nevland	0 (1)	0
Gary Pallister	33	0
Kevin Pilkington	2	0
Karel Poborsky	3 (7)	2
Peter Schmeichel	32	0
Paul Scholes	28 (3)	8
Teddy Sheringham	28 (3)	9
Ole Gunnar Solskjaer	15 (7)	6
Ben Thornley	0 (5)	0
Raimond van der Gouw	4 (1)	0
Ronnie Wallwork	0 (1)	0

1998/99

MIDDLESBROUGH
9th in Premiership
Manager: Bryan Robson
League: 26 games, 0 goals
FA Cup: 1 game, 0 goals
Total: 27 games, 0 goals

LEAGUE

	Appearances	Goals
Alun Armstrong	0 (6)	1
Steve Baker	1 (1)	0
Mikkel Beck	13 (14)	5
Marlon Beresford	4	0
Marco Branca	0 (1)	0
Andy Campbell	1 (7)	0
Colin Cooper	31 (1)	1
Michael Cummins	1	0
Brian Deane	24 (2)	6
Gianluca Festa	25	2
Curtis Fleming	12 (2)	1
Paul Gascoigne	25 (1)	3
Jason Gavin	2	0
Dean Gordon	38	3
Craig Harrison	3 (1)	0
Vladimir Kinder	0 (5)	2
Neil Maddison	10 (11)	0
Paul Merson	3	0
Alan Moore	3 (1)	0
Robbie Mustoe	32 (1)	4
Keith O'Neill	4 (2)	0
Gary Pallister	26	0
Hamilton Ricard	32 (4)	15
Mark Schwarzer	34	0
Phil Stamp	5 (11)	2
Robbie Stockdale	17 (2)	0
Mark Summerbell	7 (4)	0
Andy Townsend	35	1
Steve Vickers	30 (1)	1

1999/2000

MIDDLESBROUGH
12th in Premiership
Manager: Bryan Robson
League: 21 games, 1 goal
FA Cup: 1 game, 0 goals
League Cup: 3 games, 0 goals
Total: 25 games, 1 goal

LEAGUE

	Appearances	Goals
Alun Armstrong	3 (9)	1
Marlon Beresford	1	0
Andy Campbell	16 (9)	4
Colin Cooper	26	0
Michael Cummins	0 (1)	0
Brian Deane	29	8
Gianluca Festa	27 (2)	2
Curtis Fleming	27	0
Paul Gascoigne	7 (1)	1
Jason Gavin	2 (4)	0
Dean Gordon	3 (1)	0
Paul Ince	32	3
Juninho	24 (4)	1
Sean Kilgannon	0 (1)	0
Neil Maddison	6 (7)	0
Carlos Marinelli	0 (2)	0
Robbie Mustoe	18 (10)	0
Keith O'Neill	14 (2)	0
Tony Ormerod	0 (1)	0
Gary Pallister	21	1
Hamilton Ricard	28 (6)	13
Mark Schwarzer	37	0
Phil Stamp	13 (3)	0
Robbie Stockdale	6 (5)	1
Mark Summerbell	16 (3)	0
Andy Townsend	3 (2)	0
Steve Vickers	30 (2)	0
Christian Ziege	29	6

2000/01

MIDDLESBROUGH
14th in Premiership
Manager: Bryan Robson
League: 8 games, 0 goals
League Cup: 1 game, 0 goals
Total: 9 games, 0 goals

LEAGUE

	Appearances	Goals
Marlon Beresford	0 (1)	0
Alen Boksic	26 (2)	12
Andy Campbell	5 (2)	0
Colin Cooper	26 (1)	2
Mark Crossley	4 (1)	0
Brian Deane	13 (12)	2
Ugo Ehiogu	21	3
Gianluca Festa	21 (4)	2
Curtis Fleming	29 (1)	0
Jason Gavin	10 (4)	0
Dean Gordon	12 (8)	1
Mark Hudson	0 (3)	0
Paul Ince	30	2
Joseph Desire Job	8 (5)	3
Christian Karembeu	31 (2)	4
Carlos Marinelli	2 (11)	0
Robbie Mustoe	13 (12)	0
Paul Okon	23 (1)	0
Keith O'Neill	14 (1)	0
Gary Pallister	8	0
Hamilton Ricard	22 (5)	4
Mark Schwarzer	31	0
Phil Stamp	11 (8)	1
Mark Summerbell	5 (2)	1
Steve Vickers	29 (1)	0
Gary Walsh	3	0
Noel Whelan	13 (14)	1
Dean Windass	8	2

GARY'S TOTALS

MIDDLESBROUGH
League: 211 games, 6 goals
League Play-Offs: 4 games, 0 goals
FA Cup: 12 games, 1 goal
League Cup: 14 games, 0 goals
Total: 241 games, 7 goals

DARLINGTON
League: 7 games, 0 goals
Total: 7 games, 0 goals

MANCHESTER UNITED
League: 314 (3) games, 12 goals
FA Cup: 38 games, 2 goals
League Cup: 36 games, 0 goals
Europe: 39 (1) games, 1 goal
Super Cup: 1 game, 0 goals
Charity Shield: 5 games, 0 goals
Total: 433 (4) games, 15 goals

OVERALL
League: 532 (3) games, 18 goals
League Play-Offs: 4 games, 0 goals
FA Cup: 50 games, 3 goals
League Cup: 50 games, 0 goals
Europe: 39 (1) games, 1 goal
Super Cup: 1 game, 0 goals
Charity Shield: 5 games, 0 goals
Total: 681 (4) games, 22 goals

GARY PALLISTER'S INTERNATIONALS

(Played in 22 out of 97 England games between April 1988 and October 1996; first two as a 'Boro player, the rest while at Manchester United).

1. Friendly. 27 April 1988 v Hungary in Budapest: 0-0.
Manager: Bobby Robson. **Team**: Chris Woods, Viv Anderson, Tony Adams, Gary Pallister, Stuart Pearce, Trevor Steven, Steve McMahon, Bryan Robson, Chris Waddle, Peter Beardsley, Gary Lineker. **Subs used**: Gary Stevens for Pearce, Glenn Hoddle for Waddle, Mark Hateley for Beardsley, Tony Cottee for Lineker.

Missed eight, including Euro '88.

2. Friendly. 16 November 1988 v Saudi Arabia in Riyadh: 1-1 (Adams).
Manager: Bobby Robson. **Team**: David Seaman, Mel Sterland, Tony Adams, Gary Pallister, Stuart Pearce, David Rocastle, Michael Thomas, Bryan Robson, Chris Waddle, Peter Beardsley, Gary Lineker. **Subs used**: Paul Gascoigne for Thomas, Brian Marwood for Waddle, Alan Smith for Beardsley.

Missed 26, including World Cup '90.

3. Friendly. 6 February 1991 v Cameroon at Wembley: 2-0 (Lineker 2).
Manager: Graham Taylor. **Team**: David Seaman, Lee Dixon, Mark Wright, Des Walker, Stuart Pearce, Trevor Steven, Paul Gascoigne, Bryan Robson, John Barnes, Ian Wright, Gary Lineker. **Subs used**: Gary Pallister for Robson, Steve Hodge for Gascoigne.

Missed one.

4. ECQ. 1 May 1991 v Turkey in Izmir: 1-0 (Wise).
Manager: Graham Taylor. **Team**: David Seaman, Lee Dixon, Gary Pallister, Des Walker, Stuart Pearce, Dennis Wise, Geoff Thomas, David Platt, John Barnes, Ian Smith, Gary Lineker. **Sub used**: Steve Hodge for Thomas.

Missed six.

5. Friendly. 11 September 1991 v Germany at Wembley: 0-1.
Manager: Graham Taylor. **Team**: Chris Woods, Lee Dixon, Paul Parker, Gary Pallister, Tony Dorigo, Trevor Steven, David Batty, David Platt, John Salako, Alan Smith, Gary Lineker. **Subs used**: Paul Merson for Steven, Paul Stewart for Salako.

Missed 19, including Euro '92.

6. WCQ. 2 June 1993 v Norway in Oslo: 0-2.
Manager: Graham Taylor. **Team**: Chris Woods, Lee Dixon, Gary Pallister, Tony Adams, Des Walker, Lee Sharpe, Carlton Palmer, Paul Gascoigne, David Platt, Teddy Sheringham, Les Ferdinand. **Sub used**: Ian Wright for Sheringham.

7. US Cup. 9 June 1993 v USA in Boston: 0-2.
Manager: Graham Taylor. **Team**: Chris Woods, Lee Dixon, Gary Pallister, Carlton Palmer, Tony Dorigo, David Batty, Paul Ince, John Barnes, Lee Sharpe, Nigel Clough, Les Ferdinand. **Subs used**: Des Walker for Palmer, Ian Wright for Ferdinand.

8. US Cup. 13 June 1993 v Brazil in Washington: 1-1 (Platt).
Manager: Graham Taylor. **Team**: Tim Flowers, Earl Barrett, Gary Pallister, Des Walker, Tony Dorigo, Andy Sinton, David Batty, Paul Ince, Lee Sharpe, Nigel Clough, Ian Wright. **Subs used**: David Platt for Batty, Carlton Palmer for Ince, Paul Merson for Clough.

9. US Cup. 19 June 1993 v Germany in Detroit: 1-2 (Platt).
Manager: Graham Taylor. **Team**: Nigel Martyn, Earl Barrett, Gary Pallister, Des Walker, Lee Sharpe, Andy Sinton, David Platt, Paul Ince, Paul Merson, Nigel Clough, John Barnes. **Subs used**: Martin Keown for Pallister, Nigel Winterburn for Sharpe, Ian Wright for Clough.

10. WCQ. 8 September 1993 v Poland at Wembley:
3-0 (Ferdinand, Gascoigne, Pearce).
Manager: Graham Taylor. **Team**: David Seaman, Rob Jones, Tony Adams, Gary Pallister, Stuart Pearce, David Platt, Paul Gascoigne, Paul Ince, Lee Sharpe, Les Ferdinand, Ian Wright.

11. WCQ. 13 October 1993 v Holland in Rotterdam: 0-2.
Manager: Graham Taylor. **Team**: David Seaman, Paul Parker, Tony Adams, Gary Pallister, Tony Dorigo, Carlton Palmer, Paul Ince, David Platt, Lee Sharpe, Paul Merson, Alan Shearer. **Subs used**: Andy Sinton for Palmer, Ian Wright for Merson.

12. WCQ. 17 November 1993 v San Marino in Bologna:
7-1 (Ince 2, Wright 4, Ferdinand).
Manager: Graham Taylor. **Team**: David Seaman, Lee Dixon, Gary Pallister, Des Walker, Stuart Pearce, Stuart Ripley, Paul Ince, David Platt, Andy Sinton, Les Ferdinand, Ian Wright.

13. Friendly. 9 March 1994 v Denmark at Wembley: 1-0 (Platt).
Manager: Terry Venables. **Team**: David Seaman, Paul Parker, Tony Adams, Gary Pallister, Graeme Le Saux, Darren Anderton, Paul Ince, Paul Gascoigne, David Platt, Peter Beardsley, Alan Shearer. **Subs used**: David Batty for Ince, Matthew Le Tissier for Gascoigne.

Missed two.

14. Friendly. 7 September 1994 v USA at Wembley: 2-0 (Shearer 2).
Manager: Terry Venables. **Team**: David Seaman, Rob Jones, Tony Adams, Gary
Pallister, Graeme Le Saux, Darren Anderton, Barry Venison, David Platt, John
Barnes, Teddy Sheringham, Alan Shearer. **Subs used**: Les Ferdinand for
Sheringham, Ian Wright for Shearer.

15. Friendly. 12 October 1994 v Romania at Wembley: 1-1: (Lee).
Manager: Terry Venables. **Team**: David Seaman, Rob Jones, Tony Adams, Gary
Pallister, Graeme Le Saux, Rob Lee, Paul Ince, Matthew Le Tissier, John Barnes, Ian
Wright, Alan Shearer. **Subs used**: Stuart Pearce for Jones, Dennis Wise for Lee, Teddy
Sheringham for Wright.

Missed one.

16. Friendly. 15 February 1995 v Republic of Ireland at Lansdowne Road:
0-1. (Abandoned due to crowd trouble)
Manager: Terry Venables. **Team**: David Seaman, Warren Barton, Tony Adams,
Gary Pallister, Graeme Le Saux, Darren Anderton, Paul Ince, David Platt,
Matthew Le Tissier, Peter Beardsley, Alan Shearer.

17. Friendly. 29 March 1995 v Uruguay at Wembley: 0-0.
Manager: Terry Venables. **Team**: Tim Flowers, Rob Jones, Tony Adams, Gary
Pallister, Graeme Le Saux, Darren Anderton, Barry Venison, David Platt, John
Barnes, Peter Beardsley, Teddy Sheringham. **Subs used**: Steve McManaman for
Le Saux, Nick Barmby for Beardsley, Andy Cole for Sheringham.

Missed one.

18. Umbro. 8 June 1995 v Sweden at Elland Road:
3-3 (Sheringham, Platt, Anderton).
Manager: Terry Venables. **Team**: Tim Flowers, Warren Barton, Colin Cooper, Gary
Pallister, Graeme Le Saux, Darren Anderton, David Platt, Peter Beardsley, John
Barnes, Teddy Sheringham, Alan Shearer. **Subs used**: John Scales for Pallister,
Nick Barmby for Beardsley, Paul Gascoigne for Barnes.

Missed two.

19. Friendly. 11 October 1995 v Norway in Oslo: 0-0.
Manager: Terry Venables. **Team**: David Seaman, Gary Neville, Tony Adams, Gary
Pallister, Stuart Pearce, Rob Lee, Dennis Wise, Jamie Redknapp, Steve McManaman,
Nick Barmby, Alan Shearer. **Subs used**: Steve Stone for Wise, Teddy Sheringham
for Barmby.

20. Friendly. 15 November 1995 v Switzerland at Wembley:
3-1 (Pearce, Sheringham, Stone).
Manager: Terry Venables. **Team**: David Seaman, Gary Neville, Tony Adams, Gary Pallister, Stuart Pearce, Rob Lee, Jamie Redknapp, Paul Gascoigne, Steve McManaman, Teddy Sheringham, Alan Shearer. **Sub used**: Steve Stone for Redknapp.

Missed ten, including Euro '96.

21. WCQ. 1 September 1996 v Moldova in Chisinau:
3-0 (Gascoigne, Shearer, Barmby).
Manager: Glenn Hoddle. **Team**: David Seaman, Gary Neville, Gary Pallister, Gareth Southgate, Stuart Pearce, David Beckham, Paul Ince, Paul Gascoigne, Andy Hinchcliffe, Nick Barmby, Alan Shearer. **Subs used**: David Batty for Gascoigne, Matthew Le Tissier for Barmby.

22. WCQ. 9 October 1996 v Poland at Wembley: 2-0 (Shearer 2).
Manager: Glenn Hoddle. **Team**: David Seaman, Gary Neville, Gareth Southgate, Stuart Pearce, Andy Hinchliffe, David Beckham, Paul Ince, Paul Gascoigne, Steve McManaman, Les Ferdinand, Alan Shearer. **Sub used**: Gary Pallister for Southgate.